identity and belonging

mapping the margins

identity and belonging
mapping the margins

ABU SIDDIK

AUTHORSPRESS

Worldwide Circulation through Authorspress Global Network
First Published in 2022
by
Authorspress
Q-2A Hauz Khas Enclave, New Delhi-110 016 (India)
Phone: (0) 9818049852
E-mail: authorspressgroup@gmail.com
Website: www.authorspressbooks.com

identity and belonging: mapping the margins
ISBN 978-93-5529-311-4

Printed in India at Kensington Press

My wife Tuhina

&

our daughters Renaissance & Raisha

I never asked Tolstoy to write for me, a little colored girl in Lorain, Ohio. I never asked [James] Joyce not to mention Catholicism or the world of Dublin. Never. And I don't know why I should be asked to explain your life to you. We have splendid writers to do that, but I am not one of them. It is that business of being universal, a word hopelessly stripped of meaning for me. Faulkner wrote what I suppose could be called regional literature and had it published all over the world. That's what I wish to do. If I tried to write a universal novel, it would be water. Behind this question is the suggestion that to write for black people is somehow to diminish the writing. From my perspective there are only black people. When I say 'people,' that's what I mean.

Toni Morrison (1931-2019)

Acknowledgments

The marginals and the peripherals who refuse to dance with the frenzied rhythms of 'new' India.

Contents

Introduction

> An identity is questioned only when it is menaced, as when the mighty begin to fall, or when the wretched begin to rise, or when the stranger enters the gates, never, thereafter, to be a stranger.
>
> James A. Baldwin, *The Devil Finds Work*

Only in my Name

Let me be first freed from the big philosophical question 'who I am?' It obviously leads me to the depths of Indian philosophical queries, thoughts and pursuits. 'Know thyself' is the key motif for our existence on earth. And knowing one's self or identity is very difficult. Rabindranath Tagore, that is why, agrees, "It is not easy to know oneself. It is difficult to organize life's various experiences into a unified whole. Had God not given me long life, had he not permitted me to reach seventy years of age, I could hardly have got a clear picture of myself (qtd. in Uma Das Gupta 2010).

Radhakrishnan says, though in some sense the Upanishads are the continuation of the Vedic religion, they are in another sense a strong philosophical protest against the religion of the Brahmanas. It is in the Upanishads that the tendency to spiritual monism, which, in one form or another, characterises much of Indian philosophy, was first established whose intuition rather that reason was first recognised as the true guide of ultimate truth (qtd. in Jacob).[1] We have come from Him, and to Him we must return in the end. And our purpose is to praise Him and serve His cause. Without serving Him we cannot have access to the illumination of our soul, or to the glory and greatness of our life. So pray and praise Him day and night. On earth we will get tranquility and peace of mind, and in after life we will get a coveted entry into heaven and live with its manna and houris. Bereft of these soul-searching illuminating activities, life will lose its meaning and magnitude. It will have no mooring either. Eternally lost, we must live in chaos and anarchy and things will be falling apart before our eyes. Our ties with Him makes life worth of living. For us to receive His grace, we must be worthy of it. This worthiness comes only through bhakti. But the first thing that is needed is self-awareness. If we think highly of ourselves, where is the question of acknowledging a superior One? So the first stage in liberation is to realise our insignificance and to recognise God's greatness.... None of our other pursuits can guarantee us salvation. But introspection will help us see our faults and become humble. Once we have become humble, we become worthy of His grace.[2] Our harping on 'Vasudhava Kutumbakam' or the whole world is one family goes well with Thomas L. Friedman, one of the votaries of globalisation, who claims in his book *The World is Flat: A Brief History of Twenty-first Century* (2005) that the whole world is a level playing field in terms of commerce, wherein all competitors, except for labour, have an equal opportunity. It stresses to the perceptual shift required for countries, companies, and individuals to remain competitive in a global market in which historical and geographical boundaries are becoming increasingly irrelevant, where question of identity based on one's nationality, religion, language, colour or gender is a sacrilegious act. In 'Vasudhava Kutumbakam' you will get drenched in the spiritual light of self-illumination and self-enlightenment. And in 'borderless' world you will get showered with discounts, offers, and bonanzas on each commercial products, from a pack of pizza to a piece of land in moon.

In 2018, I wrote *Banglar Musolman* in Bangla not only to claim the unique identity of Bangla speaking Muslim of West Bengal but to withstand the waves of denial, denigration, and dehumanisation of their identity for decades. I am aware that identity is a double edged sword. It can cut from both sides. The book makes me popular especially to the readers of my community. But it also makes me an enemy to a host of my well-meaning friends within and outside of my community. What goes wrong? Obviously my identity is an inerasible stamp and it does matter. It is my strength as well as my weakness. When I, at the end of the day, return to *our* fold like the evening sheep retiring to pen after day's grazing, I feel safety, and I find a kind of harmony and peace. But returning to *our* pen also shatters me. I never want to be identified only by my religious tag. But my neighbours, my friends, my countrymen are always busy to seal me with this single communal stamp. So my identity and belonging to a particular religion or community comes first. My other multiple identities, namely teacher, independent researcher, responsible citizen, writer, motivator, etc. are always subordinate to the first one. My plural identities are not acknowledged, and even brutally subjugated by men of learning. My religious identity, and the pressure it creates on my secular and liberal self can be augmented by countless empirical evidences.

I am unable to find a suitable domestic maid for years. And my Rajasthani Marwari businessman neighbour's home is assailed by fours, sixes and so in morning and evening. My Brahmin shopkeeper neighbour is a happy go lucky aged man who keeps and kicks maids out of his door at alternate days. It is a Hindu locality. Maids are Hindus. I am a Muslim. Practicing or non-practicing who bothers? My name is my salient tag. I am a writer. I always agree to pay higher but domestic hands are not available. And you know what well of sympathy, empathy I have for domestic maids. I have written at least a dozen of poems and half-dozen of short stories where their defeats, woes, and pains find an outlet. And still I wash my dishes and clothes and wipe my floor at each day break. It happens inside my home. And interestingly one of my Hindu liberal neighbours suggests me to engage maids from *my* community. Of course I praise him for his practical suggestion. What is happening with me and my likes in public spaces you can easily imagine. You say it is too personal and needs to be validated with more facts and findings. Moreover, unavailability of maids cannot be linked with the issue of identity. You may also argue that unavailability of plot or home or flat or job or publication opportunity for the Muslims in India and abroad cannot be linked to the identity issue. Sadly, the truth is in "new" India Muslim identity is increasingly becoming a burden, a curse. It needs to be discarded to be a part of Indian mainstream or Hindu identity.

Increasing attacks on Indian Muslims by Hindu Rights in forms of bullying, trolling, rapes, riots, lynching and other ways of mob violence, and the patronage and indulgence the Hindu nationalist fanatics have from the state machinaries remind me of Ta-Neshi Coates's painful lines from his best selling personal narrative *Between the World and Me* (2015):

> Sell cigarettes without the proper authority and your body can be destroyed. Resent the people trying to entrap your body and it can be destroyed. The destroyers will rarely be held accountable. Mostly they will receive pensions. And destruction is merely the superlative form of a domination whose prerogatives include frisking, detaining, beatings, and

> humiliations. All of this is common to black people. And all of this is old for black people. No one is held responsible (9).

A black body can be destroyed in any ploy by the whites. In the same way an Indian Muslim can be destroyed in the name of anti-national activity, stealing cow, eating beef, wearing a veil or making love to a Hindu girl, and so on.

Let us hear harrowing tales of massive violence on Indian Muslims from Nazia Erum, the author of *Mothering a Muslim* (2020). She elaborates that during the course of her research she met many authentic Muslim women – a feisty hijabi principal; a burkha-clad single mother of two who was an ex-Facebook and ex-Google employee; an Urdu and paan loving 'patriarch'; a bob-haired child psychologist; a gynaecologist in a niqab; a district level swimmer; a state level basket ball player; a dentist; an advocate; an IT professional; shayara; a home-maker; a university lecturer; a civil rights advocate; a development professional; a member of parliament; an author; an activist and a feminist. She observed about the findings of her study thus:

> They were worried and fearful for their children, many of whom were targets of Islamophobia and nationalism in their classrooms and playgrounds. I was shaken by their stories....Eighty five percent of the hundred-plus children I spoke to told me that they had been bullied, hit or ostracized because of their religion....The malaise is growing but not too many people know about it as the victims' parents talk only to their circle of friends and family – and rarely to the school or media....I worried for the children facing the communal bullying all alone at school without anyone recognizing or willing to acknowledge their plight. I worried for my daughter who will be joining them tomorrow in the same playgrounds and classrooms. We need to speak, not for ourselves, but for our children.

In opinion of data-journalism pioneer Rukmini S, Hindus in particular tended to see their religious identity and Indian national identity as closely intertwined: Nearly two-thirds of Hindus (64 per cent) said it is very important to be Hindu to be 'truly' Indian. Indians may not always accept that they hold conservative positions on religion. One beloved narrative about India is that while political parties might trade in the business of communal polarization for voters, the average Indian is actually a liberal person who looks forward to his colleague's invitation for a home-cooked Eid feast and brings celebratory sweets to the office for Diwali, as the stereotype from innumberable Indian advertisements indicates. The truth is more complicated. Not every Indian might want their religion imposed on the whole country, but that does not mean they want to be friends with people from other religions, let alone accept them as part of their community or family. The housing segregation that Muslims in particular experience is borne out by data. Jains and Hindus were the most likely to not be willing to accept a neighbour from another community – particularly Muslims. Thirty-six per cent of Hindus were not willing to accept a Muslim neighbour, while the distaste for Hindu neighbours was much lower at 16 per cent among Muslims. One's religious identity can be the single biggest investment or disinvestment. For the majority community religious identity is a lucrative investment space, whereas to the minority it proves to be the biggest hindrance to their multiple socio-economic avenues of upward mobility.

Who is to be blamed? And who is not? No one can control our birth. No one can steal our caste. It is in our blood. It is our choiceless identity. I don't want to be flooded by the sophisticated, nuanced narratives and ideas of the identity theory makers of desi or foreign origin. I don't believe in social science expertise. I believe in stories – stories I love to read and tell, stories the marginal people tell, stories the voiceless attempt to voice. Is identity helpful or harmful for living a meaningful life? Is identity good or bad? Is identity to be avouched or discarded? Is identity an asset or a liability? Is identity a social capital or social liability? Does identity lead to the fertility of a greater cause or its ultimate futility? Does identity make us smaller or bigger on individual or societal or national or transnational level? Should we support politics based on identity? Besides identity are there other determiners for shared living of nonviolence and peace and harmony? Does identity really cause hatreds and violence? Does identity lead to the formation of a more just, equal, fraternal, reasoned society? Or does it lead to more violent, intolerant, toxic society? Our world is threatened by so many existential challenges of mass consumption, environmental calamities, migration, nuclear wars, rising inequalities, inerasable injustices based on gender, caste, colour, religion, language, and nationality. Has identity anything to do away with these crises and threats? Or is it simply a tool to score political leverage? The debate is endless and it will continue.

Let me quote one of my poems titled 'My Land is Nowhere' from my book *Shadows of Mourning* (2022) to show how identities and belonging are interrelated, intermingled. The interplay between identity and belonging is an agreed social reality and it works among individuals, among groups, among theoreticians, among politicians, among institutes. Our understandings of social equality or inequality, freedom or lack of it, are much coloured by our identities and sense of belonging. The poem runs thus:

I am landless.
My town is hostile to me,
Here a man is just fixed by his name.

My friends hardly know me,
My village is no longer my village,
Concretes are eating up greeneries everywhere,
The river has died, fields overused,
Delivery boys daylong parade our streets.

Our tea shops now keep country liquors
For the homecoming peasants from Bengaluru.

My colleagues and comrades are beyond my reach.
They shake earth and are shaken by the talks of the minions.

Bars are smoky, oily, overcrowded,
Filled with talks of cash and girls, projects and profits,
Outside, fair faces laugh at harrowing maids and majdoors
And gobble golgappa at busy street corners.

Street scenes –
A fakir strapped with a naked child on his back
Standing before A-Z restaurant,
Banjara boys guard a shopping mall
A madman leaning against the bars of a sweetshop,
A lanky old watchman tirelessly parking luxury wedding cars
A mad woman, stark naked, lying dead on the busy bay.

I am homeless, my land is nowhere…

The said poem is just an illustration of how our identities are continually made and remade, constructed and deconstructed, depending on multiple factors, like caste, religion, access to job, wealth or lack of it. Or simply a painful feeling for the wretchedness of the poor and the marginalised may have also coloured one's "homeless" identity and sense of belonging. Identity is thus somewhat slippery and our sense of belonging is unstable, especially in our globalised post-truth age.

American Heritage Dictionary of the English Language (3rd Edition) defines "identity" as "the set of behavioral or personal characteristics by which an individual is recognisable as a member of a group." The definition also extends to "the quality or condition of being the same as something else." It also stresses that identity is "the distinct personality of an individual regarded as a persisting entity; individuality." By "belonging" it refers to "close, secure relationship." Belonging and identity can be seen as part of the same "family" of concepts and, while both are used politically in similar ways, belonging enables a greater engagement with place and location and the structural and contextual facets of social life.[3]

Self and Identity

According to Francis Fukuyama *identity* grows, in the first place, out of a distinction between *one's true inner self* and an outer world of social rules and norms that does not adequately recognize that inner self's worth or dignity. Individuals throughout human history have found themselves at odds with their societies. But only in modern times has the view taken hold that the *authentic inner self* is *intrinsically valuable* and the outer society systematically wrong and unfair in its valuation of the former. It is not the inner self that has to be made to conform to society's rules, but society itself that needs to change. *The inner self is the basis of human dignity,* but the nature of that dignity is variable and has changed over time. In many early cultures, dignity is attributed only to a few people, often warriors who are willing to risk their lives in battle. In other societies, dignity is an attribute of all human beings, based on their intrinsic worth as people with agency. And in other cases, dignity is due to one's membership in a larger group of shared memory and experience....Because human beings naturally crave recognition, *the modern sense of identity evolves quickly into identity politics*, in which *individuals demand public recognition of their self-worth* (Fukuyama Loc 284, italics mine).

Jo Brewis' focus on the self and her struggle to resist being 'me' is an interesting study on the relation between self and identity. It is a courageous autoethnography because it lays bare her very personal struggle with identity and self. She underlies her struggles that can be felt in the construction of the self in relation to forms of power/knowledge that attempt to imprint their mark upon it. Drawing on Foucault's work on the techniques of the self, she illustrates the creative agency of the individuals to confound dominant discourses through the act of releasing one's self from oneself. She also delineates the processes of self-bricolage – the practices of liberation never reaching an end, and the pain as well as pleasure arising from engaging in this release.[4]

Swami Vivekananda put emphasis again and again on the spiritual dimension of man's soul or self. It is "the recognition of the self as our real being," and the highest purpose of human life, according to Vedanta, is "the growth of the self within man which when fully realised sees the same reality within all." It sees the Eternal, the Infinite, the Supreme. It sees this as "the secret highest self" of all, this is what it calls God, the permanent, the Real, and it sees "man as a soul." The progressive growth of the infinite consciousness of man towards this self, towards God, towards the universal, the eternal, the infinite, in a word, "his growth into spiritual consciousness by the development of his ordinary ignorant natural being into an illuminated divine nature." This is for Indian thinking the significance of life and aim of existence. This is the fundamental idea of Indian civilization and culture….In living for self's realization, as well as in pursuing the goal of spiritualising the whole of mankind, lie the secret of India's existence, as well as the perennial source of its strength which has withstood it against all types of vicissitudes (Islam and Sirswal 2013).

According to Sule Okuroglu Ozun and Mustafa Kirca, Leena Taneja's essay "Hindu Identity as a Site of Liminality" explores the luminal character of Hindu identity. Based on the well-read and popular scripture the *Bhagavad Gita* she argues that prominent Hindu sources encourage and support the concept of an "essential self," that is, "*Atman,*" "a permanent identity that provides intelligence, intuition, and intentionality to the individual person." The foundation of Hindu philosophy recognizes such an entity as a part of Brahman, the divine being, the supreme soul. She, however, claims that as different Hindu schools discover the meaning of illumination and ultimate salvation their writing reflects a purposeful change that "alters the meaning of identity from an unchanging perfect soul to a self, lost in perpetual longing for the divine." In loss and separation, not in union, is identity ultimately found, according to the bhakti writers. The liminality and rigidity of the *Gita*'s Self are deliberately and carefully subverted by the bhakti schools who sought emotion over intellectualism as a method of salvation (*B/Orders Unbound*, Loc 129).

Another extraordinary twist is thurst on the relation between *self* and *identity* by the postmodernists. Their view of the *self* was a "challenge to the individual rationalism." "Self" cannot be "subject" because it draws attention to the "subject-ed" condition of the person who is "controlled" or "constituted" by the ideologically motivated discourses of power which predominate in the society he inhabits. The subject cannot on this view ever "stand aside" from actual social conditions and judge them from a rational autonomous point of view, as moral philosophers in the Anglo-American Kantian tradition. The thoughts and expressions of the male individual, for example, are seen as part of a pattern of contaminated, patriarchal discourses, which are in any case in conflict, and of which he is the mere ephiphenomenon. This chucks out the Kantian, unifying ego in favour of a postmodernist updating of the Freudian model, of persons as undergoing an internal conflict between systems. As Seyla Benhabib, a professor at Harvard University, puts it by conflating Derridean and Foucauldian language about language:

> The subject is replaced by a system of structures, oppositions and differences which, to be intelligible, need not be viewed as products of a living subjectivity at all. You and I are the mere 'sites' of such conflicting languages of power, and 'the self' is merely another position in language (qtd. in Christopher Butler 2002).

Postmodernist fiction has been challenging the entire series of interconnected concepts that have come to be associated with what we conveniently label as liberal humanism. The focus of attention has shifted from the psychology of character (self) to the inadequacy of the concept of character, to recognition of subjectivity as the trace of plural and interesting discourses, of non-unified, contradictory ideologies. The postmodernist notion of human identity as essentially constructed like a fiction is also to be found in the visual arts.

What postmodern theory helps us to see is that we are all constituted in a broad range of subject positions, through which we move with more or less ease, so that all of us are combinations of class, race, ethnic, regional, religious, generational, sexual and gender positions. Postmodernists may not give a particularly convincing account of *the nature of the self* as it might appear in a moral philosophy concerned with responsibility, but they do very successfully adapt Foucauldian arguments to show the ways in which discourses of power are used in all societies to *marginalize subordinate groups.* For such discourses of power do not just contribute to the decentring and deconstruction of the self; they also serve to marginalize those people who do not partake in them. Under postmodern conditions, the ordered class politics preferred by socialists has given way to a far more diffuse and pluralistic *identity politics*, which often involves the self-conscious assertion of a marginalized identity against the dominant discourse.

The postmodernist self, then, is very differently conceived from the self at the centre of liberal humanist thought, which is supposed to be capable of being autonomous, rational and centred, and somehow free from any *particular* cultural, ethnic or gendered characteristcs. Postmodernists have turned away from such optimistically universalizable Kantian assumptions to see the self as constituted by language systems. The general move from a liberal emphasis on self-determination to a Marx-inspired emphasis on other determination is of immense importance. It is a sharp challenge to established post-Enlightenment, Anglo-American philosophical views, and points to the irreconcilable differences of identity between individuals. Postmodernists semm to call for an irreducible *pluralism*, cut off from any unifying frameworks of belief that might lead to common political action, and are perpetually suspicious of domination by others. Postmodernist self has turned against those Enlightenment ideals that underlie the legal structures of most Western democratic societies with their supposed focus on equality and justice. Postmodernist self tends to argue that Enlightenment reason, which claims to extend its moral ideals to all in liberty, equality and fraternity, was 'really' a system of repressive, Foucauldian control, and that Reason itself, particularly in its alliance with science and technology, is incipiently totalitarian (Butler pp. 50-60).

Belonging and its Challenges

Belonging is an emotionally charged social location. People belong together when they share value, relations and practices. To belong in the modern world means to reflexively talk about home and your sense of place. Time and again, individual and collective belonging has been encroached upon, challenged, fought about, and protected. State rule, market forces, forced displacement, transnationalisation, pluralisation, acceleration of social change, and the widening horizon of human aspirations have rendered belonging contested – from outside and from within. The more it is contested and made explicit, the less likely it is to just be, share, and join in. The value then can lie in keeping one's protected space, often at the high price of self-subjugation under the governmentality of the own collective as well as the price of excluding others and jealously guarding the boundaries of the small world of a we-collective. Bounded and exclusive belonging becomes increasingly problematic, given the pluralistic nature of contemporary societies and given the differentiated character of any given collective social space.[5]

The myth of overarching singular identity falls flat as soon as we delve into the depths of the particular contingency on which the sense of belonging is thought to be supported. In challenging times such as riots or communal clashes belonging to one's community takes primacy in the minds of the masses. But in ordinary day of everyday life the fissures with the community, within the neighbours, within the family members and even within the self become too apparent. If we look at our surroundings we can easily find that everyone is fighting against everyone. Simply put, it is no better that the world of the beasts. Everybody wants to have more choices. Everybody wants to sit at the top. In this messy race of living and livelihood nobody is friend. Foes surround us in online and offline modes of life. Our belonging to a particular set, determined by multiple social parameters which are continually changing, reshaping, reconfiguring, is a false claim. That is why we see Hindus fighting against Hindus, Muslims fighting against Muslims, women fighting against women, the rich against the rich, the poor against the poor in public spaces like buses, trains, offices, playgrounds, bars, shops, markets, malls, meetings, etc. At a given normal day motives of self-interest, self-advancement, self-comfort, self-expectation, self-ambition come to the fore, suppressing other determiners of belonging. And at a given troubled day belonging to a group in the name of caste, clan, language, religion, gender, social capital, takes the concrete shape and the motives of self-interest takes a back seat. Thus sense of belonging is not fixed, it is fragile. At the slightest opportunity people tend to break the cell of belonging. But at crisis periods the same people seek shelter under the umbrage of a particular sense of belonging, depending on the externals of that particular period. Thus, belonging is malleable, liquid, and it takes the shape forced by the external political, social, economic storms of the time. I have seen Muslims fighting against Muslims for an inch of land. I have also seen Hindus fighting against Hindus for an inch of land. I have seen Hindu women, Muslim women quarrelling at buses and trains for a seat. On the other hand, I have been witness to the sudden break of casual intimacy that often takes place between passengers during train or bus journey, because of their recognition of individual identity along their collective caste or community lines. Sometimes, identity acts as an unprecedented leverage for one's acceptance and acceleration in plural spheres of life. Sometimes, it poses a severe hindrance to one's acceptance, and fruition of desired goals in the layered networks and connectivities of life. This push and pull effects of identity and belonging is a crucial force that shapes and reshapes, configures and reconfigures, deconstructs and reconstructs one's adherence and separation to the socially approved or disapproved heterogeneous schemes of pluses and minuses.

Google's mission to organise the world's information and make it universally accessible and useful – starting with the web – changed all of our lives. There have been enormous benefits, to be sure. But for individuals it has meant that information that would normally age and be for gotten now forever young, highlighted in the foreground of one's digital identity (Zuboff 44). The notion that human material was changeable – that one's personality, identity, awareness, and capacity for self-determining behavior could be crushed, eliminated, and replaced by external control incited a new sense of panic and vulnerability (Zuboff 204). The world was rife with threats to the inner as much as to the outer man.[6] In this new digital world fixity of identity has faced tremendous challenges from all possible corners of our existence. People are haunted round the clock by surveillance operational systems. The big powers through digital penetration have unprecedented access to people's lives, even their bedrooms and balconies. No one is free. Our data can be easily used against us. So the threats to our privacy and freedom are natural corollary to our digital success. Facebook's operations are designed to exploit the human inclination toward empathy, belonging and acceptance. The system tunes the pitch of our behavior with the rewards and punishments of social pressures. It herds the human heart toward confluence as a means of other's commercial ends (Zuboff 293). Totalitarian powers and business conglomerates have been using the infinite social media platforms to steal individual's information. Many of their policies enacted to run the country or run the businesses are determined by this internet-enabled availability of personal and group data. Totalitarian powers cannot succeed by remote control. Mere conformity is insufficient. Each individual's inner life must be claimed and transformed by the perpetual threats of punishment without crime. They need a handmade terror that aims to remake every aspect of the individual from the inside out: heart, mind, sexuality, personality, and spirit. This craftwork requires the detailed orchestration of isolation, anxiety, fear, persuasion, fantasy, longing, torture, dread, and surveillance. There is a relentless process of atomisation and fusion in which terror destroys the human bonds of law, norms, trust, and affection which provides the living space for the freedom of the individual. The iron band of terror mercilessly uses men against each other so that the very space of free action disappears (Zuboff 227).

Cultural Identity

> [National] Cultural identity, like its individual counterpart, is an unconscious human acquirement which becomes consciously salient only when there is a perceived threat to its integrity. Identity, both individual and cultural, lives itself for the most part unfettered and unworried by obsessive and excessive scrutiny. Everybody living incorporates a zone of indifference with regard to one's culture, including one's language, ethnic origin, or religion [or race or land]. It is only when this zone of indifference is breached that the dimensions of ethnicity stand out in sharp relief and the individual becomes painfully or exhilaratingly aware of certain aspects of his cultural [national] identity.
>
> Sudhir Kakar, *The Colours of Violence*

Cultural groups are not only a shelter for those mourning lost attachments but also vehicles for redressing narcissistic injuries, for righting what are seen as contemporary or historical wrongs. Why people prefer 'primordial' group identities as 'Hindus' and 'Muslims' to other plural identities based on class, profession, or other criteria can be possibly analysed thus: other identities lack an encompassing worldview, are impoverished in their symbolic riches and devoid of that essential corpus of myths in which people have traditionally sought meaning, especially at a time when their world appears to have become meaningless. A core attraction and vital therapeutic action of self-consciously belonging to a cultural community lies in its claim to the possession of a future which is felt to be irretrievably lost. The cultural group which brings the 'primordiality' related to shared myths, memories, values and symbols to the fore assumes a vital healing function. One of its most vital aspects is to replace feelings of loss with those of love. This insight into the way groups work psychologically goes back to Freud who postulated eros as the vital cohesive force in a group. He believes that ties of love among members of a group come into existence through their emotional bond with the leader. Members of a group put the same object, the leader, in place of their ego ideal and consequently identify with each other. This shared idealisation gives rise to the love ties which are experienced in the feelings of loyalty, *esprit de corps*, and in the more intense moments of group life, in feelings of fusion and merger. It is a reordering and opening up of the inner world of the individual to include members of the group, who in turn, open up to include the individual in their psychological shared space. In cultural groups, the shared ego ideal may not be the figure of a single leader but many historical and mythical figures from the group's traditions, its ideals and values, and even its social and intellectual traditions.[7]

Identity Politics

> What makes identity politics a significant departure from earlier [movements] is its demand for recognition on the basis of the very grounds on which recognition has previously been denied: it is qua women, qua blacks, qua lesbians that groups demand recognition….The demand is not for inclusion within the fold of "universal humankind" …nor is it for respect "in spite of" one's differences. Rather, what is demanded is respect for oneself as different.
>
> Sonia Kruks

The terms *identity* and *identity politics* are of fairly recent provenance, the former having been popularized by the psychologist Erik Erikson during the 1950s, and the later coming into view only in the cultural politics of the 1980s and 90's. Identity has a wide number of meanings today, in some cases referring simply to social categories or roles, in others to basic information about oneself. Used in this fashion, identities have always existed (qtd. in Francis Fukuyama 2018).

In the area of cultural politics RSS shakhas are transforming the identity of Indian slum dwellers from 'poor' to 'Hindu.' Many Hindutva based organisations such as Hindu Yuva Vahini, Hindu Rakshak Sangh, and so on, have started working in slums in various cities in UP. The RSS and its affiliates like the VHP, Sanskar Bharati, Hind Mazdoor Sabha, Bharat Vikash Parishad, Sahakar Bharati, Pragya Pravah and several others are targeting these slums. On the other hand, several unofficial Hindutva-oriented outfits have suddenly emerged in these social locations. They are ambitious local leaders and they have formed small distinct groups to acquire political value. The former are working in the slums with their strategies of seva and *sahyog* (cooperation), while the newer outfits are trying to mobilise these slum populations under an aggressive Hindutva identity. While the RSS attempts to reshape the identity of the poor as Hindu citizens by inspiring them to absorb various Hindu *sanskaras* (customs), but these smaller outfits are trying to transform the slum dwellers into garvonnat (proud) Hindus. The tone and tenor of these campaigns are producing two kinds of political cultures. They may overlap sometimes, but they generate two distinct streams of Hindutva identity. One is posturing as a 'soft' Hindu, while the other posits itself as the champions of aggressive or assertive Hindu.

The intervention of the Sangh and its many affiliated outfits among the tribals in India is not new. During the 1930s, many princely states passed anti-conversion law in tribal zones. The activities of the missionaries and the rise in conversion of tribals to Christianity created situations in which Hindutva organisations got the space to work among tribal people. During the 1950s, the Vanvasi Kalyan Ashram began working in central India. It launches various projects in the areas of health, education and livelihood. And through these projects it has been slowly expanding its reach among tribal communities. It is working hard to reshape the tribal identity as the vanvasi identity as opposed to the Adivasi identity. The RSS and its allied outfits also started *paravartan* (reconversion) campaign that 'reconverted' converted tribals To Hindu religion or to their indigenous faith. In this way the RSS is not only reshaping the religious consciousness of the tribals, but it is also gradually trying tio rebuild their political consciousness. The RSS's intervention among tribal people in MP, Jharkhand and Chhattisgarh slowly weakened the Congress's strongholds among them. This resulted in a major shift in tribal voting patterns in favour of the BJP in the last few parliamentary and Assembly elections, notably in 2014 and 2019. The growing influence of the RSS in tribal zones has made many stalwart tribal leaders of the Congress irrelevant, even in their own areas.

The RSS informed NGOs to work among the tribals, to drive them towards the Sangh and to empower them as 'respectable citizens.' The Hindutva motivated NGOs started various social work projects among the tribal communities, such as creating infrastructure for good health facilities, opening schools and colleges, building temples as social-religious spaces in the villages, and so on. Alongside, the RSS has set up free schools with hostel facilities in remote areas. These schools and textbooks are based on the RSS's own pedagogy for tribes. Similarly they came up with *aarogyashalas* (hospitals of ayurveda, homeopathy, and modern medicine) there. As a ploy to support the indigenous knowledge of the tribal communities, the RSS institutes started imparting training in archery, wrestling and other traditional sports, to enable them to national level competitions. This way, while on one hand, the Sangh attracted the tribals through seva, on the other hand, it tried to cultivate a Hindu identity among them. Children trained in RSS shakhas later become role models for their communities. They learn bhajan-kirtan and other Hindu sanskaras. The Sangh support their higher education too. They maintain an ongoing relationship with them. The Sangh believes in the traditional ways of tribal living. The Sangh even offers expert advices to upgrade the trades skills of the tribals. Setting up temples of Hanuman or statues of other gods and goddesses is also a key strategy of the RSS's outreach project. At some places, many other Hindu organisations are also chipping in to reconstruct a tribal culture. Tribal deities are placed inside Hindu temples as well, forging a Hindu-tribal synergy. The RSS is also working to produce an impressive number of pracharaks from the tribal communities and using them to expand the shakha network in the tribal areas of central India, as well as in the rest of the country.[8]

The RSS is shown to be accomplishing its 'civilizing mission' through its interventions, such as replacing the tribal practices with upper caste practices which are considered as superior. The strategies adopted by the RSS as 'active agents of progress' were basically meant to differentiate between the local Oraon Christian community and their Hindu neighbours on religious grounds, for political reasons. Thus, as an antidote to the civilizing mission of the church the Hindu Right is seen introducing its own civilizing mission. The RSS is seen to be imitating and intervening in the practices of the local church and the ways of traditional tribal life (Robinson and Kujur 2010).

Identity and Violence

We are indeed largely influenced by people with whom we identify. Actively promoted sectarian hatreds can spread like wild-fire, as we daily find in Kosovo, Bosnia, Rwanda, Timor, Israel, Palestine, Sudan, and many other parts of the world. Many of the conflicts and barbarities in the world are sustained through the illusion of a unique and choiceless identity. Whether it is a homespun elemental violence or globally artful violence and terrorism, behind it works the assumption of supreme and singular identity based on religion or culture. The implicit belief in the overarching power of a singular identity can make the world thoroughly inflammable. The world is commonly taken to be a mere collection of religions or cultures or civilisations. People tend to ignore other identities that people have and value, involving class, gender, profession, language, science, morals, and politics. This unique divisiveness is much more violent than the world of plurality and heterogeneity that shape the world in which we actually live. The prospects of peace in the contemporary world may well lie in the recognition of the plurality of our affiliations and in the use of reasoning as common inhabitants of a wide world, rather than making us into inmates rigidly incarcerated in little boxes. Our shared humanity gets savagely challenged when the manifold divisions in the world are unified into one allegedly dominant identity in terms of religion, culture, community, nationality or civilisation. The uniquely partitioned world is much more divisive, violent, intolerant, bellicose and barbaric.[9] Nikki Boudreau observes that while an individual considers that their own identity is what makes them unique; their natural response is to define it by a characteristic that associates them with a larger group. An "us" versus "them" mentality results because whenever a person finds belonging with one group, it simultaneously separates from all other groups. Unfortunately, the tragedy in this need to belong is that it ultimately makes it impossible to identify with the largest of affiliations – the human race. Furthermore, this situation is becoming increasingly exacerbated as advancing communication technology encourages world cultures to grow more similar. This gives individuals even more reason to feel threatened because they feel that the qualities that are specific to their culture are coming under attack by this homogenization of world culture. This fear, this desperate need to belong, causes many people to commit fanatical and murderous crimes in the name of their identity.

Lebanese-French author Amin Maalouf in his book *On Identity*, however, eruditely analyses the problem of being identified with an individual's single self-allegiance. Anyone who claims a more complex identity is marginalised. It presupposes that "deep down inside" everyone there is just one affiliation that really matters, a kind of "funfdamental truth" about each individual, an "essence" determined once and for all at birth, never to change thereafter. As if the rest – a person's entire journey from birth to death as a free agent, her beliefs, her own individual tastes, sensibilities and affinities counts for nothing. Nowadays our contemporaries are urged to "assert their identity" meaning to seek within themselves that same alleged fundamental allegiance, which is often religious, national, racial or ethnic. They are asked to wear it as a badge of honour. But every individual is a meeting ground for many disparate allegiances, and sometimes these loyalities conflict with one another and confront the person with difficult choices….Can anyone in the US even today assess his place in society without reference to his earlier connections, whether they be African, Hispanic, Irish, Jewish, Italian, Polish or other?...so people have multiple allegiences which may conflict with one another. Their role is to act as bridges, go –betweens, mediators between the various communities and cultures. If people themselves cannot sustain their multiple allegiences, if they are being continually pressed to take sides or ordered to stay within their own tribe, then all of us have reason to be uneasy about the way the world is heading.

Individual, the author warns, is being thus "pressed" or "ordered" not by the fanatics and xenophobes, but by you and me, by each and all of us. And we do so precisely because of habits of thought and expression deeply rooted in us all [in our Selfs]. It is because of our narrow, exclusive, bigoted, simplistic attitude that reduces identity in all its varied aspects to one single affiliation, and one that is exhibited in fury. This exclusive claim to one's Self is a recipe for massacres. And people are committing crimes in the name of religious, ethnic, national identity. Each individual's identity is made of a number of elements, and these cannot be simply restricted to one's racial, ethnic or religious, or national identity.

Identity in the Age of Globalisation

The global is embedded in the local, because subjects are formed, deformed, and continually reformed by world events and therefore are not detached from the global in their more localised practices. (qtd. in Robyn Thomas, et all.)[10] People in many parts of the globe began to feel the heat of the globalisation, namely the free movement of goods, services and people, the diversification of cultures and the transcendence or crossing of borders. People were increasingly affirming their deep emotional ties with their distinctive culture, language, religion and rituals.

According to Nobel laureate Muhammad Yunus the new millennium began with a great global dream and globalisation guru Thomas Friedman marked the year 2000 as the point when the world went from being small to tiny. He claimed that several technological and political forces have converged and that has produced a global, Web-enabled playing field that allows for multiple forms of collaboration without regard to geography or distance – or soon, even language.

But Britain's withdrawal from the European Union on June 24, 2016 and Donald Trump's win as President of the United States terribly shook the world. These two events, known as 'political earthquakes', underlined a profound geopolitical and economic shifts. Trump, a controversial real estate developer and media celebrity won on the back of 'Make America Great Again' slogan. His political agenda included building border walls, instituting travel bans on individuals from seven predominantly Muslim countries, and withdrawing from global accords on climate, security and trade. The appeal of borders, separation, and exclusion in the United States, Britain and many other parts of the world put serious challenges to the hyperbolic pundits of globalisation. The twin political earthquakes were widely perceived as a revolt against globalisation and a call for strengthening national sovereignty. It was a fight between what was theoretically dubbed as nationalists and globalists. Many writers characterised the said events as a repudiation of globalism, as the emergence of ethnic nationalism, as new nationalism. Many argued that Brexit was a natural corollary of British anger at globalisation and multiculturalism.

One argument found its way in the backdrop of Britain's exit from EU and Trump's popularity as President was the reconfiguration of economic factors and cultural factors. Many experts took side with the economic woes of the poor white Americans and the Britishers. But many others sided with their alleged cultural woes. The fear of cultural displacement weighed heavily on the British. Economic deprivation was there, but the fear of being usurped by 'other' cultures was also very much in the American and British air. Fareed Zakaria argued that despite the economic grievances such as the rising inequality or the effects of global trade, most analyses of voters for Brexit, Trump, or populist candidates across Europe voted on cultural lines. People tended to forget economic woes if they were replenished by cultural bonanza.

In short globalisation brings the world closer together while varied forms of socio-cultural and political differentiation threaten to tear it apart. It is a case of coming together and the coming apart. The onrush of integration does not simply stand in stark contrast to retribalisation; it prompts, facilitates and shapes it.

Ironically, even the surge of inward-looking nationalist populism around the world has an outward-looking global dimension. Populist leaders across the globe are increasingly adopting a policy of what is known as 'a global nationalist movement' – a call for a global movement of national self-interest. And ultimately, much of what constitutes global interconnectedness is facing challenges of cultural resistance. The connectedness is not merely fuelling the resistance, it is facilitating it. Farhad Manjoo claims that social media platforms like Facebook, Twitter, WhatsApp, WeChat, and so forth, now allow billions of people to communicate more freely. Among the consequences of this communication boom is the growing social organisation and influence of once-marginalised groups, for instance, white supremacists in the United States, Brexiters in Britain, ISIS in the West Asia, and hacker collectives in Eastern Europe. Each in its own way is now wielding previously unthinkable power, resulting in unpredictable, destabilising spasms.[11]

The British writer David Goodhart has argued that in the global battle between the 'anywheres' (cosmopolitans comfortable anywhere in the world, flitting between business class lounges and five-star hotels, the votaries of globalization who thought of themselves as citizens of the world) and the 'somewheres' (those rooted in a place, a land, an ethnicity, a religion, and local assumptions and traditional prejudices), the 'somewheres' had won. Their leaders could claim an authenticity that legitimized their right to represent their peoples in all their true essence – their hopes, their drteams, their fears and hatreds. They ask people to install their people to power, and all would be well. These leaders are called themselves 'populists' from the Latin 'populus', or people, and pledged to get rid of "the plutocrats, the aristocrats, and all the other rats." In more recent years, populism was seen as a reaction to modernization, and the yearning for a simpler, rural life. Today's populism is arguably an updated version of the yearning for simplicity on the part of 'the people' threatened by the complexities of globalization. This explained both nationalism and xenophobia, both Brexit and the Hungarians sealing their borders, both Hindutva in India and the rise of alternative for Germany (Tharoor, *The Battle of Belonging*). Leaders like Donald Trump, who rose to the presidency of the United States on slogans of 'America First' and 'Make America Great Again'; Boris Johnson, who took his nation out of the European Union on a wave of xenophobic populism; Russia's Vladimir Putin, who has presided over the resurgence of Russian nationalism after the shambolic collapse of the Soviet Union; Recep Tayyip Erdogan of Turkey, and Narendra Modi of India, who successfully persuaded their voters that they were more authentic embodiments of their nations than the alleged rootless secular cosmopolitans they sought to displace; and a host of others from Jair Bolsonaro of Brazil to Viktor Orban of Hungary – who combined nationalist fervor with a determined articulation of popular prejudices, all resorted to nationalism to its place as the default model of national self-definition.

In the age of globalisation and of the ever-accelerating intermingling of elements in which we are all caught up, a new concept of identity is needed, and needed urgently. We cannot be satisfied with forcing billions of bewildered human beings to choose between excessive assertion of their identity and the loss of their identity altogether, between fundamentalism and disintegration (Maalouf 2001).

Marginal Identity

The full-fledged concept of 'marginality' entered the sociological canon through Robert Park's essay on 'Migration and Marginal Man' in 1924. Since then it proves to be a dominant field of study for social scientists. But, post-feminists and post-structuralist thinkers, in later periods, would construct this marginality in terms of 'otherness' to exemplify their marginal position with respect to the centre. The marginals hold peripheral positions in the society as they are excluded from accessing power at the centre. They are excluded by because of their social attributes such as race, caste, gender or religion. They do not fit into the normative conventions and are hence designated as the 'other.' There are varied ways of being marginal in society. Both overt and covert, incipient forms of marginality are principally observed in three main spheres – public (political) sphere, religious cultural sphere and economic sphere. The distinctiveness of the various forms of marginality in India is observable, for istance, in the prevalence of hunger in some select pockets, forcible land acququisitions and its impact on deprived sections of society, material deprivation and exclusion of religious, ethnic and sexual minorities and tribals as a result of conflicts, continuing caste discrimination, reported cases of atrocities against Muslims and Dalits and regional disparities, gendered forms of exclusion and those related to disability. The discourses on marginality and marginalisation of individual and group therefore hold relevance in a country like India, having bmyriad diversities based on region, religion, language, culture, race, class, caste, gender, sex, etc. (Bhattacharyya and Basu 2018).

Edward Said observes that the development and maintenance of every culture require the existence of another different and competing alter ego….Each age and society re-creates its 'Others'. Far from a static thing then, identity of self or of 'other' is a much worked-out historical, social, intellectual, and political process that takes place as a contest involving individuals and institutions in all societies….the construction of identity is bound up with the disposition of power and powerlessness in each society….human identity is not only not natural and stable, but constructed, and occasionally even invented out-right (Said 332). Thus, identity, whether marginal or central, is not neutral. It is constructed by geopolitical as well as economic and cultural pressures.

The minorities, the blacks, the tribals, the poor, people with deviant sexual behaviours are socio-historically considered marginal. In our Indian context the traditional focus on caste Hinduism within Brahminical or Sanskritic framework tend to put Muslims, Dalits and Adivasis on the periphery. They are bound to live spatially and culturally on the edges of the mainstream social world or Hindu social order. The tribals may live in the hills or forests, remote from the cities, the power-houses of the state. Dalits may live outside the villages, separate from caste Hindu society. The Muslims across Indian cities are increasingly pressurized either to live in ghettoes or build new ghettoes, preferably outside the posh areas of the city. The worlds of the marginals are hedged around by a variety of prohibitions too. They are taken as fringe elements and they hardly have access to the essence of the centre. And their marginality makes them the target of practices of discrimination. In the eyes of the caste Hindus they are considered as lowly, impure, 'other.' The Muslims are bullied, abused, even lynched by the Hindu rights encashing on their dominant social, political and economic identity patronage. The centre is ever wary of the subversive powers of the marginals.

It seems from the notion that it is at its brink, that authority (of state, religion or dominanat social order) is most vulnerable. Of course it may be true that today marginality is becoming universal and pervasive and it is possible to be *other* within the very colon-ization that assimilates one by deflecting and therby escaping the power of the dominanat social order without leaving it. This does not nullify the idea that the dominanat social order spatially and institutionally localizes itself, assumes a place and distances itself from that which is exterior to it. This is then the proper (*propre*); indeed, one might say the nucleus where the dominant order achieves a degree of stability and establish an arrangement of positions that is relatively secure (Robinson and Kujur Loc 102). What does need to be remembered is the narratives of emancipation and enlightenment in their strongest form were also also narratives of *integration* not separation, the stories of people who had been excluded from the main group but who were now fighting for a place in it. And if the old and habitual ideas of the main group were not flexible or generous enough to admit new groups, then these ideas need changing – a far better thing to do than reject the emerging groups (*Culture and Imperialsim*).

Indianness or Hindu Militancy

> In a wide variety of cases, a political leader has mobilized followers around the perception that the group's dignity had been affronted, disparaged, or otherwise disregarded. This resentment engenders demands for public recognition of the dignity of the group in question. A humiliated group seeking restitution of its dignity carries far more emotional weight than people simply pursuing their economic advantage.
>
> Francis Fukuyama, *Identity: The Demand for Dignity and the Politics of Resentment* (2018)

Who is an Indian and who is not? What makes one really Indian? Does India have an essential national identity? Are the NRIs more Indian than the millions of poor native Indians? Is there any single big idea of India? Or is it an amalgamation of different waves of humanity, as affirmed by Rabindranath Tagore and others? Whose version is more powerful – syncretic secularists and liberals or solitarist Hindu Rights? Is race an entitlement for the majority in the definition of Indian national identity? Is it a liability for the Indian minorities? In fact, in today's India the biggest battle is going on about the idea of India? Whose India and how and why? Whose not, how and why? Inexhaustive sources of scholars prove that India is a heterogenous and pluralistic country where the age-old mantra of 'unity in diversity' resonates in every Indian heart. Indian identity is never acknowledged in the name of one's language or ethnicity; religion or geography. Shashi Tharoor humorously compares 'the idea of India' to a *thali*:

> There has never been an archetypal Indian to stand alongside the archetypal Englishman or Frenchman. If America is a melting pot, then to me India is a *thali*, a selection of sumptuous dishes in different bowls. Each tastes different, and does not necessarily mix with the next, but they belong together on the same plate, and they complement each other in making the meal a satisfying repast.
>
> The rise of Hindu nationalism as a political phenomenon in recent years has articulated an alternative view of Indian identity – one that is expliicitely narrow and definitional. Its pro-Hindu and pro-Hindi, sectarian and anti-secular views...broadened the debate. The usual chauvinists and xenophobes were joined by political opportunists of various stripes (Tharoor 2007).

Today Indian identity is increasingly and rapidly becoming coterminous with Hindu identity. Outside the Hindu fold the peripherals and the marginals, the minorities and the Dalits and the tribals should reside as second class or third class citizens. Or simply they will have to survive as 'other' in the outskirts of the Hindu centre. They are losing power even to safeguard their basic constitutional rights. They are in constant fear of being abused, ostracizsed, labeled as antinational, jailed, and even lynched in broad day light. The 'indianness' of the Indian Muslims are under constant gaze and they are, thus, kept under constant state surveillance. Anti-Muslim slogans, hate speeches, calls for Muslim xenocide are 'new normal' in Modi's 'new India.' "It is easy to think of the prospects of the Indian Muslims in gloomy terms. Long ago denied the scope, which many thought essential to their existence, and now suspected by many for their religion and regarded as second class citizens, is there any future for them other than eventual absorptionin the Hindu mass (qtd. in Laurent Gayer and Christophe Jaffrelot 2012)?"

Beyond Identity

If we imbibe a translocational lens and if we endorse a notion of solidarity based on a greater common cause we can move away from a focus of the cultural differences of "other" and, we can erase forms of marginality and exclusion more broadly. Solidarity can be applied to political struggles that construct bonds marching beyond the fetters of ethnicity, nationality, or other group and class identities.

Solitary in place of identity entails a concern with building a common future, irrespective of differences in beliefs, values and ways of life. Solidarity is forged agnostically and in relation to a common enemy. This builds on the notion of identities of action than identities of common origin or culture, unlike the focus of integration and diversity discourses. Solidarity relates to identities forged for different struggles. Such forms of solidarity have become more evident in transnational campaigns on the environment and anticapitalist campaigns as well as the antiracisms.

Veteran cultural historian Sumanta Banerjee rued for today's youth's extreme obsession with self-interest. I and my friends' political activities, he opined, our awakening, our feeling and inspiration during 1950s, 1960s and 1970s were driven by the dream of building of an egalitarian society. But present generation is committed to the cause of their professional development based on self-interested work ethics. Their life is confined to the walls of individual progress, prosperity and wealth. They are basically careerists. Their activities are not mooted by any social responsibility towards fellow citizens. Today's youth work at multinationals and they dream to hoard more and more and be rich and spend a life of ease and comfort.[12]

But Jean Dre`ze has alternative opinion. Word has it that most people are self-interested. The literature of mainstream economic theory also makes constant reference to "rational self-interest" as the prime motivation of economic agents. The assumption is so pervasive that the concept of rational self-interest is taken at face value. Consequently rationality and self-interest are often conflated. This self-interest assumption has no theoretical or empirical support. People often act on the basis of other-regarding motives – love, kindness, solidarity, compassion, reciprocity, patriotism, public-spiritedness, and more. Some even make great sacrifices for their friend, family, community or country. Human beings, by nature, are interested in each other's lives. Whether an active school teacher, a committed trade unionist, or a passionate artist are acting out of self-interest may be hard to tell. Even in animal world instances of self-sacrifice and cooperative behaviour are aplenty. Ants work hard to build common nests, migratory birds fly in formation, elephants help the wounded. Among many selfless specific motives public-spiritedness occupies a niche. It is broadly defined as "a reasoned habit of consideration for the public interest." The use of the term "habit" is recognition to the fact that we often act on the basis of habits of thought or behaviour. For example, many people are used to standing in the queue at the bus stand or railway counter, without getting into a cost-benefit analysis of the choice between joining or jumping the queue. Reasoned habit is the hallmark of public spiritedness. Public here need not refer to the society at large – depending on the context, it could mean a smaller group also.

The importance of public-spiritedness in social life, and for human development, can be conveyed with two simple examples. The first is the punctuality. When we go to a meeting there is a temptation to go a few minutes late to avoid the inconvenience of waiting for others. But then, others may also reason that way. Extending the argument further, we may end up attending the meeting very late indeed, if we stick to the self-interest reasoning. The situation has the basic structure of an "escalation game." Games theory tells us two important things about escalation games: first, things go badly out of hand in such situations, and second, many escalation games are such that there is no rational way to play. So the best option is not to play the game at all. Punctual people or societies refrain from embarking in this escalatory reasoning. They simply turn up on time, as a matter of social norm or habit of thought. The next example is voting. Every voter knows that his or her vote will not make any difference. But people even vote navigating a sea of troubles – trekking long distances, queuing for hours under the scorching sun. It is a telling example of public-spiritedness that defies the theory of self-interest. Public-spiritedness does not always require self-sacrifice or deep ethical thinking. Ethics of course can help. But we often act in a public-spirited way as a matter of habit. If public-spiritedness requires strong ethical commitments, it may not go beyond the periphery of minority principled individuals. But if it takes the form of sensible habits of thought that can be rationalised with light touch of ethical reasoning, public-spiritedness much more of a future. This is not a small step. It can help us to avoid many daily tragedies from vandalism to violence. It can also build social institutions that reconcile liberty and equality. Dr Ambedkar put it very well in his stirring speech to the Constituent Assembly on 25 November 1949: "Without equality, liberty would produce the supremacy of the few over the many. Equality without liberty would kill individual initiative. Without fraternity, liberty and equality would not become a natural course of thing." Public-spiritedness is not quite fraternity or solidarity, but it is a step towards that at least.[13]

Inerasible Stain

Indian society has so many structural inequalities. This is evident if you have a cursory glance at a matrimonial website or a matrimonial advertisement in a daily. The tentacles based on the discrimination of caste, colour, class, community, ethnicity, economic and social status loom large and have an abiding presence of each home and family. It is highly stratified and privileges are distributed according to her connection, colour, caste, moveable and immoveable assets. In India, as elsewhere, the privileged tend to nurture the illusion that they "deserve" what they have. This illusion, however, evaporates even with the most casual introspection. Sure, some rich people work hard – but so do koilawalas, construction workers and domestic helpers. Others bases of privilege have little to do with personal merit: our aptitudes, health, inheritance, social connections, and other assets derive from contingencies (such as the accident of birth), and our parents' and teachers' efforts, far more than our own. All this is without going into the fact that wealth and power often build on corruption, exploitation, and crime.[14] But the discrimination based on multiple social and economic identities is rampant and all pervasive. Inequality and injustice are taken for granted by the people at large. Those (the educated, the privileged) who are supposed to act for the promulgation of a free, just and equitable society, are acting against the interests of the lower masses. Ironically, the powerful and the privileged in every possible way manipulate the robust systems for self-interest and self-progress. Their selfish actions will never lead to the emancipation of the poor, underprivileged masses. They merely sell their privileged identities of caste, class, religion, language, etc. in the murky competitive markets, and wield huge power in the sustenance of status quo, and exploit the marginalised people. Their hypocrisy is terribly shocking. Their private life is a poor shadow of their masked public images.

Nabaneeta Dev Sen seems to highlight some of these critical concerns of contemporary India. *Ekkdike cholche metropolitan shohor kolkatay hi rise apartment ar vugorbo reler akash patal sopner bipul bastobayon, onnodike tari modhdhe lukiye ache samontotantrik mon. sabeki joutho poribar, jati-bornoved, ponprotha, shushushrom toh achei, ektu gramancholer dike pa barale tatka dasprothar gondho mele. Na hoyeche sottokar shilpayaon, na ghoteche dhromo sanskar. Nokol adhunikotar ekti mukhosh choriye deoya hoyeche amader satkele sabeki jibon-moner upore. Ei nokol asol mile mishei ajker vartiy baektitto gore utheche. Apatoto sadhinotar bohirboivober ontorale ek sodabondhon sadhinotahinota amader jatiyo boishishto hoye dariyeche jiboner pray proti khetrei.* (In one hand, mushrooming of high rise apartments coupled with the unprecedented expansion of metro railway networks has gripped the sky and soil of the metropolitan city Kolkata, leading to the realisation of much nourished dreams of millions. On the other, under its glossy surface is hidden their feudal minds. Conservative extendende family, race and caste divisions, dowry, child labour are the undeniable reality of everyday life. If we move towards the outskirts of the city there is fresh smell of slavery in the air. Our traditional suerstitious life and mind has been covered with a fragile mask of modernism. Indian identity is a part of this odd, haphazard assortment and amalgamation. On the surface there is hype of 'Azadi Ki Amrit Mahotsav', and under it rests the cruel reality of salvery, chains, poverty, hunger and thousand fangs of caste, creed, language and religion, etc., Nabaneeta Dev Sen 2022).

Brief Overview of the Book

identity and belonging: mapping the margins is divided into fourteen chapters. Each chapter focuses on a key issue of identity and idea of belonging. It attempts to cover issues of identity and belonging ranging from textual analysis to theoretical paradigms, from Indian cultural icons to empirical evidences. It attempts to mine issues ranging from assertive identity to defensive identity, from religious identity to political identity, from ethnic identity to cultural identity, from diasporic identity to nationalist identity, from the majoritarian identity to minority identity, from individual to group or collective identity. And it attempts to show how the shades of varied identity are in perpetual operation to form, deform, shape, and reshape our sense of belonging. Identity forms a boundary and at the same time it reforms and reshapes a boundary.

In chapter 1 my focus of "bordered" identity is limited to the metaphoric level, much in the thematic resemblance of Rabindranath Tagore's 1911 *Gitanjali 35* poem "Where the Mind is Without Fear," or Robert Frost's 1914 poem "Mending Wall" or Philip Freneau's 1788 poem "The Indian Student or Force of Nature." I attempt to argue here that border is everywhere and it is ever-increasing and ever-widening and it resides in our minds. In our Indian context, the ethos of cultural plurality and heterogeneity is at stake. Marathas harass wretched Biharis and Bengali labourers in paradise land Mumbai. North East students are being attacked in posh Indian cities. Muslims are getting lynched for their adherence to a particular religion. Attacks on the Dalits are on the rise. Border is everywhere in a seemingly postmodern, borderless global village. Daily print and electronic media are flooded with the good news of our frantic harping on globalisation, cultural integration, multiculturalism, cultural plurality, "unity in diversity," racial tolerance, gender equality, economic inclusion, financial freedom, and so on and forth. All these fanciful coinages are very dear to hear but too bitter to swallow. Lived daily experiences are markedly incommensurate with the media hypes. Attacks on South Asian students in "civilised" countries like US, Australia, England recur. Caste prejudices are so rampant, vulgar and dehumanising. Atrocities on the marginalised are taken for granted. Our media are deluged with daily doses of horrifying incidents – Dalits being harassed or beaten for entering a temple, the Hindutva fatwa warning Muslims either to leave the Qur'an and the habit of eating beef or go to Pakistan, rising nefarious forces like Islamic State and Hindu Taliban, killings of liberal thinkers like M. M. Kalburgi, Govind Pansare, and activist Narendra Dabholkar, Gauri Lankesh by Hindu extremists, serial unidirectional happenings from Babri to Dadri, killing hapless poor women as *dainis* in villages across India. All these macabre, inhuman happenings make the psychic border too apparent and mar the country's eternal image of tolerance and holistic sagacity. It is indeed a "land of Circe" where thousands of castes, creeds, folk and semi-folk cultural superstitions raise their hooded fangs at the slightest opportunity and such and the likes *ad infinitum* make the border too visible and inerasable and make hearts exasperating and paralytic. Border emanates from the million identical bars of caste, class, religion, race, gender etc., from our coated prejudiced and biased minds. It is irresistibly inerasable. In spite of inculcating best modern scientific education our "enlightened" minds fear to tread the territories lying beyond traditional *dharmasastras*. Our best education fails to produce best free minds. It is a tragedy. That is why I argue for the inscrutable existence of bordered minds.

Chapter 2 focuses on the crisis of identity and belonging of Bangla speaking Muslims of West Bengal. The social and cultural exclusion of Bangla speaking Muslims are taken for granted, as if they are "unwanted" and let their issues of backwardness be untouched till the declaration of another election. This cheap "vote bank" identity politics and other multiple socio-cultural issues result in their years of dehumanisation and denigration in their homeland and beyond. Their crisis of identity, however, basically emerges from two questions and their consequent subsidiaries. Firstly, being *shudra*-converted, they are treated as impure or *sherek* Muslims by the Urdu speaking urban Muslims. And next, their innate Bengali identity is never acknowledged by their co-brethren elite Bengali Hindu bhadraloks. This dichotomy creates a traumatic crisis of identity in Bangla speaking shudra-converted Muslims of West Bengal. And their absence of representation, or their derogatory presence in literature, art, culture, cinema, media together with the harping on their negative stereotypes such as, barbaric, illiterate, temple destroyers, beef-eaters, women abductors, unhygienic, polygamists, crude, *gaiya* (rustic), *katua* (circumcised) etc., adds further vituperation and vulgarisation to their already ghettoised and intolerably wretched identity. Here I argue and attempt to explore where, how, and why the plural secular identities of Bengali Muslims are suppressed with a skewed subtlety. I also try to challenge Bengali Muslims' singular *burqa, topi, dari* from socio-economic perspectives.

Chapter 3 is another fresh attempt to show how Bangla speaking Muslims of West Bengal are stereotyped and misrepresented by the Hindu bhadralok writers. The stereotypical representation of Muslims includes such obnoxious and derogatory and humiliating terms as "terrorists," "polygamists," "beef-eaters," "invaders," "oppressors," "barbaric," "uncivilised," "anti-national," "illiterate," "ignorant," "poor," "unhygienic," "drug-traffickers," "burglars," "hate makers," and what not. It is a gross vulgar misrepresentation of identity and living experiences of Indian Muslims in general and Bengali Muslims in particular. They are poor and uneducated, but most of the other derogatory terms are forcibly inflicted on them, resulting in their years of pain and pathos, dishonour, dehumanisation and denigration. The true identity of Bengali Muslims is never reflected in art, literature, journalistic writing, media, and even in the public discourse of everyday life. They earn their livelihood by the sweat of their brow. They do "manual and menial jobs." They are farmers, daily labours. They are hands at kilns and farms and factories. They are rickshaw-pullers, toto-tuktuk-drivers, tailors, vegetable-sellers, masons, bidi-workers, village-vendors, leather-goods makers, and so on. They are voiceless backwood mass scattered in varied pockets throughout the hinterland of all the districts of West Bengal. They are poor, ill-housed, ill-clad, ill-fed, meek people with hearts of pure gold. They are hard-working, resilient and embrace woe and evil alike in the transaction of their everyday life. They are kind and hospitable to their Hindu neighbours and Hindu guests. They are bereft of any kind of superstitions or prejudices found in abundance among caste Hindus of Bengal. And most importantantly, they cannot speak Urdu or Arabic, languages thought to be the sacred medium of Muslim cultural ethos. They speak in rural Bangla dialects, and the pronunciation and intonation of which are markedly different from the *Shantipuri Bangla,* spoken by the Bengali bhadralok elites. Here I want to stress and unfold the layered avenues where Bengali Muslims are being deliberately misrepresented and their authentic identity and daily raw living experiences subjugated by the politics of pen, resulting in their inerasable humiliation, excruciating psychic pain and their lifelong denial, dishonour, deprivation and even death.

In chapter 4 the focus is on the survey of post-independence Bengali Muslim literati and their literature. Its stress is on the identity formation of Bangla speaking Muslims of West Bengal through their own writing. Chapter 3 strives to show how and why Bengali Muslims are stereotypically represented by Hindu writers. But here the focus is exclusively fixed to the key post-independence Bengali Muslim writers and the literature they produce, and how their literature forms and shapes their identity and sense of belonging in Bengali society. Literature is a continual striving toward the attainment of the essence of life. But from a pragmatic perspective divisional heterogeneity and plurality of literature have indeed been serving many desired and cherished goals and aspirations of the people of designated literature. Indeed this plurality is an inerasable strength of literature. If a community is incapable of sustaining and flourishing its own language and literature, that community is bound to lose the sheen of its unique gust of life. In this context comes the issue of Bengali Muslim literati and literature and their undeniable existence of mesmerising gaze to life's visceral and cerebral horizons from a distinct Bengali Muslim perspective. This chapter, therefore, attempts to shape Bengali Muslim identity through the works of Bengali Muslim litterateurs like Syed Mujtaba Ali and Syed Mustafa Siraj, Abdul Jabbar and Kabirul Islam, Abul Bashar, Afsar Ahmed and

Sohrab Husain, to name only a few. They took both in content and imagery the local Bengali environment and its uniqueness as the theme of their creativity which was quite different from the pure and pristine Islamic culture. And their writings focus more or less on the local and immediate reality of Bengali Muslim. Their writings are influenced by their Hindu neighbours' syncretic and mystical tradions and its liberal ways of ideas and thoughts. These writers have been votaries not of a pure and prescriptive Islamic voice, but of a shared Bengali Muslim perspective and Bengali Muslim identity, based not on their sole religious affiliation, but on their mother tongue Bangla and the literature written in it.

Chapter 5 elaborates and explains how the tea tribals of Western Dooars of West Bengal have been victims of multiple migrations which directly lead to their diaspoic condition – rootlessness and a sense of 'in-betweenness'. Duars or Dooars had been historically a part of the Bhutanese domain and was a densely forested area. Plantation and scientific forestry came only after the British occupation by defeating the Bhutanese kingdom. And with the establishment of the colonial rule, came the colonial economy. The British set up Zamindari system to garner revenue. They destroyed the rural base of Indian economy. And for their industrial needs they started indigo plantation. Like indigo they also started to further their colonial enterprise tea and forestry economy in Jalpaiguri, Darjeeling and the upper Assam. With the launching of tea plantation in the mid-1870s a large scale migration of tribal peasants, particularly Oraons, Mundas and Santals from Chhotanagpur and Santal Parganas to the Dooars whom they call Bhutan, took place. They were recruited in tea gardens run by the British. Before the settlement of other communities they converted the forests into villages and *busties*. The remnants of these tribal people form a majority of the population in Western Dooars.

These immigrants have unique ways of life and each sect has its particular culture and religious inclinations. The Oraons or Kurukh are victims of multiple migrations and they have a proneness to roaming. They have a rich range of folk songs, dance and myths. They played traditional musical instruments such as Mandar, Nagara and Kartal. Both men and women participate in dace during festivals or any social celebrations. They follow the 'Sarna' Dharma. They worship Mahadeo, the other name of Dharmesh, their supreme god. They believe that everything in nature has its own deity or god. They perform religious rituals under a sacred grove. They speak 'Sadri,' commonly regarded as a sister language of Bengali, Oriya, and Angika. They believe in supernatural spirits and practise sorcery and witchcraft. They have their distinct cultures which do not conform to the majority of the people of Dooars. And this leads to their diasporic identity and their crises of belonging.

Chapter 6 basically reflects on Vivekananda's concept of God and his views on Hindu-Muslim syncretic religious identity. Vivekananda is not only a religious visionary he is a great orator, writer, social reformer, a patriot, and a maker of modern India. This dynamic multifaceted personality has been far ahead of his time. He believed in the assimilation of the best from each and every religion – Christianity, Islam, Jainism, Buddhism, Judaism and so on. His concept of God is akin to that of Islam. Islam considers God as omnipotent, omniscient, omnipresent, shapeless, pure power, who is immune from the cycle of birth and death. God is eternal, anadi. "Say: He is Allah, the One. Allah, the Unique. He does not give birth. Nor was He given birth to. There is no equal to Him" (al-Ikhlas). God is supreme who sits in the driver's seat and the entire cosmos is regulated by His holy power. Vivekanada's concept of God or Bramha is the same.

Today Vivekananda has been hijacked by the BJP and its affiliated intellectuals for political mileage. His saying – say with pride that I am Hindu is being misinterpreted by taking it out of context. Vivekananda equals a Hindu with an Indian citizen. He never believed in sectarianism. His famous story of the well in his Chicago lecture is reminiscent of his syncretised religious vision. Though he is a Hindu monk, he is cannot be confined to Hinduism only. His vision is universal religion and particulary this line of thought has deeply influenced Tagore. He is energetic, revolutionary, and extremely conscious of colonial Bharat's maladies of untouchability, poverty, superstitions, illiteracy, and pathetic position of women in society. He has shown the West through his1893 Chicago lectures the mystic and ennobling eternal power of Hinduism. My argument is that Vivekananda is for the whole humanity, and not for the Hindus only. And after Vivekananda there are perdurable similarities between Hinduism and Islam, especially as far as the cardinal concept of God is concerned. Religious identity cannot be denied as it is done by the Left. It has a crucial role in fostering one's sense of belonging, be it harmonious or communal. And most interestingly, to sepak for the religious identiy of the minorities is to sepak for justice and equality.

Chapter 7 is exclusive to the dominanat thoughts of Rabindranath Tagore about nationalism and patriotism. He asserted that the history of India does not belong to one particular race but to a process of creation to which various races of the world contributed – the Dravidians and the Aryans, the ancient Greeks and the Persians, the Mohammedans of the West and those of central Asia. Now at last has come the turn of the English…and we neither have the right nor the power to exclude this people from the building of the destiny of India.

The history has come to a stage when "the moral man," the complete man, is more and more giving way, almost without knowing it, to make room for the political and the commercial man, "the man of the limited purpose." The process, aided by the wonderful progress of science, is assuming gigantic proportion and power, causing the upset of Man's moral balance, obscuring his human side under the shadow of "soulless" organisation. We have felt, he has affirmed, its iron grip at the root of our life, and for the sake of humanity we must stand up and give warning to all, this *nationalism is a cruel epidemic of evil* (italics mine) that is sweeping over the human world of the present age, and eating into its moral vitality.

To him Truth comes first. It can *transcend* the boundaries and barriers of place, space and time. His religion is humanity. It is inclusive. It never matches with the exclusionary ideas of Hindu nationalist thinkers. And the politics based on hate is a severe hindrance to the inclusive Indian ways of life. Tagore's celebration of Man irrespective of his caste, class, religion, region, language, and other markers of identity is an appeal to universality of human dignity. And it leads to a sense of universal belonging, Man's place in the world.

In chapter 8 I try to argue the key role one's mother tongue plays in sustaining and rejuvenating one's innate literature, culture and heritage with the help of Kenyan author Ngugi wa Thiong'o. Each language has its unique rhythm, essence and nuances. Language may be a bare medium of communication in the fields of science and commerce. But in literature it is a powerful demonstration and reflection of one's culture, one's identity, one's self. A language because of its poor global reach, limited scope as a bearer of cultural legacy, and other such alleged hindrances cannot be simply rejected by its native tongues. For Ngugi, Gikuyu, his mother tongue, is a weapon of resistance to the cultural hegemony of English language. His desertion of English and espousal of Gikuyu is a giant step to claim his cultural root, racial identity and kind of freedom he urges for his peasantry and working class countrymen. It culminates in his anti-colonial belligerent stand as well as reclaiming his unblemished African self.

Chapters 9, 10 and 11 are textual analyses of three texts, one is novel, and the rest are short stories – B S Tyagi's 2019 novel *Afzal*, Syed Waliullah's partition story *Ekti Tulsi Gacher Kahini* or *Story of a Tulsi Plant* and William Faulkner's 1931 short story *Dry September*. The stories are from America, India and Bangladesh and they are written in different period of time. But there is an underlying cohesive thread that ties them together. The setting is different; the tone and texture is different. But the theme of identity or crisis of identity and the quest for belonging are the bases on which the stories are built. Afzal is an Indian Muslim youth, Waliullah's protagonist is a Hindu woman, and Faulkner's Will Mayes is a Negro. Racial identity is a distinguished marker of everyone's existence. Racially and culturally they belong to the minority. So discrimination, denial, hatred, enmity, violence are some of the bonuses they get from the virtually majoritarian state. Will Mayes is killed by the white supremacists; Afzal is jailed because his religious identity is suspected to have terrorist links, and the Hindu lady is made to flee from her *own* country because of her religion. If all the three characters would belong to the majority culture, the stories would have different shapes and dimensions. In fact, identity has been a burden to their existence. And their minority identity is coterminous with their convoluted or tortuous sense of belonging.

At Mukti Ashram Afzal's name was suitably changed into Vedant. Why? A Muslim was not allowed to stay as a member of the Ashram. At the judge's house Afzal's name was again changed into Narayan. Changing Muslim names into Hindu ones to save a job or a life is not at all an unprecedented phenomenon in contemporary India. Muslims are stereotypically represented in cultural or daily living space as villains, betrayers, terrorists, anti-nationals, rapists, and what not. They are systematically denied entry into the Indian cities' posh housing areas. They are hardly included in country's mainstream decision making bodies or opinion making platforms or recruitment commissions. The novel raises many disturbing questions about identity. Why did the police target Muslim boys as 'terrorists'? Why were they discriminated because of their Muslim name? Afzal had to sacrifice his Muslim name in order to have access to Hindu spaces. *Afzal* was very much critical about identity and belonging issues. The novel is not identity-neutral, and the novelist never intends so, I argue.

Chapter 10 focuses on a partition story of Bangladeshi writer Syed Waliullah, *Ekti Tulsi Gacher Kahini*. Partition stories are generally ripe with stories of suffering, indecency, rape and sexual violence, loot, murder, torching of houses, decay and deaths. Multiple sources find over 75000 women were abducted, raped, mutilated during partition. But Syed Waliullah's *Ekti Tulsi Gacher Kahini* or *Story of a Tulsi Plant* is a clear departure from this mainstream narrative of gory details of violence, fears and killings. While in stories such as Banaful's *Dangar Samoy* or Samaresh Basu's *Aadab* we are shuddered with the horrific, brutal details of partition-tragedy and its inherent cruelties, in Waliullah's *Ekti Tulsi Gacher Kahini* only some bare hints of violence are offered. In this chapter I try to argue that *Story of a Tulsi Plant* is a story of the unsaid woman. Invisible Hindu woman of the house is visible in each turn and twist of Waliullah's dexterous narrative. Colours of partition violence can be unearthed in the images of the "dying tulsi plant" and the invisible lady's "glossy black sari with red border dangling from a pole in a slum in Asansol, Baidhyabathi, Lilua or Howrah." Guarding one's religious identity and the fear of losing that identity haunt the entire narrative. Identity acts as a powerful tool of belonging. The Hindu invisible lady had to flee from her country simply to protect his life and identity. "Can't you see the tulsi plant standing awkwardly there? It has to be uprooted. No trace of Hindu culture will be put up with," Modabber, one of the usurpers of the white Hindu house heatedly argued. Look at the source of the rage of Modabber. It centres on religious identity.

In chapter 11 we have racial identity issue in William Faulkner's classic short story *Dry September*. It is a terrible fact that in America racism continued long into the twentieth century despite the constitutional abolition of slavery. The disregard for the freedom guaranteed under the law, and the concomitant Jim Crow laws that enforced a 'racialised code of behaviour' along with racial segregation in public places speaks volumes about the position of the blacks and the African American or mixed race people in the America. It is reflective of the various forms in which violence and racial hatred would manifest itself in both obvious and insidious ways. In the present story Negro Will Mayes is a victim of racial hatred and violence. The story is about the assertive identity of the white supremacists McLendon and his cohorts. A black man is lynched because of the colour of his skin. And Minnie Cooper cannot lie because of her white racial entitlement. This lynching tale is a bizarre manifestation of America's ugly reality of racial identity issues and the violence based on this racial discrimination. Faulkner's story highlights race as a major source of identity marker. Race is a coin of endless privileges for the whites. It is also a coin of denial, depravity, and dehumanisation for the blacks. This chapter has mined the racial prejudice, racial hatred, inequality, inhumanity, and violence that run at the background of enlightened American society.

Chapter 12 takes us to the plain of religious festival. It shows how a community festival unconsciously or consciously makes a field of value identity among the participants and at the same time it devalues the identity of the non-participants. The question of identity and belonging based on religious festivals, irrespective of communities, takes a prominent shape in our discourses of daily life and politics. During religious festivals a plain argument like 'the things that touch you, may not touch me' takes a back seat. We are too clever to accept the truth. In the name of universality of the religious occasion, it ruthlessly separates people on the basis of religious identity. Each religious ritual has its own set of practices. Celebration of a particular religious practice does not necessarily mean the celebration of all religious practices. So, religious celebration, in its scope and reach, is always limited to a set of people. It is not inclusive. It is not universal or *sorbojonin* as always propagated by the festival enthusiasts and their political gurus. It is particular. Identity, whatever colour it may assume, is both adhesive and non-adhesive. It unites people on basis of race, caste, gender, colour, creed, religion, region, nationality, language, profession, and ethnicity. It also acts as a potential factor of disunity. From this point, religious festival, be it the festival of Hindus, Muslims, Christians, etc., champions a particular identical stand. It also relegates the non-participatory religious people to the passive plains of segregation and separation. Thus religious identity may boost a particular community's sense of belonging. But it at the same time disorients people of other non-participating communities, and makes them conscious of their separate and segregated identity.

The focus of chapter 13 is on the myth of Hindu-Muslim identical relation and the issue of contested belonging. Die-hard Gandhians hold that Hindus and their Muslim counterparts are brothers and sisters. The belief in Hindu-Muslim bhai-bhaism is a key to understand the credentials of Indian cultural identity. They argue that we [Indians] are children of the one God who is Ishwar and Allah, Ram and Rahim. Hindus, Muslims and Christians are brothers. But the harsh reality, according to Khushwant Singh, is that *wherever people of different races, religions, languages and cultures have co-existed, instead of bhai-bhaism there is tension and turmoil. And if land, property or business is involved, the tension often explodes into uncontrollable violence* (italics mine). Another canard is that in India there were no communal riots before the introduction of divide and rule policy by the British. The truth is that Hindu-Muslim tensions have existed since Islam came to India. And before Islam there were conflict between Hindus and Jains, Hindus and Buddhists, Dravidians and Aryans. This chapter debunks the myth of Hindu-Muslim brotherhood with relevant psychoanalytic inputs and empirical evidences.

Chapter 14 is my abridged version of Chapter 4 (pp.134-168) titled "The Myth of Damaging Identity Politics" from *the Guardian* columnist Nesrine Malik's book *We Need New Stories: Challenging the Toxic Myths Behind Our Age of Discontent* (2019). According to the author basically there are two definitions of identity politics. The first is the effort to secure the rights denied to some on the basis on their identity – defensive identity politics. The second is that which seeks domination on the basis of identity – aggressive identity politics. Aggressive identity politics espoused by the majority is thought to be "natural and benign." And identity politics as practiced by the blacks, the Asians, the minorities and the disadvantaged is thought to be "dangerous, indulgent and damaging."

Thus, 14 chapters of the book in its entirety broadly demonstrate multiple aspects of identity issues and the varied nuances of the quest for belonging. Chapters are varied in range and reach but their primary target is to focus on the issues of identity or lack of it, and how one's plural identities or singular identity, one's individual identity or collective identity, affect her in the varied transactions of life. The majority champions it while the minority defends it. Identity, the book argues, determines as well as unsettles one's sense of belonging. And identity is coloured by issues of race, religion, caste, class, colour, gender, nationality, ethnicity, language, region, etc. Identity is a marker of freedom, but at the same time it is a sign of boundary too. The book attempts to survey the isuues of identity and the search for belonging of the marginalised people like the Indian Muslims, Indian tribals, black Americans, Africans, women victims of the partition both with empirical evidences and textual analysis. It also attempts to debate and delve into the myriad issues of race, religion, languague, literature, culture, nationality, patriotism, identity politics, the idea of India, etc. through the eyes of Bengal's two greatest thinkers Vivekananda and Tagore, and the Kenyan author Ngugi. The centralities of the issues that configure, disfigure, and reconfigure one's identity and sense of belonging in our rapidly changing globalised world, and their subtle treatment and in-depth engagement overwhelmingly in Asian-African environment give this book its saliency.

Works Cited

1. Jacob, Father T. R. *Concept of Self in Indian Thought.* https://www.marquette.edu/library/theses/already_uploaded_to_IR/jacob_t_1975.pdf. Web.
2. https://www.thehindu.com/features/friday-review/religion/Know-yourself/article15690241.ece. Accessed Feb 10, 2022, Web.
3. Anthias, Floya. "Identity and belonging: Conceptualisations and reframings through a translocational lens". https://www.researchgate.net/publication/325204712_Chapter_6_Identity_and_Belonging_Conceptualizations_and_Reframings_through_a_Translocational_Lens accessed on 26th Jan. 2022. Web.
4. Ibid.
5. Pfaff-Czarnecka, J. "'From "identity" to "belonging" in social research: plurality, social boundaries, and the politics of the self'". (Working Papers in *Development Sociology and Social Anthropology*, 368). Web.
6. Zuboff, Shoshana. *The Age of Surveillance Capitalism: The Fight for a Human Future at the New Frontier of Power.* New York: Public Affairs, 2019. Print.
7. Kakar, Sudhir. *The Colours of Violence.* New Delhi: Penguin Books, 1996. pp. 189-90. Print.
8. Narayan, Badri. *Republic of Hindutva: How the Sangha Is Reshaping Indian Democracy.* New Delhi: Viking, 2021. pp. 76-86. print.
9. Sen, Amartya. "Preface". *Identity and Violence: The Illusion of Destiny.* [Kindle Basic Version]. Retrieved from amazon.com.
10. Thomas, Robyn, et all. "Introduction: Resisting gender, gendering resistance" in *Identity Politics at Workplace: Resisting gender, gendering resistance.* Eds. Robyn

Thomas, et all. London & New York: Routledge, 2004. [Kindle Basic Version]. Retrieved from amazon.com.

11. Croucher, Sheila. "Introduction". *Globalisation and Belonging: The Politics of Identity in a Changing World.* Second Edition. Lanham: Rowman & Littlefield, 2018.Print.
12. Banerjee, Sumanta. *Nishir Daak: Smriti Niyey Chhelekhela.* Kolkata: Thema, 2014. p. 3. Print.
13. Dre`ze, Jean. *Sense and Solidarity: Jholawala Economics for Everyone.* Ranikhet: Permanent Black, 2017. pp. 306-10. Print.
14. Ibid. p. 2. Print.
15. Maalouf, Amin. *On Identity.* Trns. Barbara Bray. Vintage Digital, 2011. [Kindle Basic] Retrieved from amazon.com.
16. Maalouf, Amin. *In the Name of Identity: Violence and the Need to Belong.* New York: Arcade Publishing, 2001. Accessed 28 May, 2022. https://www.facinghistory.org/civic-dilemmas/new-concept-identity. Web.
17. Tharoor, Shashi. *The Battle of Belonging: On Nationalism, Patriotism, and what it Means to be Indian.* Aleph Book Company, 2020. [Kidle Basic] Retrieved from amazon.com. [Loc 72]
18. Boudreau, Nikki. "Violence in the Name of Identity". https://www.csustan.edu/sites/default/files/honors/documents/journals/entries/Boudreau.pdf Accessed May 28, 2022. Web.
19. Rukmini S. *Whole Numbers and Half Truths: What Data Can and Cannot Tell us about Modern India.* Context, 2021. [Kindle Basic] Retrieved from amazon.com. [Loc 531].
20. Ozun, Sule Okuroglu and Mustafa Kirca. "Introduction" in *B/Orders Unbound: Marginality, Ethnicity and Identity in Literature.* Peter Lang Edition, 2017. [Kindle Basic] Retrieved from amazon.com. [Loc 129].
21. Robinson, Rowena and Joseph Marianus Kujur (ed.). "Introduction". In *Margins of Faith: Dalit and Tribal Christianity in India.* Sage Publications, 2010. [Kindle Basic] Retrieved from amazon.com. [Loc 329].
22. Erum, Nazia. *Mothering a Muslim: The Dark Secrets in Our Schools and Playgrounds.* Juggernaut Books, 2020. [Kindle Basic] Retrieved from amazon.com. [Loc 48].
23. Bhattacharyya, Asmita and Sudeep Basu. "Situating Marginalities in India: An Introduction." In *Marginalities in India: Themes and Perspectives.* Springer, 2018. [Kindle Basic] Retrieved from amazon.com. [Loc 280].
24. Islam, Merina and Desh Raj Sirswal. *Philosophy of Swami Vivekananda.* Pehowa (Kurukshetra): Centre for Positive Philosophy and Interdisciplinary Studies (CPPIS), 2013. [Kindle Basic] Retrieved from amazon.com. [Loc 318].
25. Gayer, Laurent and Christophe Jaffrelot, eds. *Muslims in Indian Cities: Trajectories of Marginalisation.* Haryana: Harper Collins Publishers, 2012.p. 311. Print.
26. Tharoor, Shashi. *India: From Midnight to the Millennum and Beyond.* Penguin Books, 2007. [Kindle Basic]. Retrieved from amazon.com. [Loc 250].

27. https://www.youtube.com/watch?v=7HK_0WGcC-E Accessed June 3, 2022.
28. https://thewire.in/communalism/process-of-genocide-already-underway-in-india-experts-at-global-summit Accessed June 4, 2022.
29. https://sabrangindia.in/article/dalits-and-adivasis-suffered-violence-and-discrimination-even-2021 Accessed June 4, 2022.
30. https://www.thehindu.com/news/national/dalits-adivasis-muslims-worst-off-says-indian-exclusion-report/article18427801.ece Accessed June 4, 2022.
31. Said, Edward. "Afterword". *Orientalism.* New Delhi: Penguin Books, 2001. Print.
32. Coates, Ta-Neshi. *Between the World and Me.* New York: One World, 2015. Print.
33. Said, Edward. *Culture and Imperialism.* "Introduction". Vintage Books, 2014. [Kindle Basic] Retrieved from amazon.com. [Loc 419].
34. Butler, Christopher. *Postmodernism: A Very Short Introduction.* Oxford: Oxford University Press, 2002. Print.
35. Sen, Nabaneeta Dev. *Iswarer Pratidwandee Ebang Anyanya Prabbandha.* Kolkata: R B Enterprises, 2022. p. 159. Print.
36. Gupta, Uma Das, ed. Rabindranath Tagore: My Life in my Words. Penguin Books, 2010. [Kindle Basic]. Retrieved from amazon.com. [Loc 106].
37. Fukuyama, Francis. *Identity: The Demand for Dignity and the Politics of Resentment.* Profile Books, 2018. [Kindle Basic]. Retrieved from amazon.com. [Loc 227].

CHAPTER 1

Bordered Mind and Mind Bordered

> It is just when people are all engaged in snooping on themselves and one another that they become anesthetised to the whole process. Tranquilisers and anesthetics, private and corporate, become the largest business in the world just as the world is attempting to maximize every form of alert. Sound-light shows, as new cliché, are in effect mergers, retrievers of the tribal condition. It is a state that has already overtaken private enterprise, as individual businesses form into massive conglomerates. As information itself becomes the largest business in the world, data banks know more about individual people than the people do themselves. The more the data banks record about each one of us, the less we exist.
>
> Marshall McLuhan, *From Cliche to Archetype* (2011)

Introduction

Border in the physical or geographical sense refers to boundary, frontier, limit, etc. These nouns all denote a line or an area separating one piece of territory from another. A border is basically a line that separates political, spatial, and territorial entities. Border in the figurative sense, however, means margin, edge, verge, brink, rim, brim, etc. And all these words refer to the line or narrow area that marks the outside limit of something. There has also been unprecedented growth of surveillance mechanisms to monitor migrants in the wake of Covid-19 pandemic. Digital border is in. Growing anti-migrant xenophobic sentiment, justification of surveillance and online media monitoring under the guise of security and public health, and the rise of extreme right and neo-fascist groups or political organisations globally impacts how migration management technologies function….Far-right groups have been engaged in violence again migrants around the world, including in the US, mainland Europe, Canada. In border frontiers such as Greece, far-right extremism and anti-migrant sentiments reached boiling point, with the island of Lesbos becoming an epicentre for extreme right groups across the EU….These groups have also been blatantly calling for the establishment of so-called 'deportation squads' using algorithms to identify potential targets.1 So, digital surveillance is making the much hyped digitally borderless world into millions of detailed surveillance domains.

Here I, however, refrain from intervening into the areas of the specialist political geographers discussing and debating multiple layers of the idea of physical borders across the world. I also refrain from analysing and interpreting the domain of digital border. My aim is limited to the metaphoric level, much in the thematic resemblance of Rabindranath Tagore's 1911 *Gitanjali 35* poem "Where the Mind is Without Fear," or Robert Frost's 1914 poem "Mending Wall" or Philip Freneau's 1788 poem "The Indian Student or Force of Nature."I attempt to argue here that border is everywhere and it is ever-increasing and ever-widening and it resides in our minds. In our Indian context, the ethos of cultural plurality and heterogeneity is at stake. Marathas harass wretched Bihari and Bengali labourers in paradise land Mumbai. People are getting lynched for their adherence to a particular religion. North East students are being attacked in posh Indian cities. Border is everywhere in a seemingly postmodern, borderless global village. Daily print and electronic media are flooded with the news of our frantic harping on globalisation, cultural integration, multiculturalism, cultural plurality, unity in diversity slogan, racial tolerance, gender equality, economic inclusion, financial freedom, and so on and forth. All these fanciful words and coinages are very dear to hear but too bitter to be swallowed. Lived daily experiences are markedly incommensurate with our hypes. Attacks on South Asian students in "civilised" countries like US, Australia recur. Caste prejudices in India are so rampant, vulgar and dehumanising. Atrocities and attacks on the marginalised are taken for granted now. Our media are deluged with daily doses of horrifying incidents – a dalit being beaten for his entry into a temple, the Hindutva fatwa warning Muslims either to leave their sacred book Qur'an and become vegetarian or go to Pakistan, open calls for Muslim genocide, rising nefarious forces like Islamic State and Hindu Taliban, killings of liberal thinkers like M. M. Kalburgi, Govind Pansare, and activist Narendra Dabholkar and Gauri Lankesh by Hindu extremists, online abusing of public intellectuals, serial unidirectional happenings from Babri to Dadri, killing hapless poor women as *dainis* in villages across India. All these macabre, cruel, inhuman happenings make the psychic border too apparent and mar the country's eternal image of tolerance and holistic sagacity. It is indeed a "land of Circe" where thousands of castes, creeds, folk and semi-folk cultural superstitions raise their hooded fangs at the slightest opportunity and such and the likes *ad infinitum* make the border too visible and inerasable and make hearts exasperating and paralytic. Border emanates from the million identical bars of caste, class, race, religion, politics, gender etc., from our coated prejudiced and biased minds. It is irresistibly inerasable. In spite of inculcating best modern scientific education our "enlightened" minds fear to tread beyond our "own" territories. Our best education fails to produce best free minds. It is a tragedy. Even our scientists are not freed from the issues of patriotism, religion, race, gender, intolerance, hatred. Scientists are also human beings and they are not beyond the said emotional ties and proclivities (Rabin Majumdar 16). That is why I argue for the inscrutable existence of bordered minds. Minds are increasingly becoming restrictive and exclusionary, creatining layered borders.

Psychic Landscape

Every man is isolated and living in his mental border. Border exists in the mental and psychic landscapes and not in the physical territories only. With the explosion of information technology in 21st century we are always under the surveillance of our big brothers. Where is the life of spirit? Where is the life of freedom? Our data are being constantly monitored. And we are being controlled and even persecuted by state apparatuses. The greatest hindrance to enjoy a life of freedom is the multiple barriers and boundaries imposed by our different markers – castes, languages, religions, cultures, creeds, rituals and customs. There is no way to be minimally freed or become borderless. We are bounded by physical maladies, economic wounds, racial or religious inheritance, state supervisions, educational inertness, racial clashes, communal riots, and climatic calamities, and so on. We cannot be freed from all the dehumanising norms and laws and practices of the land. All these prescriptions erect dangerous and irksome borders. To cross one border is to invite multiple others. And who wants to live a troubled life for being borderless. We all want a hassle free, cashless, paradisiacal life on a wretched bordered earth. We are bounded by thousand don't and do's prescribed by ignoble, unnamable coteries of self-appointed moral hooligans produced by the staunch nexus between gory religions and crude politics. And we are compelled to swallowing the bitter pills of their amoral perversities and vicissitudes. I am not enthusiastic about Sule

Okuroglu Ozun and Mustafa Kirca's argument for "border violations," "border crossing," or borderless world by "transgressing borders and destabilizing hierarchical orders." The authors painstakingly argue for "blurring the borders" by questioning "the given limits and orthodox beliefs." They are hopeful for alternative realities when "the established boundaries are liberated" (*B/Orders Unbound* Loc 93). But I think, given the current trends of religious and political identity issues, crossing borders or liberation from multiple borders and boundaries is hardly possible. Instead of crossing borders and enjoying a "hybrid" life, we are creating more and more borders in the name of religion, race, language and nationality. People are being bored with the ideas of pluralistic society secularism and multiculturalism so dearly uphold by the secularists and liberals. Ethnic muscular identity with its strong desire for customized boundary is the order of the day.

Reterritorialisation

Globalisation simply means that different parts of the world become and more similar and dependent on each other. Researchers have discussed the possible disappearance of the borders due to globalisation, but have come to the conclusion that even if physical borders are uprooted (as in the case of European Union) borders still exist in the minds of the people. What 31st January 2020 Brexit offers the borderless scholars and academics and enthusiasts? Border scholars are, however, more focused on the mental borders of the people. In our postmodern, post-truth world, however, many boundaries have seemingly become more permeable for people, goods, capital, and a revolutionised information technology that recognises no boundary limitation has seen a tremendous penetration into the nook and corner of every home. This rapid movement in border functions has encouraged some scholars specialising in economy and information sciences to argue their case for a unified world of geopolitics by using phrases like "borderless world" and political "deterritorialisation." But this trend has not gained ground around the globe. For example, in the post 9/11 era, borders are being re-erected or reinforced in many developed countries. Hence, the current political situation in the world characterised by the prevalence of fear of terrorism can be interpreted as a sign for a reterritorialisation rather than a deterritorialisation. All of us have several identities and it depends on the situation and context which identity we prioritise. Nation states are never monolithic, but in it inhabit different ethnic groups. States have used certain uniting ideas to coalesce together different ethnic groups under one state ideology. The idea of the American Dream, (USA) or Unity in Diversity (India) is a mythic attempt to unifying the nation and celebrating the singularity (borderless identity) of the nation state the foundation of which lies in its common past. But the idea of homogenous India does not hold in good stead in real life situation. The idea of a borderless life seems to be a cliché now. Racism, majoritarianism, prejudice, discrimination, ignorance, superstitions parade grotesquely, nakedly, in "sivilised," to quote Mark Twain, societies. Borders are ever newly reconfigured and constructed and they are too visible. Indian literature, culture, history, politics, is mired with multiple layers of unflinching borders.

Indian literature and Indias

For instance "Indian Literature" seems to be residing calm before the tumultuous storms. There is no one India. There are multiple heterogeneous Indias. And there is no essential spirit of Indian literature. The nation is stable only on the world map. P P Raveendran has argued in his classic essay "Genealogies of Indian Literature" that there are different Indias for different authors. He cites the name of Saadat Husain Manto, Mahasweta Devi, Gopinath Mohanty, Vaikom Muhammed Basheer, LaxmanGaikwad, Bama, VKN, U R Anantha Murthy and Shashi Tharoor and others who represent heterogeneous Indias. Nation's borders "keep changing from writer to writer, from reader to reader and from subject to subject." He claims:

> No one would dare to talk about an essential Indian spirit running through the works of these writers who share the same nationality and perhaps the same period of writing, but whose histories, contexts, mindsets, experiences, lifestyles, languages and sensibilities are different, from the other. These writers dwell in different Indias, and to speak of them as sharing a common culture and a common sensibility is to beguile oneself.[2]

Thus Hinduized grand narrative of India's mythic past as a *Aryabarta* is a self-defeating, self-delusory, and even suicidal. India is a multilingual, multi-ethnic country, where a unified history asserted by national grand narrative is always contested by different groups, such as women, or ethnic minorities. India has a checkered history where religious plurality and heterogeneity rule the roost, as argued by

Amartya Sen and many other scholars. India is a "shared home" for Hindus, Buddhists, Jains, Jews, Christians, Muslims, Parsees, Sikhs, Baha'is and others.[3] And though toleration of the diversity is always recognised, intolerance is never given up by India and her violent fanatics. Border in the name of religion, caste, language, nationality is the undercurrent running through nation's rhythmic tensed pulses. Border is bare not to the virtual and filmy fashionable India, but the India of ill clad, malnourished, educated but ignorant billions, where they fight in the name of Allah, Ram, Buddha, Jesus, etc. where ethnic clashes and cleansing, gory communal riots raise their poisonous fangs. Why are we afraid to recognise the truth? Why are we sugarcoating the bitter pills? Let us recognise the border. The sooner, the better. Why are we busy with the politics of writing by manufacturing and multiplying falsies such as "borderless" world or so to say homogenous India. A morning daily with matrimonial advertisements will slap you hard over your morning cup of tea for being a borderless personality.

Psychic Reterritorialisation

Pirouz Mojtahed-Zadeh citing Jean Gottmann, the internationally respected political geographer of the late twentieth century and who is often claimed to be the father of modern Geography, has stressed on the inscrutable existence of psychic border which is ever increasing and ever widening and which cannot be erased at all. Physical border can be transgressed, but not the border of the minds. The author cites Gottmann who claims:

> The most stubborn facts are those of the spirit, not those of physical world … And while history shows how stubborn are the facts of the spirit, geography demonstrates that the main partitions observed in the space accessible to man are not those in the topography or in the vegetation, but those that are in the minds of the people (qtd. in *Ashgate Research Companion* 397).[4]

Gloria Anzaldúa's 1987 book *Borderlands/ La Frontera: The New Mestiza* celebrates the border-crosser, the marginal figure who queers boundaries of race, class, gender, sexuality, nation, and language. Here border is a site of struggle where one seeks to assert one's identity by crossing it. Anzaldúa's theory, thus, remarkably and most interestingly differs from that of Gottmann who most persuasively and convincingly argues that, if I understand him correctly, one is proud of one's cultural, bodily, psychic and ethnic border. There is no harm in taking pride in one's bordered identity. It is man's inborn salient character. It is inerasable. Border basically champions one's inborn innate identity. To be bordered by one's special identical features is a matter of pride and nobody can completely surmount it. Bordered existence is a matter of cultural assertiveness. Anzaldúa's theory, on the contrary, suggests that to cross the border erected by multiple social, economic, political or cultural forces is to claim one's identity. There is no pride in claiming bordered life. To cross the border is to champion one's identity. She asserts her borderless identity:

> Because I, *Mestiza*
> Continually walk out of one culture
> And into another,
> Because I am in all cultures at the same time,[5] (99)

She hates to be taxonomically classified by a single identity. She rather takes pride in blurring borders and, therefore, celebrates multiple fluid borderless identities. She strives to exist in "all cultures." Her thoughts are muck akin to Tagore of Bengal.

Poems under Study

"The Indian Student"

Let us concentrate on some ordinary but powerful poems to elucidate my main argument that border is a state of mind and it is inerasable. One way we are harping on such fine coinages as globalisation, borderless world, global village etc. and, on the other, we are witness to more new borders which are being erected day and night by the state and the corporation. First I come to Philip Freneau (1752-1832), the great agnostic, who always celebrated rationality and free thinking. I try to tell the story of Shalum, the copper-coloured boy from his poem "The Indian Student."[6] Shalum has transgressed the border of "savage tribe" shepherd identity of an uncouth Red Indian. He is taken to "white-man's land" by a "wandering priest" and he exchanges his "blanket for a gown" and admitted to Cambridge College. The boy then masters Hebrew, heathen Greek, physic, law, grammar, divinity etc. Then comes his moment of recognition! The "tedious hours of study" and "heavy-moulded lecture" fail to ignite the spark of his mind, "No mystic wonders fired his mind." The shady bank, the purling stream, the woody wild has possessed his heart. He is not drifted away from what he was. Susquehanna's forest lad then leaves the gloomy walls of college halls, and "musty books." He deserts the enticement of wealth and power and runs towards the "land of shades." Now he vows: "My heart is fixed; – and I must go/ To die among my native shades." He throws away his borrowed robe "the gown" and wears again his native dress "His blanket tied with yellow strings" and goes to the forest from where he once bregan his journey. The last two lines of the first stanza, "(His blanket tied with yellow strings,)/ A shepherd of the forest came," are repeated only with a variation of the verbs "came" and "went" in the last two lines of the last stanza, "His blanket tied with yellow strings,)/The shepherd of the forest went." And that makes the poem circular. The lad came to know the white man's world which could not stir his spirit and he went back from where he came. The poem in the end is reminiscent of Gotmann's tangible phrase "stubborn are the facts of spirit." Shalum cannot cross the border and even border crossing cannot ignite, to quote A P J Abdul Kalam, his "wings of fire." Border is in the boy's mind and he temporarily overcomes it. But at the end of the day his spirit remains unchanged, and he comes back to his own fold of black people and his own land leaving the promised white man's land and education forever.

"The Mending Wall"

I now attempt to argue the power of psychic border with the help of Frost's (1874-1963) fine poem, "The Mending Wall."[7] The poem basically deals with "walling" or bordering. "And set the wall between us once again./ We keep the wall between us as we go." They "wear" their fingers "rough" with handling the boulders, loaves and balls needed for mending wall in the spring. The persona of the poem is well convinced that he and his neighbour need not any wall as there is no enmity between them. He claims:

> He is all pine and I am apple orchard
> My apple trees will never get across
> And eat the cones under his pines, I tell him.

But his neighbour remains unconvinced. He loves to remain in the border of his father's saying that good fences make good neighbours. He then most realistically argues that they need not any wall as "here there are no cows." But his neighbour only believes in his father's saying, "'Good fences make good neighbours.'"And the neighbour is seen "Bringing a stone grasped firmly by the top/ In each hand, like an old-stone savage armed" to make the wall more stable and dark. The persona's unflinching faith in "Something there is that doesn't love a wall,/That wants it down" has not found any material impact on his neighbour's stubborn spirit. He cannot cross the border set by his father. Despite the best persuasion of the poem's persona of not erecting a wall between them, he fails to get an entry into the bordered/ walled dark savage spirit of the neighbour. The persona is all humanity, "What I was walling in or walling out,/And to whom I was like to give offence." But he cannot ignite the mind of his neighbour towards the possibility of a borderless identity. He is accustomed with his bordered identity and he does not want to set his foot beyond that wall. Shalum has for a few years crossed the border of his black savage identity, but in Frost's poem the neighbour is not at all interested to cross the border set by his ancestor, his father.

"Where the Mind is without Fear"

I now come to one of Tagore's (1861-1941) moving poems "Where the Mind is without Fear …"[8] which in a word is an attestation to his heart's desire for a borderless (both physical and physic) world. He is much concerned for the world being fragmented by "narrow domestic walls" erected by caste prejudices, sectarian violence, irrational thoughts, and poverty of reasoned arguments. Much of Tagore's caustic attack is encapsulated in this adroit phrase "the dreary desert sand of dead habit." Life is aimless, deeply dried with meaningless superstitions and prejudices. It is a dull, dead, cactus land which needs to be regenerated by the supplication of "the clear stream of reason." That is why he is with utmost sincerity praying to the Almighty Father to let his country awake into "that heaven of freedom":

> "Where the mind is without fear and the head is held high
> Where knowledge is free,"…
> "Where the clear stream of reason has not lost its way
> Into the dreary desert sand of dead habit."

Tagore did understand that the questions of race, caste, class, gender, nationality, language make the border markedly visible. But he firmly believes that all these man-made manacles or hindrances are vulnerable. He craves for a world of truth, perfection, and "ever-widening thought and action." Mere thinking is not enough. It has to be translated into a fruitful action. His emphasis on the faculty of human reasoning "the clear stream of reason" indeed champions his humanity. Has Tagore's message been materialised, the earth could have tasted the bliss oozing from the heaven of freedom. The entire poem is a soulful solemn invocation for making a borderless humanity. The poet fervently believes in man's innate goodness and humanity. This poem is a paean for man's eternal desire for love and freedom and justice. Amartya Sen finds here Tagore's "emphasis on reasoning and much celebration of freedom" that can have an "enormously constructive role today [even more]." He further claims:

> Tagore wanted to overcome all these barriers [borders]. He did not quite succeed there. Yet engagement in open-minded and fearless reasoning, so strongly championed by Rabindranath, is no less important today than it was in his own time.[9]

Religious Border

Swami Vivekananda's famous lucid story of the frog in a well, delivered on September 15, 1893 at the World's Parliament of Religions in Chicago focuses primarily on the causes of religious borders. He finds the root cause of disagreement among world's major religions. He asserts:

> I am a Hindu. I am sitting in my own little well and thinking that the whole world is my little well. The Christian sits in his little well and thinks the whole world is his well. The Mohammedan sits in his little well and thinks that is the whole world.[10]

Religious border is not the only border, but it is evidently at the root of other multifarious social borders and its aggravated role behind them cannot be denied. Vivekananda's metaphor of "well" and Tagore's "wall" have the same imperatives. And till date the scenarios have not changed, rather worsen.

Conclusion

Throughout this article I attempt to establish my argument that border remains in the minds of the people. Physical borders are of course there, but border of the spirit is no less important. The poems analysed above succinctly reflect and represent the delicate nuances of the problem of figurative border and its inherent layered complexities. The balloons of "global village," "borderless world" are in every minute punctured by daily lived experiences of communal riots, threats of ethnic cleansing, murder of liberal thinkers, hate speeches, terrorist activities, fanatic hooliganism, continual digital attacks on the women, minorities and Dalits by party appointed dedicated trolls, moral policing, etc. The tension of race, caste, class, gender, nationality, language, sexuality is so pervasive and rampant that the borders of these identities make our hearts asthmatic. People are killed, denied visas to enter into a particular country, barred to enter into a prayer house, targeted, detained and persecuted, loved or hated on the basis of caste, creed, religion, sex, gender, race, and so. Where is Tagore's heaven of freedom? And to achieve that freedom we need the faculty of critical reasoning and not the blessings of *babas* and *pirs*. But the mental border is too rigid to be crossed with ease. It always needs extra energy and will power on the part of the border crosser to cross the periphery of the spirit. And crossing the fence can be both frustrating and rewarding. Henry Louis Gates, Junior's claim that "the challenge of mutual understanding among the world's multifarious cultures will be the single greatest task that we face, after the failure of the world to feed itself" (qtd. in Habib 1)[11] is indeed illuminating to encapsulate the concept of cultural wars with which the world is grappling today. Culture and the construction of the mind are inalienable. Clashes of cultures fundamentally emerge from the clashes of heterogeneous cultural moorings. The idea of a borderless world is a chimera. In our daily actual life too many barriers and borders of caste, creed, religion, race, nationality, language, class, gender, sexuality etc. make our minds' border too rigid and cemented to be crossed. Thus, Syed Amanuddin's vehement protest against bordered identity only reemphasises the heaviness of a bordered exasperated soul:

> i hate hyphens
> the artificial bridges
> between artificial values
> in the name of race religion n language
> i damn all hyphenated minds
> prejudiced offsprings of unenlightened souls
> i denounce all labels n labelmakers[12]

Border is in the minds and until and unless that minds get cleansed and purged we cannot cross the border. The *raison d'être* is spirit is too rigid. We cannot deny "label" for our penchant for psychic stolidity and fixity. We cannot proclaim what Vladimir in Samuel Beckett's *Waiting for Godot* can:

> Pozzo: Who are you?
> Vladimir: *We are men*[13] (112, italic mine)

We are stubbornly habituated to bordered existence, and old habits die hard. Nothing is to be done. "The essential doesn't change (51)," says Vladimir.

Notes

This article was originally titled "Border is in the Mind,"and was first published in *Border, Globalisation and Identity*. Eds. Sukanta Das, et al. UK: Cambridge Scholars Publishing, 2018. ISBN (10): 1-5275-0360-7 ISBN (13): 978-1-5275-0360-1. Here it is modified and updated for the present book.

Works Cited

1. Molnar P. "Territorial and Digital Borders and Migrant Vulnerability Under a Pandemic Crisis." In: Triandafyllidou A. (eds) Migration and Pandemics. 2021. IMISCOE Research Series. Springer, Cham. https://doi.org/10.1007/978-3-030-81210-2_3. Web.
2. Raveendran, P P. "Genealogies of Indian Literature." *Economic and Political Weekly,* June 24. 2006. pp. 2558-2563. Print.
3. Sen, Amartya. 2005. *The Argumentative Indian: Writings on Indian Culture, History and Identity.* New Delhi: Penguin Books, 2005. pp.16-17.Print.
4. Mojtahed-Zadeh, Pirous. "Borders and Territorial Identity: Persian Identity Makes Iran an Empire of the Mind." In *Ashgate Research Companion to Border Studies*, edited by Doris Wastl-Walter, 397. England: Ashgate Publishing, 2011. Print.
5. Anzaldúa, Gloria. *Borderlands: La Frontera.* Accessed 14 November, 2015. https://www.sfu.ca/iirp/documents/Anzaldua%201999.pdf. Web.
6. Freneau, Philip. "The Indian Student or Force of Nature." Accessed 15 November, 2015. http://www.bartleby.com/96/96.html.Web.
7. Frost, Robert. "Mending Wall." *The Norton Anthology of Poetry,* 5th Edition, edited by Margaret Ferguson et al. Print.
8. Tagore, Rabindranath. "Where the Mind is without Fear…" *Literatures of India*, edited by Anna Kurian. Bangalore: Foundation Books, 2008. Print.
9. Sen, Amartya. *The Country of First Boys*, edited by Antara Dev Sen & Pratik Kanjilal. New Delhi: Oxford University Press, 2015.pp. 215-216. Print.
10. *Works of Swami Vivekanand.* Meerut: Tulsi Sahitya Publications, 2015. Print.
11. Habib, M. A. R. *A History of Literary Criticism: From Plato to the Present.* USA, Malden: Blackwell Publishing, 2005. Print.
12. Amanuddin, Syed. "Don't Call Me Indo-Anglian." *Literatures of India,* edited by Anna Kurian. Bangalore: Foundation Books, 2008. Print.
13. Beckett, Samuel. *Waiting for Godot*, edited by Javed Malick. New Delhi: Oxford University Press, 2002. Print.
14. Majumdar, Rabin. *Acharyay Prafullachandra.* Kolkata: Charchapada, 2013. Print.
15. Ozun, Sule Okuroglu and Mustafa Kirca (eds.). *B/Orders Unbound: Marginality, Ethnicity and Identity in Literature.* Peter Lang Edition, 2017. [Kindle Basic] Retrieved from amazon.com.

CHAPTER 2

Crisis of Identity of Bangla Speaking Muslims of West Bengal

Na kisee kee aankh ka nor hoon
Na kisee key dil ka quaraar hoon
Jo kisee key kaam na aa sakey
Main v eek musht-e-ghubaar hoon

Bahadur Shah Zafar (1775-1862)

Bare Words

In West Bengal more than one fourth of population is *Bangla* speaking Muslim. Despite their numerical density and their participation in different socio-economic activities their identity is basically singular, based only on their religious tag. They are solely "Muslims." Their other identities are never acknowledged, and most interestingly often suppressed by the state, popular lazy media, and concocted by unscrupulous religious and political bigots, leading to their age-old abysmal marginality, subjugation and terrible crisis of identity. An unperturbed eerie silence and voicelessness covers them in all fronts of life – economic, political, educational, cultural, occupational, etc. Media hardly cover disturbing stories of their hard manual and menial life. The social and cultural, economic and political exclusions of Bangla speaking Muslims are taken for granted by the Bengali Hindu babus, as if they are "unwanted" and "unwelcome" issues, to be kept within the Muslim periphery. Tey are merely "vote bank" to the political opportunists irrespective of their party colour or ideology. This cheap "vote bank" identity politics and suppression of the Bangla speaking Muslims' political and economic ambitions, willingly if not forcefully, result in their years of dehumanisation and denigration in their homeland and beyond.

The crisis of identity of Bengali Muslims, however, basically emerges from two questions and their consequent subsidiaries. Firstly, being *shudra*-converted, they are treated as impure or *sherek* Muslims by the urban Urdu speaking Muslims. And next, their innate Bengali identity is never acknowledged by their co-brethren elite Bengali Hindu *bhadraloks*. This dichotomy creates a traumatic crisis of identity in the mind of Bangla speaking shudra-converted Muslims of West Bengal. And their absence of representation, or their derogatory presence in literature, art, culture, cinema, media together with the harping on their negative stereotypes such as, barbaric, illiterate, katua, temple destroyers, beef-eaters, women abductors, unhygienic, polygamists, crude, *gaiya* (rustic) and so, adds further vituperation and vulgarisation to their already ghettoised and intolerably wretched identity. I will argue in this article to explore where, how, and why the plural secular identities of Bengali Muslims are suppressed with skewed subtlety. I also try to challenge Bengali Muslims' singular *burkha, topi, dari* identity which is gnawing at their marrow at present day India.

The Invariable Fallacy

Amartya Sen in his *Identity and Violence* (2006) penetrates with conviction the global problem of identity politics and its vicious aftermath on our thought processes thus:

> Indeed, many of the conflicts and barbarities in the world are sustained through the illusion of a unique and choiceless identity. The art of constructing hatred takes the form of invoking the magical power of some allegedly predominant identity that drowns other affiliations and in a conveniently bellicose form can also overpower any human sympathy or natural kindness that we may normally have. The result can be homespun elemental violence, or globally artful violence and terrorism.

In fact, a major source of potential conflict in the contemporary world is the presumption that people can be uniquely categorised based on religion or culture. The implicit belief in the overarching power of a singular classification can make the world thoroughly inflammable. A uniquely divisive view goes not only against the old-fashioned belief that all human beings are much the same but also against the less discussed and much more plausible understanding that we are diversely different. The world is frequently taken to be a collection of religions (or of "civilisations" or "cultures"), ignoring the other identities that people have and value, involving class, gender, profession, language, science, morals, and politics. This unique divisiveness is much more confrontational than the universe of plural and diverse classifications that shape the world in which we actually live. The reductionism of high theory can make a major contribution, often inadvertently, to the violence of low politics.[1]

The overemphasis on the religious identity of Bangla speaking Muslims of West Bengal "drowns" their several other important identities – Bengali, residential, economic, professional, physical, sartorial, educational, and many more. Indeed, continuous harping on their religious or cultural identity has been a much recognised phenomenon. On and off some promises of *madrasas*, *Imam Bhatas,* "Urdu Academies," and "Haj Houses" are doled out to them. By the use of such religious tokenism no material progress of Bengali Muslims has been done. And it can be convincingly argued that their *nun ante panta furai* or *din ana din khaoya* (hand to mouth living) lives will never have a materialistic fillip by indulging in such burqua-topi-dari elements by the populist political leaders . Though the treatment of Bengali Muslims as solely "Muslims" and nothing else has not yet resulted in any form of violence, it has certainly jeopardised their potency of excellence in different spheres of practical life. The act of foregrounding their singular choiceless religious identity by downplaying their other plural heterogeneous identities is itself a gross violence and misappropriation of truth and reasoning and the denial of their hard and harsh existential life.

Na Gharka Na Ghatka

The crisis of identity of Bangla speaking Muslims of West Bengal originates firstly from the prevalent contested confusion of their origin. Bengali Muslims are often alleged to be the descendants of marauding foreign Central Asian Muslims. This allegation bereft of any truth is an imposed onslaught on the root of the indigenous Muslims of Bengal. Being *shudra*-converted, they are treated as impure or *sherek* Muslims by the urban Urdu speaking Muslims. They are *namae musolman* (Muslim only by name). They are *roja namaj na koriya* (qtd. in "Bongosahitye Hindu-Mussolman") Muslims.[2] Promoth Choudhury humourously equates non-Bengali Muslims as caste Hindus and the *desi* Muslims like *Jola, Gola, Kosai, Potuya, Tirkor, Kabari* etc. as Hindu shudras, belonging to the lowest rung of the societal ladder. So, both to the non-Bengali Muslims and the Bengali Hindu bhadraloks there has been a sustained and amazingly agreed belief in the "low" status of Bangla speaking Muslims. Bengali Muslims cannot speak Urdu or Arabic, commonly considered to be the sacred medium of Muslim cultural ethos and ideologies. They are, thus, assumed with a certain certitude that their cultural wells have dried up, as they are removed from the daily resurgent global waves of Arabic and Urdu religious dialogues, discourses or pure texts. They are somewhat "tainted" Muslims as their daily dealings are not as urbane and sophisticated as that of the non-Bengali Muslims. They are allegedly "hinduised" Muslims. Citing a host of western and South Asian scholars like Richard Eaton, Imtiaz Ahmed, Rafiuddin Ahmed, Francis Robinson and others Alefiya Tundawala sums up the problem of Bengali Muslims' painful difficulty in cultural assimilation process with "pure" Islam when she says that the Bengali Muslim mass having no access to the appropriate and authentic Islamic lifestyle, language and culture which are essential for the cultivation of a pure Islamic identity, face a difficulty to be linked with correct Islamic traditions. They continue to remain enclosed within the un-Islamic local traditions and affiliations which are generally thought to be the "debasement of the pristine purity of Islam."[3] The Bengali Muslims having both an "inextricable blend of foreign and indigenous elements" have demonstrated "the roots of cleavage and dualism between the opposite pulls of an exclusive Islamic identity with its extra-territorial implications and of local Bengali socio-cultural traditions."[4] The traces and remnants of the faiths of their ancestors staunchly linger on them still. They could not distance themselves from their local colour, ethnic and cultural milieu which allegedly makes them hinduised Muslims. This line of argument alienates and identifies the West Bengal Bengali Muslims as "other" Muslims in their own homeland and in the territories of global Islamic contours.

The question of "Bengali" identity of the Bangla speaking Muslims of West Bengal paves the rugged path of a highly contested territory too. There is no culture of speaking Urdu or Arabic in rural Bengali Muslim households. They cannot even speak pure "shantipuri" Bangla or the standard Bangla accepted and taught at educational institutions. A recent exclusive study on the Muslims of West Bengal (SNAP Report 2016) finds that more than 90 percent of the rural Muslims [in West Bengal] are Bangla-speaking, and only a tiny section reported Urdu to be their mother tongue. This sharply contrasts with a notion prevalent even among the literati of the urban areas that Muslims are mostly Urdu speaking.[5] "...some members of the urban 'mainstream' Bengali elites construct an idea about the Muslims which takes their religious affinity as their singular identity, completely missing all other identities the strongest among which is their being *Bangali*.[6] And such bizarre statements like "*tora ki bariteo Bangla bolis*," or "*toder barite ki Banglar chol ache*?" (Do you speak Bangla at home?) from our Hindu friends and acquaintances are daily circulated in our multiple transactions of everyday life. Among the Hindu Bengali cultural bhadraloks and the general mass, the Bangla speaking Muslims are identified as inferior "Muslims" only. Their linguistic and ethnic identities are always under their calculated questioning gaze and, hence, they suffer a painful omission in the media and cultural discourses of daily Bengali life. In spite of having "shared" homes and habits, dress and food, flora and fauna, hills and plains, rivers and waterways, hopes and dreams and destiny, they are not the "same." They are "same but not the same" because the much unwanted weightage is ascribed to their solitary religious or cultural identity, forgetting their age old inseparable practices of local language and syncretic culture. Indeed, their multiple socio-economic identities (poor, rural, landless labourer, migrant labourers to other Indian cities and suburbs etc.) are willingly negated. This calculative move leads to the phenomenon of the ghettoized existence of Bangla speaking Muslims. And it is most singularly encapsulated in the frenzied form of a digestive "religiously identical capsule."

The prevalent assumption is that a Muslim is a Muslim, as if, she cannot have other identities based on other secular parameters like language, region, profession, economy, habitation etc. And the identity of innate *Bengaliness* or *bangalitto* of Bangla speaking Muslims of West Bengal is nullified with a mechanistic and surreptitious design. In fact, there is a sustained source of textual and non-textual disbeliefs to this lucid and much needed linguistic recognition of Bengali Muslims. In this context of identity crisis of Bengali Muslims, however, Sunil Gangopadhyay's holistic comment is deeply enlightening:

> *Kolkata shohorer hindura bivinno peshay obangali musolmander dekhe ovostho bole hotat kono nobagoto musolmanke dekhe bole felen, oi lokti musolman na bangali? Ei obodhera janenna je uvoy bongo miliye banglavashider modhey musolmanrai onek beshi sonkhyagoristho. Itihaser dik diye dekhte gele, sultani amolei prothom bangla vasha dana bedhe othe. British amoleo jokhon sikshito hindu bangalira ingrejite tubri fataten, tokhon bidhansovai musolman sodosyarai prothom bangla vashai Vashon debar dabi tolen.*[7] (The Hindus of Kolkata, habituated in seeing non-Bengali Muslims living in the city, when come across a Bengali Muslim, they often ask him if he is a Musilm or Bangali. They don't understand that the number of Bangla speaking Muslims taking Bangaldesh and West Bengal together far exceed the Bengali Hindus. From the historical point of view it is in the time of Sultanate that Bangla as a separate language began to emerge. In the British period when the Bengali Hindus cackled in the Assembly House in sophisticated English, it is the the Bengali Muslim legislative members who demanded first to introduce Bangla as the medium of legislative discourses.)

Thus, Gangopadhyay unlike the common and popular mistaken societal and cultural assumption asserts with a deep poignancy the unblemished, unsullied and inherent *bangalitto* of Bangla speaking Muslims of both Bangladesh and West Bengal.

What remains unsaid till is that the pan-Islamic theoreticians with their continuous emphasis on "pure" and "correct" Islam have further played a disparaging role in aggravating the identity crisis of Bangla speaking Muslims. The path of embracing correct Islam by emphasising on non-local identity slowly but steadily has eroded all forms of local beliefs and myths and practices from Bengali Muslim life. Under the bewitching spell of village maulvis and mullahs' spirit of global Islamism *and* their constant harping on Urdu or Arabic "high" culture, the village Muslims apprehensively begin to shed their age old inalienable habits and customs. They begin to dispossess everything local and Bengali: local names, language, dress, habits, and traditions. The celebrated and much acclaimed Rafiuddin Ahmed summarises this painful and schematic cultural transformational onslaught and the consequent dilemma of crisis of identity of Bangla speaking Muslims thus:

> The rural masses were victims of painful cultural conflict. The constant harping on extraterritorial links created in their minds a vague, yet persistent, notion that perhaps most, if not all, Muslims were alien to Bengal. Bengal to them thus became a non-Muslim land. The consequent crisis of identity was reflected in a curious distinction: now the Hindus alone were 'Bengalis', the Muslims being only 'Muslims', liberated from all local ethnic affiliations. This odd dichotomy became a part of the Bengali Hindu vocabulary as well.[8]

Amadpur: The Big Exclusion

Now with the help of a photograph book I attempt to show the process of "distancing" Bengali Muslims from the greater and bigger cultural picture of a typical Bengali life, the space where entry of Muslims is punitively unwanted or forbidden. According to the Census 2011 the Memari block I under Bardhaman district of West Bengal has 79 per cent Hindu and 18.3 per cent Muslim population and the rest are Christians, Sikhs, Buddhist, Jain and others. (SNAP 147). The Mumbai based photographer Chirodeep Chaudhuri has photographed his ancestral village [Amadpur under Memari I] in Bengal for twelve years, visiting annually during the festival of Durga pujo," as the jacket of his *A Village in Bengal: Photographs and An Essay* (2012) confirms. The photographer has done a wonderful job by "selling" the village with his mesmerising photographs. The book contains more than ninety photographs of which seventeen or so are of idyllic rural scenes with paddy fields, village paths with cattle, fishermen catching fishes, preparation of fields for sowing seeds, bamboos' withered foliages heaped as a soft bed on the soil on which a mother and her child are sleeping on a homespun *chatai* made of dry date leaves, while yonder the cattle grazing on pasture. Indeed, each picture is a powerful book on Bengal rural life. But here is also a great miss perhaps to make the project a perfectly "Bengali" [Hindu] one, and to "sell" it smoothly to the civilised as if any harsh scene from rural Bengali Muslim life with ploughing *lungi* clad ill fed farmers will be an eyesore to the beautification of the pristine images of "Zamindari" and "elite" Bengali Hindu sensibilities with images of Durga pujo, Khepa Kali, Radha Madhob Temple, and other moribund cultural elitism. Only the penultimate photograph with a lungi clad villager with his homebound goats and a mid-photograph displaying the daily fish and meat bazaar can be assumed with pain and difficulty to have the local touch of the rugged and poor rural Bengal Muslim peasant life.

A Bengal village life without the covert or overt portrayals of rural Muslim poor peasants and their innate cultural affinities and local practices is unimaginable and unthinkable. It can only be possible to the tourist photographers like Chaudhuris to whom "Amadpur was exotica." And rural Bengal was "pretty exotic with its mud huts, swaying palm trees, bullock carts, ponds, paddy fields, and open skies, a Durgo pujo in progress inside the house of an old zamindar family."[9] Almost three-fourth of Chaudhuri's photographs are heavily tinged with elite Hindu ritual items – zaminadri dalan with elderly *babus* in spotless dhotis and panjabis, immersion of Durga pujo with much fanfare, evening *aaroti* before maa Durga, drawing intricately designed *alpona* on the floor, blowing conches with *uludhoni* by domestic housewives wearing vermillion and *sakhas and saris*, beatings of dhols, purohits with holy threads reading holy books or papers, burning of multiple clay-made oil lamps, dilapidated ancient temples by the side of the zaminadari dighi, and so on. This Amadpur village the name of which is suggestive of conveying the message of the possibility of having Muslim inhabitants is denied an entry to Chaudhuri's intentionally "made" elite project on Bengal representation. The village contains not a single picture of Bangla speaking Muslims with *topi*, *dari*, thatched mosques or madrasas, or any Islamic signs. Neither has it portrayed poor Muslim peasants or labourers with his bullock carts, or sowing fields. They are uprooted from their village Amadpur by the biased lens of exotic Chaudhuri. But he cannot be blamed for his "miscarriage" of Bengal Muslims from his ambitious project because of his candid recognition that Amadpur has never been his home, "Amadpur isn't home to me. In fact, even Kolkata is not. Amadpur isn't home even to my father. It never was." He is exactly a travel agent who doesn't have the inner eye to soak the tears and sorrows of a remote village life of common multitude. He is a Durga pujo tourist enthusiast to grasp the exotic and idyllic Amadpur of zamindar Choudhuris:

> Amadpur – placid through the year – experience a wave of excitement in the days leading to the Pujo. In the Chaudhuri household, there is a sudden flurry. Mattresses and pillows are aired, utensils come out of cupboards and are washed and furniture is dusted in anticipation of the family's arrival. After that, the five days of the festival are a meandering adda session. Endless cups of tea are downed. Morning passes into afternoon debating the virtues of Mercurochrome over tincture of iodine or trying round up cousins to go for a swim in the dighi.[10]

This painted idyllic Amadpur with its exclusive exclusion of "other" cultures and the conscious negation of the ways of their different lives is an attestation to the hegemonic cultural tyranny over the plurality and heterogeneity of Bengali mass. This exhilaration of one culture and the schematic annihilation of others in art, literature, media, photography, cinema, and public discourses have also been playing a crucial destructive role in the marginalisation of others leading to their painful and writhing crisis of identity. And the Bangla speaking Muslims of West Bengal are not immune from these crude and savage onslaughts from its opportunistic, dishonest and selfish intellectual or cultural predators.

Another interesting example of Bengal's exclusionary cultural project is given by Moumita Alam in her recent article "Exclusion of Muslim women writers in West Bengal Textbooks." She writes:

> Only Begum Rokeya, Sufia Kamal have got some attention. The writings of Khayarennesa, M Rahaman (to whom Kazi Nazrul Islam dedicated his poem '*Bisher Banxi*') , M Fatema Khanam, Nurunnesa Khatun (she is considered the first Muslim novelist of Bengal) , Sayeda Khatun (wrote two novels: '*Niyantrita*' and '*Maranbaran*'), Fazlitunnesa, Mahamuda Khatun Siddiqua, Razia Khatun Choudhury, Samusnnehar Mahamud, have remained forgotten from our academic discourse, our textbooks. Their contribution to literary genres was not less than their Hindu sisters. But a patriarchal, religious framework guiding in designing curriculum have pushed them to the dungeon of oblivion.

Representation and Reality

Print, electronic and social media, literature and art, as earlier stated, are playing a disparaging role in creating a severe crisis of identity for Bengali Muslims. They are so lazy and facile that they miserably fail to investigate the everyday hard naked reality faced by Bengali Muslim peasants. Their stereotypical representation of Muslims includes such obnoxious and derogatory terms as terrorists, beef-eaters, invaders, oppressors, barbaric, uncivilised, anti-national, illiterate, ignorant, poor, unhygenic, drug-traffickers, burglers, and so. It is a sheer and vulgar misrepresentation of the true identity of Bengali Muslims. Bengali Muslims may be poor and uneducated, but most of the other insulting terms are forcibly and purposely imposed on to to dehumanise and denigrate their holistic rural and poor status. Their sordid socio-economic backwardness and their local cultural identities are poorly reflected in Bengali art, literature, journalistic writing, media, or in the intellectual public debates and discourses of everyday Bengali life. Bengali Muslims earn their livelihood by the sweat of their brow. They are God's own men. They do multifarious manual and servile jobs. They are farmers, rickshaw-pullers, tailors, vegetable-sellers, masons, labourers, biri-workers, village-vendors, poor, meek mass. Why are Bengali Muslims being misrepresented? The reason is the indulgence in the politics of writings or representations by so called intellectuals, journalists, media anchors. Nirad C. Chaudhuri, who claims to be an astute Bengali bhadralok and who hails from East Bengal (Bangladesh) spreads venom and vituperation against Muslims when he utters that "the Muslims had once ruled and oppressed us, that they spread their religion with the Koran in one hand and the sword in the other, that the Muslim rulers had abducted our women, destroyed our temples, polluted our sacred places" (qtd. in Ahmed, 127).[11] His pejorative assessment of Muslims or his line of vicious and vilifying thoughts is more or less shared and supported by Hindus in general. But he consciously forgets that his neighbouring poor rural peasant Bengali Muslims who eke out a living by ploughing a plot of land or by the work of their bodies, have nothing to do with such horrendous atrocities. He refuses to admit their simple rural farming life because of wearing opaque glasses. Muslim subaltern mass and the Muslim rulers cannot be equated as abominable force. Barring a few exceptions all Hindu historiographers, litterateurs have recurrently painted Muslims with derision and animosity and pollution. Chaudhuri, however, condescendingly came to recognise the true identity of Bengali Muslims with adequate reason and clarity of thought when he uttered:

> I was quite familiar with the normal features and expression of the peasants [Bengali Muslims]. I always saw them in large numbers on the two weekly market days we had at Kishorganj, once when they went towards the bazaar with the heavy load, and again in the evening when they returned home chatting and halooing.[12]

This schematic dichotomy of Bengali Muslims of what they actually are and how are they being represented in variegated cultural studies is a serious hindrance to the holistic and reasoned recognition of their identity as "pichiye pora" (backward) in educational, economic, social and cultural fronts. And what culminates their crisis of identity is a lack or apathy to view the Muslims from not a singular religious perspective but from a multidimensional socio-economic parameters. The inadequacy of informed engagement has not only had its effect on the continually depressed socio-economic status of the Muslims of West Bengal, but also on the imagination of the Muslim identity that is being [invariably] framed solely on religious line, ignoring multiple other facets of their lives.[13]

The crisis of identity of Bengali Muslims was not because of being Bengali and Muslim. It is the result of a long historical process. And the role of Bengali Renaissance Hindu intellectuals like Bankim Chandra and others in the subjugation of Bengali Muslim identity cannot be denied. *Unish shotoker renesha bole je kothati procholito aache se kothati bivromattok. Eder karo abedon-e nimnborner occhut hindu somajer proti chilo na, eder abedon kolkatar baire bangladesher somogro onchole prosarito chilo na, ebong musolman somaj eder chintay sompuronovabe onuposthit chilo.* (What was known and thought as 19th century Bengali Renaissance was indeed a confusion. Bengali Renaissance intellectuals were Kolkata centric. Their ideas could not spread beyond Kolkata. And the lowly Hindus were hardly influenced by them. And the Bengali Muslim society was completely absent in their thoughts.)[14]

Conclusion

The crisis of identity of Bengali Muslims of West Bengal, thus, basically emerges from two or three main twisted fronts and its consequent subsidiary affiliations. Firstly, in one hand, being *shudra*-converted, and having a mixture of foreign and indigenous elements in popular habits and beliefs, they are historically in the habit of being treated as impure or *sherek* or debased Muslims by the urbane Urdu speaking Muslims and the majority Bengali Hindus. On the other, to our greatest surprise and bewilderment we see that Bengali Muslims are perennially identified under the garb of their solitary "religious" or what I call as "burkha-topi-dari" identity. The continuous emphasis on this choiceless identity is much avowed and adored by the dishonest, power-hungry, opportunistic, corrupt, and cowed political party bossess of variegated shades and intelligentsia of myriad hue of West Bengal. And next, their innate contiguous Bengali identity is never duly or even perfunctorily acknowledged by their co-brethren elite "cultural" Bengali majority Hindus and their life-enhancing literatures, art, journalism and media. This designed and doctored dichotomy together with their cultural dilemma manufactured by Mullahs' over emphasis on extraterritorial authentic Islamic ways of life create a traumatic crisis of identity for Bangla speaking shudra-converted indigenous Muslims of West Bengal. And their absence of potentially redolent representations or their nauseating presence of vulgar and shocking representations in literature, art, culture, cinema, media together with the unbridled harpings on their negative stereotypical imposed identities such as, barbaric, illiterate, temple destroyers, beef-eaters, women abductors, unhygienic, polygamists, child producing machines, *katua*, *nere,* crude, *gaiya* etc. add further vituperation and vulgarisation to their already ghettoised, marginalised, traumatised, and intolerably wretched identity in their land of hope and desire, remorse and sorrow, pride and sacrifice, love and dream and death.

Notes

This article, originally titled, "Crisis of Identity in 'Bangla' Speaking Muslims of West Bengal: An Overview" was first published in *Perspectives: A Collection of Essays on Language, Ethnicity and Identity*, Eds. R Mohan & M Choudhury.

Tinsukia (Assam): Tinsukia College, Dept. of English, 2018. ISBN 93 80247-79-3. Print. It is revised and enlarged for the present book.

Works Cited

1. Sen, Amartya. "The Preface." *Identity and Violence: The Illusion of Destiny*. Penguin Books, 2006. [Kindle Edition]. Retrieved from Amazon.com.
2. Choudhury, Promoth. "Bongosahitye Hindu-Mussolman." *Masik Bosumoti*. 1331 bangla sal. N list programme, Falakata College, Accessed 13 Dec. 2016. <http//www.southasiaarchive.com/Content/sarf.120001/200026/010>. Web.
3. Tundawla, Alefiya. "Multiple Representations of Muslimhood in West Bengal: Identity Construction Through Literature." *South Asia Research*, Vol.32 (2): 139-163. 2012. Print.
4. Ibid. pp. 139-163.
5. "Introduction". *Living Reality of Muslims in West Bengal: A Report*. Kolkata: Association SNAP and Guidance Guild in association with Pratichi Institute, 2016. p. 6. Print.
6. Ibid. p.6.
7. Gangopadhyay, Sunil. *Ami Ki Bangali*. Kolkata: Potrobharoti, 2015. pp. 205-206. Print.
8. Ahmed, Rafiuddin. *The Bengal Muslims 1871-1906: A Quest for Identity*. Delhi: Oxford University Press, 1996. pp. 111-112. Print.
9. Chaudhuri, Chirodeep. "Amadpur and me," In *A Village in Bengal: Photographs and An Essay*. India: Picador, 2012. n.p. Print.
10. Ibid.n.p.
11. Ahmed, Rafiuddin. *The Bengal Muslims 1871-1906: A Quest for Identity*. Delhi: Oxford University Press, 1996. Print.
12. Nirad C. Chaudhuri. *Autobiography of an Unknown Indian*. Ahmedabad: Jaico Publishing House, 2013. p.38. Print.
13. "Introduction." *Living Reality of Muslims in west Bengal: A Report*. Kolkata: Association SNAP and Guidance Guild in association with Pratichi Institute, 2016. p. 3. Print.
14. Mukul, M. R. Akhtar. *Kolkata Kendrik Budhijibi*. Dhaka: Ananya, 2014. p. 15. Print.
15. Alam, Moumita. "Exclusion of Muslim women writers in West Bengal Textbooks." Available at https://peoplesreview.in/women/2021/ 03/exclusion-of-muslim-women-writers-in-west-bengals-textbooks/ Accessed June 24, 2022.

CHAPTER 3

Bengali Muslims of West Bengal: Writing, Representation and Experience

> Enlightened society is a finite complex of centre and margins, opposed to one another. The outside remains what it was in Kant: unknowable, in the shadow of silence, mute, and beyond the reaches of enlightenment.
>
> Ajit Chaudhury, et al., *margin of margin* (2011)

Bare Words

Numerically of every four people of West Bengal one is a Bengali Muslim. Despite their numerical density and active participation in different socio-economic activities their identity is basically singular, based only on their religious affiliation. They are solely "Muslims." Many other identities based on their language, profession, education, economic condition or residential status is never acknowledged. The stereotypical representation of Muslims includes such obnoxious and derogatory and humiliating terms as "terrorists," "polygamists," "katua," "beef-eaters," "invaders," "oppressors," "barbaric," "uncivilised," "anti-national," "illiterate," "ignorant," "poor," "unhygienic," "drug-traffickers," "burglars," "hate makers," "cattle-thieves" and what not. It is a gross vulgar misrepresentation of the identity and experience of Indian Muslims in general and Bengali Muslims in particular. Bangla speaking Muslims of West Bengal are of course poor and uneducated, but most of the other derogatory terms are forcibly applied resulting in their years of pain and pathos, dishonour, dehumanisation and denigration. The true identity of Bengali Muslims is never reflected in Bangla art, literature, journalistic writing, media, or even in the public discourses of everyday life. They earn their livelihood by the sweat of their brow. They do "manual and menial jobs." They are farmers, daily labourers. They are hands at kilns and farms and factories. They are rickshaw-pullers, toto-tuktuk-drivers, tailors, vegetable-sellers, masons, bidi-workers, village-vendors, leather-goods makers, and so on. Only 13 per cent of Muslims have regular salaried jobs in West Bengal, while the corresponding figure for India is 22.1 per cent. Around 34.3 per cent of Muslims in West Bengal work as casual workers, while the figure for India is around 26 per cent. In other words, compared with the rest of India, greater numbers of Muslims are engaged in precarious casual employment or self-employment in West Bengal. As a result, the earnings of Muslims in West Bengal are lower than those of Muslims of other states.They are voiceless backwood mass scattered in different size throughout the hinterland of all the districts of West Bengal. They are poor, ill-housed, ill-clad, ill-fed, meek people with hearts of pure gold. They are hard-working, resilient and embrace woe and evil alike in the transaction of everyday odd life. They are, however, kind and hospitable to the Hindu guests and neighbours, and bereft of any kind of superstitions or prejudices found in abundance among the caste Hindus of Bengal. And most importantly, they cannot speak Urdu or Arabic, languages thought to be the sacred medium of Muslim cultural ethos. They speak in rural Bangla dialects, and the pronunciation and intonation of which are markedly different from the *Shantipuri Bangla,* spoken by the Bengali Hindu *bhadralok* elites. Through this article I want to stress on the wretched conditions of Benagli Muslims. I also attempt to unfold the layered avenues whereby Bengali Muslims are being deliberately misrepresented and their unique identity and daily raw living experiences being subjugated by the politics of pen resulting in their inerasable humiliation, excruciating psychic pain and agony and their lifelong denial, deprivation, dehumanisation, and even death.

Who are Bengali Muslims?

Let us ask a simple question. Who are "Bengali Muslims?" Does it mean all the Muslims living in West Bengal? I use the term to refer only to all the Bangla speaking Muslims of West Bengal. Are they foreigner, or descendents of Emperor Babur as often alleged by non-Muslims? Is there any deeper relation, barring religious tokenism, among Bangla speaking Muslims and UP, Tamil, Nepali, Syrian, Arabian, Pakistani, Afghanistani, Palestinian, Indonesian, Kashmiri or say Egyptian Muslims? There is absolutely nothing in common among these world Muslim variants. It is further interesting to note that variants among the Muslims even in India are inter-state, intra-state, inter-district, intra-district, and so on and forth, depending on the economic and social structure of the region, and its climate, major land forms, and biodiversity. For example, the Bengali Sheikhs have nothing in common with Arabian Sheikhs' wealth, status and luxury. A few Bengali Sheikhs do also the job of a scavenger in Arabian Sheikhs' home or office for a few *rials*. Neither the Indian Muslims nor the Bengali Muslims are a homogenous stock. Bengali Muslims are Bengali at the core as that of the Bengali Hindu *babus*. They are the son of the soil, born here and will die here. They are *shudra* converted because of Brahmanic tyranny as many texts and history itself is a witness to this often willingly forgotten fact.[1] They are culturally, socially, financially excluded from the so called mainstream "bhadralok" Hindu "babus." They are "pichieye para" (backward) underprivileged base mass of rural folk. They are the cheap labourers of West Bengal. I reiterate "Bengali Muslim" here does neither refer to all the Muslim inhabitants of West Bengal, nor the Bangladeshi Muslim whose mother tongue is Bangla. The term is strictly applied only to the Bangla speaking Muslims living in the state of West Bengal. They speak Bangla and follow Islam. That is why they are called "Bengali Muslim," or *banglavashi musalman*.

Against Stereotypical clichés

1. Bengali Muslims cannot speak Urdu. They speak only local Bengali dialects and the intonation of which makes the urban Bengali Hindu elites often utter "gaiya voot," (rustic).
2. Bengali Muslims are not giving births like street dogs, as often alleged. "Unlike the socially constructed belief that there is 'Muslim population explosion,' the recent Census data [2011] show a decreasing trend in growth among the Muslim population across the state.[2]
3. The students of Bengali Muslim households are not madrasa-centric. Their enrolment in public school and colleges are increasing day by day. Govornment's apathy to the educational and infrastructural development in highly Muslim concentrated districts, blocks is as clear as daylight. "That the rate of enrolment in schools was very high in the areas with Muslim preponderence clearly showed that not only they were not averse to moden education but also that there was a clear lack of educational infrastructure in those areas."[3]

4. "Khariji" madrasas with a tin or thatch roof, a few broken chairs, tables and benches, no toilets or supply of running water, a few half-naked, emaciated Muslim boys and girls from poor households who call their master not "sir" but "*chhaarr*" can never be the sponsors of terrorism or "hub of terror" as alleged by self-defeating Hindu babus. If one is human and sane, I am quite sure, that seeing such sorry and pathetic conditions of the remote Khariji madrasas in the villages of West Bengal one must be shocked.
5. Bengali Muslims are not responsible for the destruction of Hindu temples, and they cannot marry a Hindu girl by force judjing their "nun ante panta furai" (hand to mouth) condition. Anisujamman wrote that during Bengal Renaissance a revival of Hinduism based on ancient Hindu texts and scriptures took place. Its overemphasis on past glory of Hinduism and *Bharat* made the Bengali Hindus see the Indian medieval history as shameful, repulsive, "an age of darkness." And the wrath naturally fell on the foreign Muslims who came to India as destroyers and plunders. And most surprisingly they immediately forget to differentiate the shudra-converted indigenous Bengali Muslims and the power-hungry marauding foreign Muslims.[4]

So there are reasons to be proud as a Bengali Muslim. Unlike the central Asian Aryans, the Bengali speaking Muslims can take pride in their identity as sons of the soil, indigenous, truthful and grateful to their own land and culture. But instead of tasting power and wealth they are marginalised in literature, media, and society and by the Hinduized public and private discourses of daily life. For example, if a suicide attack takes place in Syria, Kabul, Islamabad, Paris or Spain, media and our non-Muslim "close" neighbours become agog with a new zeal for Muslim bashing in Bengal. And the Bengali Muslims often become available soft target of the popular Hindu rage, anger and hatred and, thus, they suffer silent humiliation and mortification though they are in reality far away from any misdeeds happening across the world in the name of Islam.

Writing, Representation and Reality

Iswar Chandra Gupta, Bankim Chandra Chattopadhyay, Nabinchandra Sen, Nirad Chandra Chaudhuri, Hem Chandra Sen, to name only a few Bengali literati, have been well known for anti-

Muslim writing or Muslim bashing. Nirad C. Chaudhuri, who claims to be an astute Bengali bhadralok and who hails from East Bengal (Bangladesh) spreads venom and vituperation against Muslims when he utters that "the Muslims had once ruled and oppressed us, that they spread their religion with the Koran in one hand and the sword in the other, that the Muslim rulers had abducted our women, destroyed our temples, polluted our sacred places" (qtd. in Ahmed, 127).[5] His pejorative assessment of Muslims or his acrid line of thoughts as to his Muslim neighbours is more or less shared and supported by Hindu intellectuals in general. But he consciously forgets that his neighbouring poor rural peasant Bengal Muslims who eke out a living by ploughing a plot of land have nothing to do with such vilifying atrocities. He refuses to admit their simple rural farming life because of wearing Hindu opaque glasses. Muslim bashing has, thus, been an acknowledged phenomenon in literature by Nirad Chaudhuri and his cohorts.

Along with literature print elctronic and social media are playing a disparaging role leading to the extreme marginalisation of Bengali Muslims further. They are so lazy and one-sided that they fail to investigate the every day hard reality faced by Bengali Muslims in their multiple transactions of daily life. Their stereotypical representation of Muslims is vulgar misrepresentation of the true identity of Bengali Muslims. Bengali Muslims may be "poor" and "illiterate," but most of the other terms are forcibly applied to them to dehumanise and denigrate their holistic status. The true identity of Bengali Muslims is never reflected in Bengali art, literature, journalistic writing, media, and the educated public discourse of everyday Bengali life. Bengali Muslims earn their livelihood by the sweat of their brow. Why are Bengali Muslims being misrepresented? The reason behind is the indulgence in the politics of writing/ representation by so called intellectuals, journalists, media anchors, bloggers for some vested interests. The moot point is that as the most of Bengali Muslims are landless illiterate labourers, a powerless poor mass, they are unable to represent themselves. They must be represented and of course with a tinge of malice, hatred and vituperation in order to make them Saidian "other."

Socio-Economic Condition and Politics

Let us have a cursory look at Sabir Ahmed's report on Muslims of West Bengal published in *The Anando Bazaar Patrika*. The report is a tip of an iceberg, and most important aspect of it that it does not separately delineate the status of the Bengali speaking Muslims. However, the report is an eye-opener to the pathetic socio-economic condition of the Muslims of West Bengal.

State Govt. Employee	
Year	**Percentage of Muslim Employee**
2007	2.1 (in higher ranks 4.7)
2015	5.47

Kolkata Police	
Year	**Percentage of Muslim Employee**
2007	9.13
2015	9.44

Kolkata Municipality	
Year	**Percentage of Muslim Employee**
2007	4.47
2015	4.79

These statistical records, though only suggestive, reflect only the poor sordid condition of West Bengal Muslims in the area of Government employment.[6] In villages 80 percent Muslims' monthly income is below Rs.5000, whereas in the urban areas the percent is 65. Jeremy Seabrook and Imran Ahmed Siddiqui comment:

> Muslims are not a matter of concern for the State unless they disturb or disrupt the existing order. It is only when they try to turn their eyes on wealth and power their activities become the interest of the State. If Muslims destruct one another it is of nobody's concern. The word 'Muslim' has become synonymous with poverty and crime. They are antisocial elements. They will find a redressal mechanism for their cause.[7]

The State Government's lackadaisical attitude towards the development of Muslims is quite evident. Muslims are not a matter of serious introspection, and the maintenance of the status quo of their marginality in all public spheres seems to be desirable. The problem arises when the Muslims try to assert their demands for equal rights as citizens by highlighting their multiple parameters of backwardness. They are then invariably harassed in the name of criminal or terrorist activities or other antisocial behaviours. All the political parties irrespective of their creed and colour are in the habit of claiming that unlike the other Indian states Muslims in Bengal live in security and peace. At least there is no fear of riots and other communal fumes and flares. The writing on the back cover of the book *people without history: india's muslim ghettos* unmasks the masks of political shrudeness and dishonesty of Bengal leaders:

> Kolkata's Muslims live in a city that for 33 years was governed by the Communist Party of India [Marxist]. It has been the proudest boast of the Communists that they have been guided by a secular ideology, and that as a result, Muslims in West Bengal have been spared the excesses of communalists in Gujrat, Maharastra, Orissa and elsewhere.[8]

Muslims in Bengal need not freedom from the pain of hunger and poverty, but freedom from communalism! Bengali Muslims belong to the lowest rung of any societal parameter, spending their inner resources and bodily strength to eke out a bare living. They are T. S. Eliot's hollow men, in the literal sense, "Leaning together/ Headpiece filled with straw" without hope of being nearer to "death's dream kingdom." Is the fear of communalism more overpowering than their recalcitrant fear of daily hunger and poverty?

There is a serious dearth of able and decisive Bengali Muslim political leaders in Bengal politics. Bengali Muslim leaders are "item" leaders, used and abused, bereft of any potency of their own. "...the pre-dominantly rural and socio-economically backward status of the Muslims has resulted in their poor representation in the social platforms – academic, political, cultural and so on, and this has created sort of social ignorance about the Muslims."[9]

Saliency of Bengali Muslims

The Bengali Muslims embrace Islam as an escapade in the hope of not being inflicted inhuman tyranny by the Brahmins further. But by mere conversion they cannot forsake their earlier ethnicity, indigenous language and culture. Thus, though in religious practices they follow Islam, their inherent Bengali identity remains the same. And this ethnic Bengali identity makes them markedly different from all the major practitioners of world Islam.

The rural Benagli Muslims are generally thought to be weak and meek as compared to non-Bengali Muslims. They are taken as inferior *sherek* Muslims because of their history of origin which is entirely different from that of the non-Bengali urban Muslims. My friends and acquaintances' casual remarks like, "you are not 'aggressive' like the Bihari Muslims" attest to the said claim. And I am witness to such claim during a weekend visit to home from my working place Falakata. I was in Teesta Torsha. When the train stopped at Kishanganj, a group of ill fed, dwarf Bengali Muslims, all wearing either *lungi* or pajamas, *topis* and ruffled soiled *panjabis* with rubber or plastic slippers, huddled into my coach. They were returning home from a *tablig jamat*, a religious practice of educating Islam in practical to people of a chosen area. Having seen them the Hindu bhadrolok sitting beside me said to his son indignantly, "Fie! They are enfeebled Bengali Muslims. Muslims of Ajamgarh are not comparable with them. UP Muslims are aggressive, strong, dangerous, etc." This derogatory, however, apparently nonchalant remark is very suggestive to the identical saliency of benevolent, hospitable, meek, generous, peaceful, poor, rural Bengali Muslims. Bengali Muslims are not "aggressive," and it is one of their salient qualities of which they are very proud. Who can claim that a Bengali Muslim is equal to aggression or barbarism often linked to the violence of temple-destruction, plunder and loot, women-abduction, pollution of places of worship. They are so poor and wretched that their entire life is spent to light their cooking pots twice a day. And they are gentle, and amicable, meek but resilient rural folks. Those who accuse Bengali Muslims for some one reason or other are seriously suffering from poverty of thought. They need healthy food and good health to make them freed from myopia. The meekness of Bengali Muslims is a coveted gift, I claim. They should not be ashamed of it; rather they should believe that this singular trait is the hallmark of their identity. And the gentleness and meekness of Bengali Muslims remind me of my much loved poem of William Blake "The Lamb" where he solemnly says, "He [God/ Christ] is called by thy name, for he calls himself a lamb." If Bengali Muslims are lambs, it is their greatest gift from Allah. And they should take pride in it. They are nonviolent and peaceful. It is their inalienable behavioural asset.

Bengali Muslims are immune from the squalor and squabble of the gory sectarian clashes between the *Shias* and the *Sunnis*. The Shias, after the death of the Prophet Muhammad in 632, took Ali (656-61), Muhammad's cousin, and son-in-law as the Prophet's successor, whereas the Sunnis chose Abu Bakr (632-4 C.E.), the Prophet's closest advisor as their leader. The Muslims of West Bengal with the exception of a negligible per cent are all Sunnis, and resultantly the sectarian violence and killings do not take place here. The sectarian bloodbath is totally absent among the Bengali Muslims, making them the most unique Muslim community in the history of Islam which is allegedly mired today with the avalanche acts of terrorism, suicide bombings, sectarian killings, hate killings, horrendous *fatwas* by religious bigots, etc. The most admirable spirit of Islam, that is, the spirit of peace and brotherhood is literally followed by the poor Bengali Muslims. They have been able to keep the image of Islam untarnished, unblemished, and immaculate.

Bengali Muslims are immune from the four *varna* system prevalent among the Bengali Hindus. The Rigveda's division of humanity into four strict castes – *Brahman, Kshatriya, Vaishya, Shudra* is a gross exploitative and inhuman mechanism created by the *Aryan* texts and co-texts for the benefit of the Aryans themselves. Unlike the Vedas the Qur'an lays emphasis on liberty, equality and fraternity among all human beings ad infinitum. Abdur Raheem Kidwai's poignant remark is an eye-opener:

> According to the Qur'an, all human beings are equal, regardless of their gender, colour, race or language. It condemns those who are guilty of fragmenting mankind into classes and subclasses, and thereby reducing vast chunks of humanity into hapless and helpless victims of oppression, inhumanity, injustice and poverty.[10]

Some writings are however, available in the public domain which painstakingly hammer to project the division of Muslims into two or three broad categories, *Ashraf*, *Ajlaf*, and *Arzal* and many more subcategories. But the missing point is that the Qu'ran is not permissive to all these man-made divisions, based on mainly one's social status, wealth and asset, and power. And what is more revealing is that, unlike the Hindu community, all Muslims, irrespective of his socio-economic status, have an equal access to all kinds of professional and religious-cultural activities.

Bengali Muslims should never be ashamed of their manual and menial job. Their manual work is in consonance with the God's inner design. When they work in sun and shower in agriculture, construction, or any small enterprise or industry, they keep the wheel of civilisation moving. It is their supreme sacrifice towards the earth. The acclaimed Lebanese poet Gibran says:

> "...that when you work you fulfil a
> part of earth's furthest dream, assigned to you when
> that dream was born,
> And in keeping yourself in labour you are in
> truth loving life.
>
> And to love life through labour is to be intimate
> with life's inmost secret." [11]

The Bengali Muslim rustics and labourers are doing their best part of work assigned. And keeping "life through labour" they have been the "intimate with life's inmost secret." Their manual and menial job whether in native villages or India's growing suburbs and cities is not a matter of shame; it is a matter of supreme sacrifice and they should take pride in nation building project.

The Conundrum

Bengali Muslims are, however, merely triumph cards at the hand of dishonest and unscrupulous political leaders who use, misuse and abuse them only for their political mileage. The upper caste Bengali Hindus irrespective of party colours who are at the helm of affairs never want their co-habitant Muslims at par with them in multi sectored perspectives. And the local *maulvis* and their madrasas is a severe hindrance to the educational and social competence of the Bengali Muslims. To defeat the said corrosive designs, they must assert their Bengali identity and refuse the path of Urdu speaking urban Muslims. Moreover, an economic and educational revamp and a change of stolid mindset of hackneyed Muslims, and a cleansed heart of their haughty and egoistic co-brethren can allay their pain of being marginalised.[12]

Conclusion

In contrast to the national trend, where more than one third of the Muslims live in urban areas, in West Bengal Muslims share less than one fifth of the urban population. Given the urban-centric power structure dominated by upper caste Hindu elites, the rural root of the Muslims of West Bengal has led to their being almost invisible in urban public domain – educational institutions, public services, media, cultural platforms, and other podiums of importance. Nevertheless, notwithstanding a general silence on the issue, some initiatives, however limited, were seen to be taken by part of the intelligentsia. This had contributed, in its limited way, to the strengthening of a Muslim agency, the seeds of which could be seen in the social efforts at organising schools, healthcare facilities, and so on taken up by sections of the Muslims.[13]

Surprisingly and shockingly any discussion on Bengali Muslims has been almost an unsolicited inhibition. While, thanks to certain constitutional guarantees and other public measures, unfair treatment against the Adivasis and the Dalits is at least acknowledged, discussion on the socio-economic handicaps of the Muslims remains almost a taboo. And even after the publication of the Sachar Report (2006) that has clearly brought out the depressed status of the Muslims as regards capability-enhancing opportunities, debates and deliberations on the issue in West Bengal are far from adequate. The inadequacy of informed engagement has not only had its effect on the continually depressed socio-economic status of the Muslims of West Bengal, but also on the imagination of the Muslim identity that is being [invariably] framed solely on religious line, ignoring multiple other facets of their lives.[14] For the true development of Muslims the first and foremost condition is to separate them from what I call their *Burqa-topi-dari* line. Muslims should have to be thought as a democratic citizen with all the constitutional rights and duties of the nation. Religious tag is not to be tantalised to aggravate their existential pain and suffering further. But at the same time it is to be kept in mind that assertion of identity is not always harmful. It may be one of the ways to achieve jutcice and equal rights in the inequal rugged hegemonic social terrains. Let me conclude by quoting Gibran again to address the much needed self-pride and self-assertion the Bengali Muslims lack:

> I have cried over your humiliation
> And submission; and my tears streamed
> Like crystalline, but could not sear
> Away your stagnant weakness…
> ……………………………………
> I hate you, My Countrymen, because
> You hate glory and greatness. I
> Despise you because you despise yourselves.
>
> "My Countrymen"[15]

Bengali Muslims must face the reality thrust upon them. Mimicking the Bengali babus and at the same time mimicking the maulvis will not in any way help them to construct their identity. Whatever good they have will be diluted if they fall into the traps of the said two sects. Bengali Hindu bhadraloks will never support

Bengali Muslims' cause. And the village maulvis' coiled self can never bring light to the pool of darkness the Muslims are striving to ferry to reach to the shore of the rising sun. *Bangali musolmaner mon ekhno adim. Eti tar bangali O musolman hoyar jonno noi. Dirghodiner oitihasik poddhothitir dorun tar moner upor ek garo mayajaal bistrito royeche. Soggane tar baire se beriye aste pare na. Manosik viti e ei somajke chaliye thake.* (The mind of Bengali Muslim is primitive even now. It is not for being Bengali or Muslim. It is because of many years' historical processes. His mind is covered with a thick magical spell. Mental timidity acts as the driving force of this society.)[16] What is needed is to rationally analyse the bases, the pillars, the contours, the proclivities of his mind. Then if not in two or four years, but one day he can come out of his mental stasis, psychic cocoon or his recoiling self. Then he can achieve what is deliberately denied to him for ages – political and cultural empowerment. And of course with honour!

Works Cited

1. Mojumdar, Atindra. *Arabic, Persian and Turkish Words in Bengali Literature.* Kolkata: Ekwsh Shatak, 2012. pp. 10-12. Print.
2. "Introduction."*Living Reality of Muslims in west Bengal: A Report.* Kolkata: Association SNAP and Guidance Guild in association with Pratichi Institute. 2016. p. 7. Print.
3. Ibid. p. 7.
4. Anisujamman. *Muslim Manos O Bangla Sahitya (1757-1918).* Dhaka: Charulipi Prokashan, 2012, p.340. Print.
5. Ahmed, Rafiuddin. *The Bengal Muslims 1871-1906: A Quest for Identity.* Delhi: Oxford University Press, 1996. Print.
6. Ahmed, Sabir. "Sachar Commeettee Reporter Dosh Bochor Pore." *Anando Bazaar Patrika*, 24.01.2016, p.4. Print.
7. Seabrook, Jeremy Seabrook. *people without history: india's muslim ghettos.*New Delhi: Navayana, 2011. p. 19. Print.
8. Ibid.
9. "Introduction". *Living Reality of Muslims in west Bengal: A Report.* Kolkata: Association SNAP and Guidance Guild in association with Pratichi Institute. 2016. p. 6. Print.
10. Kidwai, Abdur Raheem. *The Quran: Essential Teachings.* Mumbai: Jaico Publishing House, 2007. p. 65. Print.
11. Gibran, Kahlil. "On Work". *The Prophet.* New Delhi: Full Circle Publishing, 2011, pp. 47-48. Print.

12. Siddik, Abu. "Bengali Muslims as Marginals: An Overview." In *Representation of the Marginalised in Indian writings in English*. Ed. Abu Siddik. Falakata: Falakata College Publication Cell, 2015. pp. 183-184. Print.
13. "Introduction". *Living Reality of Muslims in west Bengal: A Report*. Kolkata: Association SNAP and Guidance Guild in association with Pratichi Institute. 2016. p. 4. Print.
14. Ibid.p. 3. Print.
15. Kahlil Gibran. "My Countrymen." *Secrets of the Heart*. New Delhi: UBSPD, 2006. Print.
16. Sofa, Ahmed. *Bangali Musolmaner Mon*. Dhaka: Hawladar Prokashani, 2018. p. 44. Print.
17. Chowdhury, Subhanil and Saswata Ghosh. "Condition of Muslims in West Bengal: A reality check", available at https://frontline.thehindu.com/the-nation/condition-of-muslims-in-west-bengal-a-reality-check-ahead-of-west-bengal-assembly-elections-2021/article33887344.ece Accessed May 21, 2022.

CHAPTER 4

Post-Independence Bengali Muslim Literature: Issues of Identity and Belonging

"One is known by the language one speaks."

O. V. Vijayan, *Khasakinte Ithihasam*

Bare Words

Literature whether it is regional, national or global always inspires, invigorates, and energises us to look at life's greater mystery and miracle from multitude heterogeneous contours. It deepens the meaning of life in its colourful and painfully beautiful foliages – splendours and glories, hopes and aspirations, loves and expectations, sorrows and tears, strength and endurance, death and doom, diseases and pathos, the courage and resilience of a sea of humanity. And Bengali Muslim literature aims at giving many of the said life's innate shades to humanity in general and to the Bengali Muslim in particular. From the aesthetic and idealistic perspective there cannot be a strict division among the so called Hindu literature, Muslim literature, Christian literature, Buddhist literature, Jewish literature and so on. But that does not mean that literature is always universal, and it is always community, caste or gender neutral.*Upojukto karone keu mukh fute na bolleo 'hindu sahityo' ebong 'muslim sahityo' e dhoroner ekti ghotona lokkho kora jabe. Kothati sthulo vabe bolle ekta nojir dite hoi. Hinduder sompadito potro-potrika jemon durgo pujo upolokkhe sharodiyo sonkha prokashito hoi, temni tar dekha dekhi muslimder sompadito potro-potrikar eid sonkha beroy. Fole dekha jacche bangla sahityer shorir theke dhormer alkhalla khule fela somvob hoi ni. Eki songe etio lokkho korar bishoy bangali Muslim shardiyo potro-potrika jotota vokto bangali Hindu eid sonkha potro-potrikar proti tototai shitol….muslim pathokder kachei uvoy bonge Hindu lekhok jotokani sikrito, Muslim lekhok totokahni sikrito non. Ei odvut probonota ki shudhu sahityogoto utkorsher karnei? Amar ta mone hoi na.*

(Though nobody speaks out for suitable reasons, there exists a tendency of dividing literature into 'Hindu literature' and 'Muslim literature.' I am giving a common example for my argument. During Durga pujo many *sharodiyo* magazines, edited by Hindu writers, are come out. Likewise during Eid many Muslim writers publish *eid* editions. So, the removal of the dress of religion from the body of Bangla literature has not been possible. It is seen that the sharodiyo magazines are favourably read by the Bengali Muslim readers, whereas Eid editions generally get cold reception by the Bengali Hindu readers. Moreover, in West Bengal and Bangladesh Bengali Hindu writers are heartily welcomed by Muslim readers, whereas the Bengali Muslim writers are not duly recognised by Bengali Hindu readers. Is the aesthetic richness of literature sole determiner for this strange tendency? I don't think so (Biswajit Panda 2020).

Literature is a continual striving toward the attainment of the essence of life. But from a pragmatic point of view divisional heterogeneity and plurality of literature has indeed been serving many desired and cherished goals and aspirations of multiplicity of people. Indeed this plurality is an inerasable strength of literature. If a community is incapable of sustaining and flourishing its own language and literature, that community is bound to lose the sheen of its unique gust for life. In this context the issue of Bengali Muslim literati and literature and its undeniable existence of mesmerising gaze to life's visceral and cerebral horizons from a distinct Bengali Muslim perspective emerge. This article aims to establish Bengali Muslim literature not as a completely separate entity but as an added milieu to the enrichment of Bengali literature as well as to the formation of a distinct Bengali Muslim identity and their sense of belonging based on their community's literature.

Introduction

Why do we talk of Bengali Muslim Literature? Can we dissect literature into multifarious separated segments based on religion, caste, language, gender, ethnicity, socio-economic backwardness, nationality, age, space, technology, environment, and other unending list of identities and theories (isms) and ideologies? The answer is 'no' and 'yes' at the same time. Literature itself is self-referral, self-sufficient and cannot have any ulterior ends. It is self-contained. Literature like other arts is primarily thought to please and instruct us. Pleasure or what we more concisely call aesthetic enduring pleasure is one of the sole determiners of a good literature or a classic. From this perspective literature is for literature's sake. It cannot have plural designated specialised, bizarre technical and anatomical names. But literature is also thought to have specific roles and goals for voicing the hopes, aspirations, sorrows and pathos of the numberless divided and bordered societies across the world's vast panorama. That is why literature now comes to be more and more recognised with specialised terms and epithets. There is also the unavoidable nuisance of literary extreme theorisation which kills the essence of a literary piece, making it not the exercise of mind (as thought earlier) but simply mathematical and scientific and mechanical dry process. Whatever it may be, we cannot deny the existence of literature in the name of multiple societal determiners such as the socio-economic disadvantaged and the marginals, religion, ethnicity, language, nationality, age, environment and other plural specificities. And here comes the question of "Bengali Muslim" literature. Is it possible to divide *Bangla Vasha O Sahitya* into such strict religious miniaturisation? If there is a Bengali Muslim literature, there also should be, it may be naturally argued, a likewise "Bengali Hindu" literature. I think such division in literature written in a particular language goes against the basics of a much coveted life-enhancing discipline like literature. But simultaneously it is also true that a literature which does not reflect the hopes and aspirations, endurance resilience and magnanimity of a particular society or community is liable to be treated with discontents and suspicions by the "others."And a literature reflecting the spirit, energy, love and ardour of a community or class may be generally embraced with ease and comfort by that coterie of people. And Bengali Muslim literature aims at giving many of the life's innate shades to humanity in general and to the Bengali Muslim in particular.

Bengali Muslim Literature under Study

The Bengali Muslim literati like Mir Mosharraf Hossain and Qazi Abdul Wadud with their love and rational humanity were the stars of a unique literary flavour enunciating Bengali Muslim life in its vast panoramic hues in colonial Bengal. But the bloom could not last and only Humayun Kabir's *Chatturanga* could manage its authority over a period of time. The community losing a host of literary luminaries and many influential heroes because of India's 1947 'tryst with destiny' was in a bad shape. No literature of merit had seen the light of the day for a long period. And after this ebb came the resurgent web of celebrity writers like Syed Mujtaba Ali and Syed Mustafa Siraj. But they could not voice a radically distinct and differentiated Muslim voice because the country faced newer challenges of partition and communal riots. In this communally charged ambience it was natural for them to refrain from writing which might be considered purely Islamic in character. They both along with other Muslim Bengali litterateurs like Abdul Jabbar and Kabirul Islam writing in the first three decades of independence, and the contemporaries like Abul Bashar, Afsar Ahmed and Sohrab Husain took in content and imagery the local Bengali environment and its uniqueness as the theme of creativity which was quite different from the treatment of a imagined pure and pristine Islamic culture. And their writings focus more or less on the local and immediate Bengali Muslim nuances and peculiarities. Their writings are influenced by the tradition of, Hinduism, syncretism and mysticism, and the Bengal's local colour and flavour. These writers have been a votary not of a pure and prescriptive Islamic voice, but of a new Bengali Muslim perspective and a uniquely Bengali Muslim identity where the emphasis is laid not on Muslim identity first but Bengali one.[1]

Golam Kuddus (1920-2006) in his *Bandi* (1952) has vividly portrayed the tyrannies and tortures, oppressions and exploitations, both physical and psychological, which are inflicted upon the domestic maids and servants by their household masters. Its setting is urban, and the background is the pre-partition days of treachery and distrust. Rafik, the protagonist of the novel, comes from village to town for higher education. He takes shelter at his uncle Sadek Saheb's house. Sadek Saheb is a rich man. He is a Government employee and his in-laws are *borolok* (rich). In his affluent family Shamiron, Kulsum, Batashi, Emdad – all domestic maids and helpers – slave from generations. They have to bear with physical violence, mental oppression, verbal abuse, and even sexual violence. Rafik is a witness to these social ills and exploitative systems, but he is an unemployed youth, and he lives under Sadek's roof, at his mercy. He wants to protest against Sadek's tyranny. But he cannot. How can he? He has no financial freedom.

Apart from the detailed portrayal of inhumanity and cruelty of the rich Bengali Muslims like Sadek, *Bandi* has also political underpinnings. The communal distrust and violence between Hindus and Muslims has cast a deep shadow on Rafik's sensibility. There are issues of patriarchy and financial exclusion at his uncle's home. Rafik is disturbed as much by the tyranny of his uncle, as by the fissure in Hindu-Muslim relation, economic and social inequalities, lack of freedom in private and public life. Many confusing questions crowd him. Who is not a bandi or slave? Who is free? Nobody is free, he thinks. Shamiron, Kulsum, Batashi, Emdad are slaves, we know. But is Sadek Saheb free? His wealth is his in-laws' wealth. Is Saleha Bibi, Rafik's aunt, free? She is merely a doll in her house, and has no power to take any family decision. However, the novel ends with positive note. Kulsum has fled with Tahamina, and has achieved the life of freedom. Emdad has gained his economic freedom. Satyaban has been freed from his narrow cell of communal prejudices, and Rafik too in the end has been freed from the exploitative clutches of his uncle Sadek. *Bandi* is a radical Bengali Muslim voice as its focus centres on its attempt to establish the social, communal and economic justice in society. The preface of the text reads:

> *Bandi kono modhdho jugiyo haramer kahini noi, somokalin somaj e er potovumi. Bangali Muslim modhdhobitter asha, akankha, rajnoitik dristivongi samontotantrik chintavabnai chalito gotanugotik jibon o notun chinta chetonar unmesh o uvoyer tanaporoner ekti ontorongo alekhkho ei uponnase oti sohojvabe bidhrito hoyeche….ei uponnaser bandi namkoron amader chintavabnay ek prochond aloron sristhi kore. Bartoman somaj baebosthay meyeder bastob obostha amader chetonabibek ke tibrovabe bidhdho kore….ke bandi ar ke noi, ei prshno amaderke vabay, chintachetonake nara deay.* (*Bandi* is not a Mediaval harem story. Contemporary society is its background. It lucidly, intimately, humanely, unravels the clash between past, hackneyed feudal ways and awakened resurgence in Bengali Muslims' hopes, aspirations, and political attitudes….the name of the novel Bandi itself has unsettled our thoughts. The sketches of pathetic condition of women in contemporary society have tremendously hurt our sensibility. Who is a bandi or who is not? This question has given us food for thoughts. And it has violently jolted our stale consciousness.

Abdul Jabbar's *Ilishmarir Char* (1959) shows how easily poor and religious fishermen are being duped by the money lender *Mahajan* Torbodi's oppressive machinations. Their life gets changed only in coming contact with Ratan and Anwar who play a pivotal role in uplifting the fisher folk by providing education and raising class consciousness among them. Abul Bashar's *Surer Sampan* (1990) and *Dharmer Grahan* (1992) depict religion as the major hurdle in otherwise smooth and candid man-woman relationships. The texts recognise that true and noble passions can transcend the so called religious barriers and borders. In *Surer Sampan*, for instance, music becomes the deep bonding agency between Sohini, daughter of

Jafarullah, a music teacher, and Gopal, an unknown Hindu boy who grows up under the patronage of Jafarullah. Gopal and Sohini have a deep desire for each other but their wish for marital solemnisation falls apart not from Jafarullah's objections but from the village folk who are dead against Hindu-Muslim marriage in their locality. Sohrab Husain's *Sharam Ali's Bhuban* (2004) also raises issue of religious insincerity of a *maulvi* who advises him to be sexually restraint for he is a Muslim. Sharam Ali, contrary to maulvi's advice, dreams of beautiful female figures and craves to have Fajli's body anyhow. He steals mango from the orchard and talks like an atheist for his stomach's unruly behavioural pattern. Sharam Ali is a radical deviant from the pure Islamic code or way of life. Moreover, a recurring emphasis by these authors in their other multiple writings on the beauty and truth in the lives of Muslim *bauls* and *fakirs* who espouse a mystical syncretistic tradition of humanity and their acceptance of life's wide diversity and this particular baul or fakir way of life is detested and hated by the insular maulvis and other religious preachers. Thus, these Bengali Muslim writers mark a charismatic departure from traditional Muslim writings where the emphasis was invariably put on the myths and stories of the Prophet Muhammad and other sacred men of Islamic history and civilisation, epistles of advice, namely *nasihatnamas* and hagiographies and other esoteric materials. They, on the other, by their sheer insistence and perseverance, painstakingly endeavour to depict Bengali Muslim life in its naked and sordid immediate reality where the nexus between religious bigotry and monetary oppressions crush the poor, and the concept of Islamic Brotherhood vanishes. But the humanity and endurance exerted by the oppressed poor and marginalised beacons new directions in the history of Bengali Muslim writings and representations.

This, however, does not suggest that all Bengali Muslim writers of post-independence have criticised normative Islam and distance themselves from the revivalist spirit of pristine Islam. A host of writers like Abdul Aziz al-Aman, Maulana Muhammad Tahir, Abdur Raquib and Abu Atahar have indeed manifested Islamic values and principles through their numerous writings. They are not believers in religious syncretism or cultural reconciliation. They are Muslim in orientation and they firmly hold the Islamic cultural beliefs, values and ethos. Their contribution to Bengali Muslim writings is to either translate some Arabian or Persian books into vernacular language or to write fresh biographies of the prophet and other holy men of Islam. Their writings are encomiastic of Islamic past glories and have an Islamic moral vision and they imbibe Arabic words in Bengali literary structure also. They basically try to write about Islamic thoughts and philosophy and thereby inject a dose of pure Islam into the body of Bengali language, literature and culture. They have been able to make even the pious Muslims understand the need for vernacular language in disseminating Islamic knowledge and belief. They are in many respects pioneers in championing the cause of Bengali Muslim identity and restoring a sense of Muslim pride and prestige in the realm of Bengali (Hinduised) literary and cultural history.

Portrayal of Rural Landscape

Bengali Muslim literati have presented an immaculate portrayal of the nature and rural landscape striped with evocative and mesmerising vignettes of Bengal rural life such as ploughing, sowing, hunting, milking, catching fish, etc. These writers have themselves endured poverty and the odd sway of rural haphazard but idyllic life. And their writings often attest to their deep bonding and innate emotional love to the land of their birth and growth. Thus, it is quite natural for their writings to have a unique and exquisite rural flavour with all its wonders and oddities and trajectories.

Syed Mustafa Siraj has vividly portrayed the rural landscape of Bengal and more interestingly he has also based his novels on rural setting. *Kingbadantir Nayak* (1969) encapsulates most brilliantly the unalloyed joys and sorrows of a group of unsophisticated people in a village in Uttar Rhar. They protect their fields of harvest by keeping them awake and guarding the fields in the dead of nights. *Trinabhoomi* (1970) is a perennial saga of Murshidabad folk life which exhibits the malaise of modern life, society and economy based on indiscriminate urbanisation, ever increasing construction of dams, and deforestation which forcibly push the forest people, tribals, milkmen, birdcatchers and agricultural farmers to the extreme margins of human survival race. Siraj's *Janmari* (1990) depicts various concerns of contemporary rural life, where the landless generation hurls themselves to dacoity and other criminal activities because of their disgust and disillusion with life.

Siraj's *Aleek Manush* (1988), Based in Murshidabad, a backward and Muslim-dominated district of the then undivided Bengal – it offers a vivid and real portrait of the Muslim cummunity of the time, divided by different religious cults and their leaders, and their multitude of suckers against the backdrop of independence struggle that was then brewing across Bengal. Safi, the protagonist, was a rebel, and though born of an orthodox family – his father was a "pir" (a saint) - left the family in school-going age, lived in different places, came in contact with different learned men, and studied different religious texts, literature and western philosophy to finally morph into an atheist. He was greatly influenced by the philosophy of Henry David Thoreau and strongly believed that the state is a torture machine, the officers in the administration are complicit, and the police and the military are the state-owned hooligans.

Safi got to be a mythical hero in his own right. In course of his life, Safi murdered some notorious men and lived like a sage, attracting a huge following from both Hindu and Muslim communities. Finally, when he was going to kill his hypocrite father, someone called in the police and got him booked. He was subsequently tried and hanged. Massive crowds attended his cremation (Mrinal Bose). Siraj affirms: "One of my chief convictions has been that of not believing in any particular religion. I am free of religious belief. But I also understand that most people are religious and I am, therefore, tolerant towards anybody's religion. I would consider to have succeeded in my role as a writer if I have been able to spread this message (Farida Shaikh)." That may be the one reason he strives to paint Safi of *Aleek Manush* as 'mythical man', though he has a very active life. Man wants freedom of spirit. But he is ever confined within the chains of family, society and state. He also cannot deny the existence of religious life, life of shared myths. Collective Hindu-Muslim rural life cannot be analysed with the lens of Western individual identity and individual freedom.

As Ziya Us Salam commented, "Though Siraj wrote for adults as well, and lately for children, he always strived to bring the scent of the soil to his works. His was a realist narrative, quite removed from the mysticism and romanticism that characterised much of contemporary Bengali literature. No self-aggrandisement, he was a master of the unsaid word."

Gulam Abdullah Rasool's novel *Aabad* (1969) demonstrates a peasant movement in South 24 Parganas. Afsar Ahmed's *Shanu Alir Nijer Jami* (1989), Abul Bashar's *Sparsher Baire* (1995) and Sohrab Husain's *Sharam Alir Bhuban* (2004) are also in the same pattern and genre and all are marvelous portrayal of rural life and landscape with all micro and macro layers of human complexity. Abdur Raquib's vigorous stories also portray the rural Bengali Muslim's simple and hardworking peasant life with strong moral and ethical concerns. However, Afsar Ahmed's *Metiaburujer Kissa* (2003) is a notable exception for its colour and flavour is urbane and it sets another note of urban Muslim life.

Afsar Ahmed about his parentage and creative leanings observed:

> *Haorah jelar Koriya grame ami janmechi. Amader barita adidigonto dhanjomir ga chuye. Aat dosh kilomitar khet doure cholegeche. Amader barir uthontholay charti aam gaach chilo. Baranday rate tebil pete bose ei gaachgulike oboyobe uther moto dekhtam. Onnanno gaachgachali jure jonakir jhikimiki. Ekhane amar kolpona kagoj-kolome vor korto. Nirupai daridro o obohelar vetor nijeke khuje paoya amar shuru hoye jai. Hoito amio nije kichu likhte pari…baba khete kaaj korto, dhanvanga kole kaaj korto, emonki chaibasar chinematir khonite kaaj niye koyek bochor katiye eseche Bihare. Tarpor to Kolkata bondorer shromik. Onek bochor porjonto oniomitoh kormi…* (I lived at Koriya village in the district of Howrah. My home bordered the endless paddy fields. Greenary ran for eight, ten kilometers. There were four mango trees at our yard. At night the trees looked like camels from our verandah. Fireflies danced around other trees and shrubs. Here imagination rested on my pen and paper. I found myself amid abysmal poverty and utter neglect. I might write something. Such belief came…my father worked in fields, at rice mills, at china clay mining at Chaibasa in Bihar. Then he worked as a casual hand at Kolkata port for many years…)[2]

His childhood and upbringing paint the separate landscape of Bengali Muslim literature which is distinctly alien to drawing room and laptop-palmtop friendly urban elite or middle class public and private life of West Bengal. It sheds light to inner sanctum of Bengali Muslim livelihood, their living life, their community feeling, their relation to mother earth, their peripheral fringed rustic existence. It is quite understandable why bhadralok literati of Kolkata and other district towns (mainstream) find no aesthetic value in Bengali Muslim voices which are generally discarded by Bengali babus as community specific.

Representation of the Poor Peasants

Bengali Muslim writers have also been very vocal against the plight of the poor peasants, and they championed the cause of the poor peasants against zamindars' atrocities and cruelties. Their writings focus on the plight of the peasants making them conscious of their rights and, thereby, spearheading a protest against the evils of zaminadari system. Indeed, these writers have been a game changer in the day to day lives of the hard working poor peasants. The effect is that the peasants become more resilient and energised to protect their livelihoods. Such novels as Abdul Jabbar's *Ilishmarir Char*, Abdullah Rasool's *Aabad,* Mustafa Siraj's *Niranjan Ganga* (1980) and Abul Bashar's *Bhorer Prosuti* (1991) depict a heartless picture of the peasants' daily living experiences of the *mahajan* atrocities and tyrannies. These texts are sympathetic to the cause of the peasants and they are indicative of a long term solution toward the amelioration of peasants' problems. A pungent twist is supplied to the theme of mahajan atrocities by Sohrab Husain's *Math Jadu Jane* (2004) which encapsulates the protagonist Qausir Ali's heart-rending struggle to rescue his two *bigha* field from the clamped fists of the mahajan whose lust cannot be quenched until he gets the body of Ali's wife Sabera. One of the most striking features, however, of these writings, is that they are a departure from the perspective of colonial writings where the peasants are always Muslims and the zamindars are invariably Hindus. Here community based relationships (Hindu-Muslim) is overpowered by the class interests among the same community members themselves. Afsar Ahmed's *Atma Parichay* where the poor sharecropper Gafoor and the mahajan Haji Sahib is an attestation to this thematic paradigm shift.

Socio-cultural Issues

Bengali Muslim writings have also drawn our attention to the prevalent socio-cultural problems which are plaguing the lives of Muslim women who are becoming easy victims to the cumbersome practices of *pardah,* polygamy and triple *talaq.* Afsar Ahmed's writings throw a serious challenge to the concept of *shari'at* (the code of laws regulating the spiritual and temporal aspect of Muslim life) itself. These man-made laws are fetters which stunt a Muslim woman's hope of exploration of her full individual potency in every walk of life. His *Kaalo Borkhar Bibi o Kusumer Gandha ebong Challees Jan Lok* (1996) shows pardah as exploitative and inhuman custom which empowers men over women. The implication is that women are sexually vulnerable and they must be kept in guard. On the first night of her third marriage, Rehana comes to know about her husband's madness. The novel depicts Rehana's two worlds – one behind her veil and the other external to it, inhabited by forty men not immune to the desire for sexual gratification. The scent of flowers behind the veil intoxicates these men and Rehana becomes an enticing article of consumption. His *Ek Ascharya Bashikaran Kissa* (1998) is a virulent attack against polygamy. Maulavi Malukha is a powerful, respected and torch bearer of religious piety and sacredness. But he is obsessed with his physical quenchless desire of bringing home a fourth wife. *Ditiya Bibi* (1997) captures the trauma of an ordinary man who because of shari'at approval marries two women but he fails to look at his two wives at par, as directed in the Islamic laws, and ultimately leaves one. His *Bhang Jyotsna* (1993) and *Bibir Mittha Talakh o Talkher Bibi ebong Halud Pakhir Kissa* (1995) are severe attacks on the custom of easy and thoughtless divorce. This theme of talaq and polygamy is also deftly enunciated in Abul Bashar's *Phoolbou* (1988), a narrative of a Musilm widow's pathos. Razia is Millat's love, but she is married as the fourth wife of his father, the old Haji. And at the death of his father Millat cannot marry his mother. And thus Razia, Millat's love and mother eventually commits suicide having failed to have Millat's love. What emerges as one of the dynamics of these writings is the desire and demand for emancipation of Muslim women from the clutches of man-made shari'at which is at odd with the holy Qur'an, the supreme authority in Islam and Islamic way of life.

Another facet of perspective is added to this genre by Kamaal Husain who depicts most evocatively the sense of fear, insecurity, mistrust and alienation of the Bengali Muslim society of contemporary West Bengal. His *Param Biswaser Gandha*, *Shikarer Prabaha* and *Swatantra Baranda* (1990-2005) is a massive trilogy narrating the growing up of a young ordinary Muslim girl Sufia from adolescence to menopause. The texts are besmeared with her story of successes and failures, hopes and aspirations, dreams and desires, struggles and afflictions – all are part of her project of survival and recognition of her minority identity amid all odds and obstacles and prejudices. In a word Sufia's story is somewhat representative of the strive for the establishment of Bengali Muslim's unique identity facing and overcoming all odds in a Hindu majority land. Husain's hero Dr. Haneef in his novel *Taeefa* is afraid of being accused in the name of terrorism, treason. There is a fear psychosis playing unconsciously on his inner self without any rhyme or reason. The text raises a host of holistic concerns of Bengali Muslims' identity and dignity in the backdrop of increasing attacks on Muslims. If a Muslim terrorist is caught, the whole society has to pay price for it. They are then needed to prove their nationality and patriotism. His short stories *Anuprabesh* and *Bhay* also enunciate the perennial fear and anxiety of being identified with terrorists, ISI agents, Bangaldeshis, under which the Muslims of Bengal have to survive. Husain's writing has created a niche for him in the oeuvre of Bengali literature and culture.

Shahzad Firdous (b. 1950) in his classic novel *Vyasa* (1995) has transported us to the realm of a phiolosophical quest for knowledge. His Vyasa was widely known as the maker of division of the *Vedas* for which he was credited with the title Vedavyasa. He authored monumental *Mahabharata* as well as most of the *Puranas*. The epic *Mahabharata*, however, has not chronologically depicted the life of Vyasadeva or Vedavyasa or Krishnadwaipayana. And Firdous has given a clear and chronological life-sketch of Vyasadeva. Moreover, in his adroit hand the wall between the writer and his wrting, the creator and his creation gets blurred. It seems to map the outlines of Vyasa's life is to seek the knowledge itself. The novel also raises questions about knowledge and how it can be achieved. Subrata Kumar Das has critically analysed the novel. Let us have a look at his critical appreciation of the text. What does the Mahabharata say about the life of Vyasa? He was the son of Satyabati, begot by the sage Parashara. Satyabati, when a maiden, would row her boat across the river. One day Parashara happened to be her passenger and incidentally the knowledgeable person felt affinity with the black boatwoman. He soon gave way to desire and after their sexual union the sage gave her the boon that the child to be born out of the union would be the wisest man under the sun. This man was to be Krishnadwaipayana. Firdous delineates the bringing up of this black boy and his growing up in youth. We find that at some time Parashara leaves Satyabati and takes away Krishna to a faraway ashram to provide him with proper teaching. But he does not become a commoner; he raises questions and thus turns disobedient to his father too. And thus Firdous makes the sage an ordinary man for which the novelist deserves much appraisal. Firdous' *Vyasa* runs through the maze of the Bharata family where Krishna's mother had been married to Shantanu. Crossing all these, the story moves through historic events, such as the Kurukshetra War and even after that Vyasa is alive to console Gandharai, the mother bereft of all her one hundred sons. And what a miracle that in between all these stories come the final chapters of the Mahabharata where we get

Vaishampayana narrating the historical story to Janamejoya, the great grandson of Arjuna.

As an ordinary human, Firdous' Vyasa throws questions at his father Parashara; he brings up the question of the right of the Sudras. Vyasa asserts: 'All men are equal.' Very forcefully he announces: 'The learning of the wise is for the wise, the learning of the illiterate is for the illiterate. The illiterate will never know the learning of the wise. Similarly, the wise, too, will never know of the learning of the illiterate' (p 17). To his father's face Vyasa declares: 'If the entire world abandons me I shall bow my head before the Sudra, I shall bow my head before the particles of dust, I shall bow my head before the worm in the mud for the sake of knowing life' (p 20). And thus he denounces the entire establishment, all the truths established in society and so becomes the wisest. Let us not forget that it is Vyasa who puts questions to Parashara about the legality of the relations that Parashara had with the fish-smelling Satyabati. Vyasa bursts forth with the eternal truth: "No wealth in the universe belongs to any one individual. Everybody has equal right to all things" (p 44). Firdous makes a modern man out of the mythological sage character.

There are many notable Bengali Muslim writers, and their literary pieces, especially novels and short stories, have merit to be appreciated. All of them cannot be included in this chapter. Shamim Ahmed's *Saat Aasmaan* (2012), *Bishad Bindu* (2013); Mosarof Hossain's *Janmavischo* (2012), *Poribartan* (2012), *Ekhno Alo* (2013); Musa Ali's *Mukhosher Aarale*, *Ochena Aakash* (2012); Nurul Amin Biswas's *Osomoyer Japannama*, *Din Bodoler Gaan*; Dr. Nazrul Islam's *Bokul*, *Vumiputro*, *Roktolekha*, *Gopon Chokher Gochore*, *Somporko*, *Bishonno Pran*, etc.; Abdur Raqib's *Kobitar Feriowala*; Hasan Azizul Huq's *Aaghunpakhi* (2008); Murshid A M's *Akkharshahi*; Ismail Darbesh's *Talashnama* (2021) Short Story anthologies of Sourav Hossain (*Komred O Onnanogolpo*), Lutfor Rahaman (*Nishipaloner Prohore*) Abu Siddik (*Bihotojoner Upakhyan*) and many more need to be studied for the enrichment of the project this chapter attempts to map.

Unique Contribution of Bengali Muslim Writers

Bengali Muslim literature with its emphasis on its local elements such as language, dress, food habit, indigenous customs and rituals, beliefs and creeds, daily living hardships and strivings, dreams and desires of immediate life along with its focus on conciliatory and assimilatory aspects of Islam is a much avowed phenomenon to be reckoned with grace and magnitude in the growth and development of the overall oeuvre of Bengali literature and culture. It is neither purely Islamic nor Muslim in orientation nor is it entirely divorced from its immediate local colour and setting, flora and fauna, people and customs, hopes and dreams, struggles and failures. These writers seem to have been less concerned with pristine Islam with its strict rules and regulations. Rather they have found elements of synthesis and reconciliation in Islam with other venerable cultures, especially the Hinduism for their context and treatment. The authors, however, despite their seemingly non-Islamic credentials can never be alleged to have imbibed a leniency toward Hinduized form of writing. Most of them have been vocal against plural societal, economic cruelties and malaise, religious dogmas or *fatwas* about talaq and pardah.

Bengali Muslim literature is primarily an unprecedented approach of treating Bangali *musalmans* as the core subject of their literature for the exploration and encapsulation of a missing theme. It deals with the daily living experiences as well as their somewhat ambivalent imitation of Islam in a land which is far away from its origin. This literature touching some amorphous religious issues of Islam has laid its heavy weight of preponderance to the depiction of West Bengal and its marginal Muslims in its myriad array of hued tapestries. And this literature has been well accepted and recognised by the Hindu and Muslim alike. They in no way can be called community writers, writing particularly for a specific community. In fact, their writings have added an extra mileage to the richness of Bengali literature. And their critics include such notable Hindu writers as Manas Majumdar, Ameya Bhushan Majumdar, Sadhan Chattopadhya, Atin Bandopadhya and many more. Their writings with their powerful and vigorous representation of the marginal Muslims of Bengal have indeed paved a bridge to reaching Hindu-Muslim reconciliation and emotional closeness of Bengali people as a whole. The Bengalis irrespective of caste, class, or religion should take pride in this literature which cannot be relegated to the lower status as merely one of the offshoots of mainstream Bengali literature. Bengali Muslim literature has indeed injected a rich mosaic of local colours and flavours with its existential reality to the texture and the matrix of the *Bangla vasha o sahitya* both in its thematic orientation and stylistic representation.

Unlike the Urdu literature which is besmeared with the images of pristine Islam of Arab origin, Pan-Islamic theorisation and Islam's past glory and present decadence, the Bengali Muslim writers are much less concerned with the concept of pure Islam and Pan-Islamic fervor. They are primarily preoccupied with their immediate environment and culture. Their resources of inspiration emerge first from the land of their birth and death, poverty and marginality, its flora and fauna, rivers and fields, forests and hills, daily living experiences and haphazard attempts of acculturation. And then come the issues of religion, faith, creeds and customs – all are more or less influenced with the images of Hindu culture and ethos. Basically they are regional writers and their focus is only on the land of their inhabitation and its people. They write both in simple colloquial Bangla and the standard Bangla. Their readers are not limited to a few Muslim literate only. Their works are loved and admired by the vast Hindu readers. Their writings are never meant for Muslim community only. It is dedicated to the Bengali community by and large. Bengali is their mother tongue. And as Bengali they are proud of their inheritance of language, culture and literature. But they face identity crisis only when they are asked by some ignoble Bengali Hindus such callous question as 'Are you Bengali or Muslim?', their innate pride of being a Bengali faces a severe jolt of consciousness. But such exceptional happenings do not deter them from supporting their unbiased and unconditional loyalty to their mother tongue Bangla. And Bengali Muslim writers seem to be increasingly happier in not using Arabic or Persian words in their body of literature. Certainly some words relating to Islam and Islamic code of life surface on their writings. But they do not put any hindrance to the sweetness, smoothness and richness of a free flowing language like Bangla.

Conclusion

The entire literature under review is a search for Bengali Muslim identity and sense of belonging which is not solely based on pure Islam or Pan-Islam and this literature has no ulterior motive for the construction of pure Muslim identity. It is much concerned with a search for the assimilation of Islamic concepts and ideas to their innate Bengali identity in its indigenous locale, colour and setting. Islamic theme is an added advantage to their cultural exploration in its rural poor but elegant beautiful Bengal setting. Their writings border the marginal poor rural Muslim folk of West Bengal with all their vicissitudes of life, pain and hunger, joys and sorrows, hopes and frustrations, intra and inter community heterogeneous nuances. With its strict theological ignorance and its leniency to the mythic and esoteric interpretations of Islam of *pirs and bauls and fakirs* coupled with the land's beauty and people's poverty Bengali Muslim literature has created a permanent niche of its individuality and uniqueness in the oeuvre of Bangla vasha o sahitya.

Works Cited

1. Tundawla, Alefiya. "Multiple Representations of Muslimhood in West Bengal: Identity Construction Through Literature." *South Asia Research*, Vol.32 (2): 139-163. 2012. Print.
2. Mukhopadhyay, Arunkumar, ed. *Kaler Puttalika: Hundred Twenty Years of Bengali Short Story 1891-2010*. Kolkata: Deys's Publishing, 2016. p. 568. Print.
3. Panda, Biswajit. *Swadhinata-Uttar Chhotogalpe Paschimbanger Muslim Manas*. [Kindle Basic]. Retrieved from amazon.com. [Loc 288].
4. Kuddus, Golam. *Bandi*. Available at https://archive.org/details/in.ernet.dli.2015.454759/page/n3/mode/1up?view=theater. Web.
5. Islam, Aminul. *Bangla Sahitye Muslim Ouponayasik*. Kolkata: Patralekha, 2015. pp. 242-91. Print.
6. Salam. Ziya Us. "Voice of the 'other' India Falls Silent." Available at https://www.thehindu.com/news/national/voice-of-the-other-india-falls-silent/article3859575.ece Accessed June 23, 2022. Web.
7. Bose, Mrinal. "Reading: ALEEK MANUSH by Syed Mustafa Siraj (Bengali Novel)." Available at https://awritinggeek.blogspot.com/2012/08/reading-aleek-manush-by-syed-mustafa.html Accessed June 22, 2022. Web.
8. Shaikh, Farida. "Man of nature and poetry." Available at https://www.thedailystar.net/news-detail-249757 Accessed June 23, 2022. Web.
9. Das, Subrata Kumar. "A Sage, a boatwoman, and a river." Available at https://www.thedailystar.net/news-detail-172829 Accessed June 24, 2022. Web.

CHAPTER 5

Dooars Tea Tribals' Diasporic Identity and the Question of Belonging

Neka nortai bara lognai bala paira sohor baire
Na ga pur ti nagpuria
Bar lagnai bala pahera sohor bai
E raji nendar raji choi
Eangraji bhotang ragi koi
Hare moto chutira lagi

(part of a Kurukh song)

Introduction

The Dooars or Duars are the foothills of eastern Himalayas in North-East India around Bhutan. Duar means door and the region acts as the gateway to Bhutan from India. There are 18 gateways through which Bhutanese and the people living in plains can enter or exit. The region is divided by the Sankosh River into the Eastern and the Western Dooars. The Western part is known as Bengal Dooars and the Eastern as Assam Dooars. The altitude of Dooars ranges from 90 to 1750 metre. From the mountains of Dooars innumerable streams and rivers flow through Dooars, the major is Teesta. Monsoon here usually starts from mid-May and continues till the end of September. Winters are cold with foggy days and nights. Summer is mild. Its economy is based on three "T"'s – tea, tourism and timber. With the launching of tea plantation in the mid-1870s a large scale migration of tribal peasants, particularly Oraons, Mundas and Santals from Chhotanagpur and Santal Parganas to the Dooars, known to them as Bhutan, took place. They were recruited in tea gardens run by the British. Before the settlement of other communities they converted the forests into villages and *busties*. The remnants of these tribal people form a majority of the population in Western Dooars. My article is, however, linked to the diasporic identity of this forcedly displaced tea tribal community of Western Dooars and their question of belonging in Bengal and beyond.

Diaspora

The term 'diaspora' has a catastrophic origin. It derives from a Greek word meaning dispersion and it presumes that there exists a homeland to which the diaspora will eventually return (Tatla xviii).[1] And the term is often used by historians to describe the Jewish people's search for a home after their uprooting from the Holy land.

But today the term gains wider ramifications. According to Vijay Mishra Diasporas are people who are "precariously lodged within an episteme of real or imagined displacements, self-imposed sense of exile" (Mishra 1).[2] He shows that in seeking a common theory for the diverse phenomena of human migrations, the researchers have suggested diaspora to capture the most experience of displacement associated with migration, homelessness, painful memories and a wish to return to the land of origin. Some writers are, however, reluctant to extend the term 'diaspora' to migrant groups. They insist that a diaspora condition represents a unique, a mythically experience of the Jewish exile. They argue that the term diaspora should be reserved for groups forced to disperse, and whose members conscientiously strive to keep memories, maintain their heritage, and are involved in a survival struggle. They refer to the classic case of Jewish, Chinese, Armenians, Palestians diasporas (Tatla xix).

Robin Cohen in his classic study *Global Diaspora: An Introduction* (2008) emphasises on nine salient characteristics of diasporaic community:

1. dispersal from an original homeland, often traumatically
2. alternatively, the expansion from a homeland in search of work, in pursuit of trade or to further colonial ambitions
3. a collective memory of myth about the homeland; an idealisation of the supposed ancestral home
4. a return movement or at least a continuing connection;
5. a strong ethnic group consciousness
6. a troubled relationship with host societies
7. a sense of co-responsibility with co-ethnic members
8. the possibility of a distinctive creative, enriching life in tolerant host countries.[3]

Moreover some theoreticians single out genocide and ethnocide as a part of the diasporic experience. And many others do not favour voluntary migration as a part of the diasporic condition at all.

My Argument

My basic argument is that migration whether forced or voluntary can result in some diasporic incongruity, anomalies, a sense of displacement, painful memory of the ancestral past, a strong sense of ethnic bond, and a cultural impasse among the immigrant groups. Certainly, the uprooted chunks of tribals fail to fulfil the classic mode of diasporic criteria prescribed by Cohen and analysed by other theoreticians. They are not the victims of genocide or ethnic cleansing. But they are uprooted, displaced, dislocated from their land of origin, their homeland. I think migrations whether transnational or inland automatically impose some diasporic experiences, such as, a sense of exile, alienation, inhibition, rootlessness upon the immigrants. Diasporic condition from my point of view can never be celebratory. Though the postmodern celebration of diaspora, as in the case of NRIs is now well recognised. I, rather, agree with Mishra that diasporas are basically unhappy. "All diasporas are unhappy, but every diaspora is unhappy in its own way" (Mishra 1). E.J. Hobsbawm rues, "wherever we live in an urbanised society, we encounter strangers: uprooted men and women who remind us of the fragility or the drying up of our own families' roots (qtd. in Mishra 6). Thus, migration directly leads to diaspoic condition, that is, in other words, rootlessness, and a sense of 'in-betweenness', a sense of problematic uneasy belonging among the migrant groups. From this migratory point of view I try to focus on the diasporic identity or the diasporic condition of the Dooars tea tribals who mainly comprise of Oraons, Mundas and Santals.

Dooars Plantation History in Brief

Duars or Dooars had been historically a part of the Bhutanese domain and was a densely forested area. Plantatation and scientific forestry came only after British occupation by defeating the Bhutanese kingdom. And with the establishment of the colonial rule, came the colonial economy and colonial mode of production. They set up Zamindari system to garner revenue. They destroyed the rural base of Indian economy. And for their industrial needs they started indigo plantation. Like indigo they also started to further their colonial enterprise tea and forestry economy in Jalpaiguri, Darjeeling and the upper Assam. With the launching of tea plantation in the mid-1870s a large scale migration of tribal peasants, particularly Oraons, Mundas and Santals from Chhotanagpur and Santal Parganas to the Dooars which is known to them as Bhutan, took place. They were recruited as coolies in tea gardens run by the British. Before the settlement of other communities they converted the forests into villages and *busties*. These tribal coolies form a majority of the population in Western Dooars.

Dooars Tea Tribals

These tribal immigrants have unique ways of life and each sect has its particular culture and religious inclinations. The Oraons or Kurukh are victims of multiple migrations and they have a proneness to roaming. They have a rich range of folk songs, ritual dance and tales. They played traditional musical instruments such as Mandar, Nagara and Kartal. Both men and women participate in dace during festivals or any social celebrations. They followed the 'Sarna' dharma. They worship Mahadeo, the other name of Dharmesh, their supreme god. They believe everything in nature has its own deity or god. They perform religious rituals under a sacred grove. They speak 'Sadri,' commonly regarded a sister language of Bengali, Oriya, and Angika. They believe in supernatural spirits and practise sorcery and witchcraft. They have their distinct cultures which do not conform to the majority of the people of Dooars. I here cite a few sentences from a song written in Kurukh to refer to their diasporic condition and the pain it involves:

Neka nortai bara lognai bala paira sohor baire
Na ga pur ti nagpuria
Bar lagnai bala pahera sohor bai
E raji nendar raji choi
Eangraji bhotang ragi koi
Hare moto chutira lagi. (*Kirat Bhumi*: *Jalpaiguri Jela Sankalan* 666-667)[4]

It roughly means during our arrival to Bhutan (Duars) from Chhotanagpur we have to leave our relatives and even husbands behind. It is an unknown land or 'porar desh' and our lives are sordid indeed. This song attests to their diasporic condition and the pain and a sense of exile and hopelessness oozes out of it. So the Oraons address Duars as desh or another country, where everything is alien or unfamiliar and this unfamiliarity induces in them a feeling of exile, rootlessness, and unease and these characteristics are integral to any diasporic phenomenon. Like the Oraons, Santals and Mundas have experienced the same pain and agony because of their uprootedness from their original homeland.

The Santals believe in supernatural beings and ancestral spirits. Their rituals consist mainly of sacrificial offerings to the spirits or bongas. They have their own myth of creation. The story runs like this. The two heavenly birds Pilchu Haram and Pilchu Buddhi were first created by God. One day the birds made a nest and laid two cosmic eggs and out of the two eggs came the males and females of the earth. This myth is integral to the Santal worldview as it uniquely connects the life of humans to animals. The Santal have a high regard for the flora and the fauna and they decorate the mud walls of their houses with figures of animals and plants, known as 'fresco.' They express their joys and happiness through group dancing and singing. The three most quintessential instruments in Santali music are: two kinds of drums, Tumda and Tamak and the Tiriao or flute. Men and women together take part in dance and it has a wide variety of types and is attuned with the ceremony and social celebration. Similarly they have a variety of songs which are generally accompanied by dancing. Today many Santals have accepted Christianity, but still they retain some vestiges of their unique separate cultural identity. Even today the Santals of Samuktala, a santal majority locality in the district of Jalpaiguri (now Alipurduar), arrange annual 'Shikar Baithak' or 'La Bir-Baisi' (*Jela Sankalan* 642). Indian cast system is alien to them and, hence, Santal society is free from the maladies and violence of untouchability and other rigid societal wrongs and prejudices. They have no written form of language. Ol Chiki, the Santali script is a 1925 innovation by Pandit Raghunath Murmu.

The term Munda designates the name of the leader of the tribal community. The Munda call them 'Hodoko' which means 'human beings.' Like the Oraons and Santals, the Mundas have also a unique cultural affinity. Indian multifaceted caste system is alien to them. Buried ancestors are memorialised as 'Guardian' spirits or symbolised by burial stone 'sasandiri' and the bones of the deceased are placed under it. Once a year all members of the family are required to pay homage to sasandiri. Endogamous marriage is common among the Mundas. Like the Oraon, they follow the Sarna religion. Mundas converted to Christianity do still retain some of their intrinsic values though their life style has much been modified by the advent of modernity and globalisation.

These tribal immigrants barring few differences have nourished a strong ethnic unity. Duars is a foreign land to them. They were peasants and now have been tea labourers and coolies. They migrated to Duars in the hope of a better life. Their destitution and precarious condition of existence in their homeland made them fall to easy prey to the alluring prospect in the tea gardens as promised to them by the British hiring agencies. They, however, on their arrival to the unknown region saw themselves duped and victimised. At the time of recruitment they were given advance to apparently pay off debts in their country but actually to ensnare them. They were required to put their thumb impressions on an agreement bond for work for a period of at least six months in the tea estate. Before despatching these 'coolies' to the tea gardens they were kept in a concentration-camp like situation. No complaints could be made to the managers or the sarders who were law unto themselves. Physical coercion, beatings and flogging [as we found in Afro-American slave narratives] were common. Incidents of death due to physical torture were not unknown. There were unrecorded accounts of troublesome workers being thrown into furnaces of garden factories. Besides, tiny plots of land were given to them for cultivation either free or at a nominal rent. It was a means of allurement with a view to binding them to the garden. Universal Sunday open markets were organised so that the labourers of a particular garden could not get scope of contacting and meeting their kindred coolies recruited in other adjacent gardens. They had to work hard from dawn to dusk under the piercing eyes of an Indian subordinate staff such as sardar, dafadar, chaprasi, munshi and the like. The wages were too meagre to support a whole family. In consequence, the women and the children had to labour also. As a means of coercive practices, the British also introduced North Bengal Mounted Rifles (NBMR) to curb militant elements. Thus the planters devised various direct and indirect methods to these coolies on the garden and to hold them virtually in a state of captivity and servitude. They were in fact reduced to a semi-servile status.[5] They passed their days in exile. They could not and did not integrate themselves with the majority of the people. They lived a life of segregated or isolated existence clinging to their mythico-magical ancestral past. So their unhappy condition was indeed diasporic.

Dooars tea tribals' traditional life came to be severely dislocated because of their migration. They were pushed out of their traditional habitat and livelihood of a peasant in an unknown land. They were the most exploited groups of tribals. Their exploitation in colonial period by the sahibs and now by the various entrepreneurs lead to their social exclusion, backwardness, malnutrition, poverty and diseases. Poor standard of living with minimal health facility is noticeable everywhere. So what is seen is remarkable in our diasporic context. They migrated from their homeland to seek a better life. But on arrival their hopes and dreams were dashed. These peasants-turned tea labourers were herded together in a totally unfamiliar surroundings and this particular aspect itself put a restriction on their movement and freedom. The whole labour system involving their recruitment from their long distance home, the separation of workers from their known environment, their total isolation from their native surroundings because of geographical locations, social, cultural and language distances and barriers and various forms of open as well as hidden compulsions imposed on them by the sahibs are some of the major causes for their diasporic identity. All these factors coupled with their unforgotten past create a sense of alienation, aloofness, and exile among them. They have a strong ethnic sense. And Das Gupta mentioned that these tribal groups in the early decade of their migration maintain a close link with their village homes. In course of time the majority of them settled permanently in Duars but their link to their original home has never been completely cut off. Over the years as a result of diverse influences, their customs and cultures came to be modified. A very large section was subjected to the impact of Hindu religion and Hindu social practices, while another section embraced Christianity. However, "both segments retained their religious beliefs and social practices to a substantial extent" (Das Gupta 24). It was seen that in various spheres of Dooars social life there was an intermingling of Rajbansi Hindus and Muslims creating condition for the growth of a composite culture with elements of syncretism at base level. But the "immigrant tribals, particularly the plantation workers led practically a life of segregated existence and their points of contact with the other population groups remained minimal" (Das Gupta 25). They were cut off from the mainstream of Jalpaiguri and national freedom movement. They exhibited a strong sense of xenophobia, witchcraft and other cheap amusement. So they can be called diaspora like Tobago, Trinidad and Fiji and any other form of labour diasporas. However, by the second and the third generations the settlement patterns led to the development of at least some working relationship. Haats and other market places gradually became meeting points for economic and social intercourse between the local people and the immigrant tribals. But the Bengali middle class belonging to the higher castes as well the Marwaris with their widespread social networks bypassed and indeed looked down upon the indigenous autochthonous such as Meches, Rajbansis, Garos, Rabhas, Totos and the immigrant tribals.[6] They lead now a life which is quite different from the indigenous people or bhatias or other immigrant groups such as Nepalis, Marwaris etc. They stick to their basic cultural root and socio-cultural moorings. Economically, socially, historically and culturally they exist quite separate from the majority too. They have their own pain, suffering, alienation and aloofness. They indeed did not experience the trauma shared by the Jewish. But their hope of better life has been betrayed in an alien land. And their present condition, though some developments have obviously taken place, cannot be said better than their previous one. Poor housing and shocking health facilities, malnutrition, abysmal poverty still surround their ghettoised life.

"Chathuurtha Panipather Juddho"

Now to bolster my view of Dooars tea tribals' diasporic identity I cite a Bengali short story "Chathuurtha Panipather Juddho" by noted writer Subodh Ghosh.[7] Stephen Horo, the principal character is a Munda student who has both physical prowess and intellectual calibre to mark his stamp on both academic and non-academic activities. He is, thus, the cynosure of attraction of the whole class but at the same time, he is also a cause of fear and anxiety for his tribal origin. He is, however, admired by both teachers and his mates for his ability. As his name indicates, he has been converted to Christianity. But in course of time his proximity with Buro Sokha, the mentor of tribal culture has made him conscious of his ancestral past. Awakened as he is, he strives to free himself from the clutch of alien cultures. The author has provided a good example of his renunciation of the majority culture by not joining to a picnic arranged by his friends at Shiloarar jungle where palatable dishes are ready to be served. Instead, to show his defiance, he kills a squirrel to eat. This single incident proves his tribal root and he is very proud to exert his tribal identity. In the end we come to know that he has changed his name to Runnu Horo and, he is very conscious of his reclaimed identity. Thus, we see Horo to exert his defiance against the alien culture and at the same time to return to his root. But we can add from our diasporic context that he has experienced some diasporic existential dilemma in his attitude to both the alien culture and to that of his own. Once in school he takes Sanskrit as his optional subject and gets the highest marks. He can easily quote from the New Testament to please Father Lindon. Thus, he assimilates some traits of Hindu and as well as Christian cultures. But ultimately he forsakes them and comes back to the fold of his *own* people. Now the basic question is, is his condition diasporic? I think so. We discern in him the 'in-betweeness' as he strives to exist between two strands of culture, one of his own and the other, the imposed one. He is a Christian but he has not forgotten his ancestral past. His original identity is elaborated by Tudu, Horo's classmate. Horo beats drums in 'akhra,' drinks haria, a local brew, and makes love with a girl of their clan, Chirki Murmu. In moonlit night he killed a deer with his bow. He dances with frenzy with other tribals with a 'tangi' in his hand to celebrate their festivals. He cuts a burning simul tree first and when he is burnt Chirki Murmu embraces him. He knows English, Sanskrit but he does not neglect his mother tongue. He is civilised as well as primitive. He did not throw away his ancestral cultural moorings. Had he heard the Father, he could have easily managed an honourable job. Instead, he lends his hand to the tribal cause and thus convicted. During his school days he sometime proves himself sullen, aloof, and in a state of exile in the midst of alien land and culture. His friends Kalko, Besra, Tigga not to mention the Bengali Indu fail to understand the cause behind Horo's alienation and whimsicality. I argue that it is his diasporic identity which pains him and instills in him a sense of homelessness and rootlessness. The sense of aching unease, difference, exile, alienation, deprivation, discrimination and deterritorialisation can be discerned in Stephan Horo.

Diasporic Features

Now I present the following characteristics in brief in support of Dooars tea tribals' diasporic identity:

1. They have been dislocated from their original homeland, namely, Chhotanagpur and Santal Parganas
2. They have a strong ethnic group consciousness based on a distinctiveness, a common history and the belief of a common fate

3. They have a collective memory and shared myth about the homeland
4. The Duars is a foreign land to them in that the people, the occupation and the region is quite unfamiliar and different from their land of origin
5. a troubled relationship with the host societies marked their history too. That is why they try to keep a segregated existence of their own. Now they begin to voice their hopes and aspirations in the banner of Akhil Bharat Adivasi Vikash Parishad (ABAVP)
6. They cling to their mythico-religious past in the form of their various rituals and festivals
7. Culturally they still maintain some pristine characteristics in which individuality and structure of independent personality cannot take root
8. They exhibit existential dilemma and unilinear material development. They cannot, thus, relate themselves to history in process and literature as a social testimony.
9. A sense of unease, difference, exile, discrimination and rootlessness still reign over their lives.

Conclusion

Thus, the Dooars tea tribals' condition in strict compliance with Cohen and other diaspora theoreticians may not qualify as diasporic. But with some limitations the term can be used to the 'coolies' of Dooars in reference to their multiple migration, displacement, rootlessness, shared ethnic sense, a belief in common fate, idealisation of the ancestral past, sense of exile, and homage to rituals. Though much has been changed in their life styles, they still cannot and do not integrate themselves neither with the majority and the minority of the Duars nor with other immigrants such as Nepalis and Marwaris. And from this disintegration much of their diasporic identity emerges. Most of them cannot read Bengali, the language of the majority, till now. A Sense of strong ethnic affinity still acts as a cohesive agent among these tribal labourers. But before the face of dominant Bengali language and culture they feel marginalised. Their rootlessness, their existential pain among the aliens, their ghetto life and xenophobic anxiety make them a diaspora community of Dooars.

Notes

This article was originally titled "Dooars Tea Tribals' Diasporic Identity", and was first published in *Criterion e-journal* 4:2 (2013), 1-8. ISSN. 0976-8165. It is revised and enlarged for the present book.

Works Cited

1. Tatla, Darshan Singh. *The Sikh Diaspora: The Search for Statehood.* London: UCL Press, 2005. Print.
2. Mishra, Vijay. *Literature of the Indian Diaspora: Theorising the Diasporic Imaginary.* London & New York: Routledge, 2008. Print.
3. Cohen, Robin. *Global Diasporas: An Introduction.* 2nd Edition. London and New York: Routledge, 2008. p. 17. Print.
4. Kar, Aurobindo. *Kirat Bhumi: Jalpaiguri Jela Sankalan.* Vol. 2. 2004. Print.
5. Gupta, Ranjit Das. *Economy, Society, and Politics in Bengal: Jalpaiguri 1869-1947.* New Delhi: Oxford University Press, 1992. pp. 66-67. Print.
6. Ibid. pp. 24-25.
7. Ghosh, Subodh. "Chaturtha Panipather Juddho."*Bangla Choto Golpo.* Ed. Bijit Ghosh. Kolkata: Granthathirtha, 2009. Print.

CHAPTER 6

Religious Identity and Belonging: Vivekananda's Way

In a world marked by the existential challenges of mass consumption, environmental degradation, the unprecedented flow of humans, ideas and goods across boundaries, the threat of nuclear weapons, growing inequalities within and between countries, and enduring injustices based on gender, nationality, colour and creed, it is important to interrogate the role of religion and culture, and to examine whether they are part of the problem, and potentially at least part of the solution.

Joseph Camilleri & Sven Schottmann,
Culture, Religion and Conflict in Muslim Southeast Asia (2013)

Swamiji always stressed the fact that the best approach to Hindu mind and one sure to move it was through religion. So he put the organised and devoted service to the masses for their all-round regeneration in intellectual, religious, moral, and material conditions, not as a political programme, but on a religious basis as a means of salvation to every individual in accordance with the neo-Vedanta or practical Vedanta preached by him.

R. C. Majumdar, *Swami Vivekananda: A Historical Review* (2013)

Bare Words

Swami Vivekananda is not only a religious visionary he is a great orator, writer, social reformer, a patriot, and a maker of modern India. This dynamic multifaceted personality has been far ahead of his time. He believed in the assimilation of the best from each and every religion – Christianity, Islam, Jainism, Buddhism, Judaism and so on. His concept of God is akin to that of Islam. Islam considers God as omnipotent, omniscient, omnipresent, shapeless, pure power, who is immune from the cycle of birth and death. God is eternal, anadi. "Say: He is Allah, the One. Allah, the Unique. He does not give birth. Nor was He given birth to. There is no equal to Him" (Kidwai 1). God is supreme who sits in the driver's seat and the entire cosmos is regulated by His holy power. Vivekanada's concept of God or Bramha is the same, I claim.

Hijacking Vivekananda

Today Vivekananda is hijacked by political parties and by intellectual like Swapan Dasgupta who recently authored *Awakening Bharat Mata* with pejorative selections from Hindu nationalist writers, (Vivekananda being one) for their vested interests. His saying – 'say with pride that I am Hindu' is being misinterpreted by taking it out of context. Rafiq Zakaria observes:

> He [Vivekananda] never associated himself with the campaign of hate against them [Indian Muslims]; it is a pity that some Hindu communalists are whipping this up in his name. The protagonists of Hindutva are spreading canard that Swami Vivekananda is their inspiration and mentor for promoting aggressive and militant Hinduism and for promoting ethnic and economic cleansing of the Muslims. From my study of the teachings and the activities of the great Swami I find what they contend about the Swami totally incorrect. He was, on the contrary, a convinced champion of good relations between Hindus and Muslims. As for his involvement in Hinduism, he was more an iconoclast than a revivalist; more a unifier than a divider; more a universalist than a sectarian (*Communal Rage in Secular India* 162-63).

Vivekananda equals a Hindu with an Indian citizen. He never believed in sectarianism. His famous story of the pond of well in his Chicago lecture is well reminiscent of his syncretised religious vision. Though he is a Hindu monk, nowhere he is confined to Hinduism only. His vision is universal religion. He is energetic, revolutionary, and extremely conscious of the maladies of untouchability, poverty, superstition, illiteracy, and pathetic position of women in society of colonial India. He has shown the West through his1893 Chicago lectures the mystic and ennobling eternal power of Hinduism in its true sense. Through this paper I want to stress that Vivekananda is for the whole humanity, and not for the Hindu nationalists or Hindus only. And after Vivekananda there are perdurable similarities between Hinduism and Islam, especially so far as the cardinal concept of God is concerned.

Vivekananda's Hinduism

According to Vivekananda the ultimate aim of Hinduism is to have *moksha* or salvation so that rebirth is checked and man could have an eternal life by mingling *Jeeebatama* with *Paramatma* or God. How can it be achieved? There are roughly four ways – Knowledge, Work, Prayer and Meditation. We can restrain our inner and external anxieties by following one or all the ways. If we can practise the said ways with extreme admiration of God we can reach Him, *Bramha*, which is the ultimate truth. The basic concept is that if we follow the ways wholeheartedly, our affinity of this *maya* world will get day by day loosened, and there will come a day when we can be freed from the affection of this earthly world and our ego will perish and we will be capable to get transported to the Eternity. So far we are affectionate to this earthly world and earthly ways of life; we are 'jeebatma.' It is a kind of coarse life. And when we will be able to negate our ego or *ahang*, we will be 'Shiv' or Brahma. And one who can shed his ego which centres on I, he will be a Bramha. So, jeebatma which is mundane, ordinary, coarse will be transformed into the ultimate and eternal paramta, which is shapeless, pure, omniscient, omnipresent and omnipotent.

Vivekananda offers that our minds are always hankering after earthly pleasures. This is natural. We are all materialistic. In words of English Romantic poet William Wordsworth, the world is too much with us. We are madly pursuing materialistic inert objects. This apparent world is a hindrance towards the goal of achieving moksha. That is why we have to strive hard to follow the four ways to concentrate and tame our minds towards the God. One can do it by work, knowledge, prayer, by meditation, by visiting temple, church or masjid. These are all externals but supportive paraphernalia to reach to the ultimate destination God. All religions take the support of externals in its own way to cross the uphill road to God. Vivekananda has shown us with a simple example how the roads to the God is different from one religion to other. We all eat food, but one eats by sitting on an *asson*, (mattress), one eats on dining table, one eats with hands, and one eats with spoons. The aim is the same, to nourish the body. So each religion has its own specialities and externalities, but the aim is the same. This is the syncretic religious vision of Vivekananda. All religions are true, only the ways and praxes differ. This is the true imitable version of Vivekananda vision of religion. It is a common man's religion.

Vivekananda opines that man should work, whatever work it may be, with sincerity and devotion. God should have to be loved for love's sake only, not for any ulterior motives, namely, earthly prosperity or life – afterlife bliss and divinity. But man is doing that, and there is no harm in it. But the best way is to love God for God's sake only. That's why our ideal prayer should be like this: hey God I don't want asset, son or knowledge, I will go through innumerable trials and tribulations but my only prayer is to love you for love's sake. He opines that superstition is man's hardened enemy. But the worst is bigotry which rules the roost of contemporary world religions. About idolatry of Hinduism he explains that to Hindus idols are merely images which help them to concentrate on God. An idol is not God, or Iswar, Vivekananda's favourite word, and he or she is not omnipresent or omniscient. He opines that idolatry is the first step towards god. "It is the attempt of undeveloped minds to grasp high spiritual truths" (*Vivekananda Rachana Samagra* 20).[1] The next step is mental prayer or meditative prayer, that is prayer sung by the minds only, and the last is the vision of God. Here I think Islam is doing the second one that is prayer to God without external images. But who does not love the computerised photos of Mecca and Medina. In every mosque there is an arched shape structure placed to the west, though there is not an idol inside it as is customary to the way of the Hindus. Does not the structure indicate something or not? He says that worshipping idol is only a means to reach to the ultimate truth. And if one can internalise God without the externals it is good, but idolatry is not to be considered as something horrible. It is not that the help is necessary for everyone, but that those who do not need it have no right to say that it is wrong. "Nor is it compulsory in Hinduism." (20). So in pure Hinduism idolatry is not a must. Here Islam and Hinduism go hand in hand.

Vivekananda also opines that Hinduism is a universal religion whose sun will shine upon the followers of "Krishna, and of Christ, on saints and sinners alike; which will not be Brahminic or Buddhistic, Christians or Muhammeden, but the sum of total of all these" (20). Hinduism will be a religion which will have no place for "persecution or intolerance" in its polity. He pities the man who "dreams of the exclusive survival of his own religion and the destruction of others" (24). To have access to God one does not need to forsake his own religion. His suggestion is that a Christian does not need to a Hindu or a Buddhist, nor a Buddhist or a Hindu to a Christian. The same analogy if we keep the spirit of the sentence is applicable to a Muslim also. What is needed is to assimilate the best of each religion, keeping his own religion intact. His address at the final session of 27th September 1893 comes to an end with "Help and not Fight," Assimilation and not Destruction," "Harmony and Peace and not Dissension" (24).

Islam and Hinduism

Now I come to Islam. The word Islam in the Arabic of the Qur'an means "complete devotion or submission to God" (Haleem xxii)[2], unmixed with worship of any other. Qur'an urges the Christians and the Jews to practise their religion. They are given the prestigious title of 'People of the Book,' and it appeals to them 'Say, "People of the Book, let us arrive at a statement that is common to us all: we worship God alone, we ascribe no partner to Him, and none of us take others beside God as lords" (qtd. in Haleem xxv). According to the author God addresses Muslims, Jews, and Christians with the following: 'We have assigned a law and a path to each of you. If God had so willed, He would have made you one community, but He wanted to test you through that which He has given you, so race to do good: you will all return to God and He will make clear to you the matters you differed about' (qtd. in Haleem xxv). By the same analogy Qur'an certainly cannot forbid the Hindus to follow their own religion. The statement can be applied to all world religions. The aim is same, namely, to surrender to God. Islam does not recognise, as the Christians do in reference to Jesus, Prophet Muhammed as God. He is like Krishna, only the messenger of God. Christians think Jesus as their supreme God. Krishna, Kali, and other deities are not Gods, in line of thought of Vivekananda. They are the ways to the ultimate God. They are the ladders to reach to the highest Paramatma. Islam considers God as omnipotent, omniscient, omnipresent, shapeless, pure power, who is immune from the cycle of birth and death. God is eternal, anadi. God is supreme who sits in the driver's seat and the entire cosmos is regulated by His holy power. Vivekanada's concept of God or Bramha does not differ from this basic tenet of Islam.

Our experience shows that Islam paves the path to true socialism. That is why, we strongly believe that without Islam Vedanta to humanity is irrelevant. We want to push humanity toward a destination where the question of the existence of the Vedas, the Bible or the Qur'an does not arise. For our country our hope rests in the assimilation of Islam and Hinduism (qtd. in Partha Banerjee 156).

Vivekananda against Intolerance

Vivekananda is dead against the notion of persecution and intolerance. Even "toleration" of other faiths was not right; it smacked of blasphemy. He said, "Why should I tolerate. Toleration means that you are wrong and I am just allowing you." His Guru Sri Ramakrishna, he pointed out, had accepted all religions are true (Zakaria 166). But what we witnessing is the persecution of minorities is happening everywhere across the globe – Israel, Iraq, Serbia, Bosnia, India, Bangladesh, Pakistan, Myanmar, Srilanka, China, not to mention the racial invectiveness of the first and second world countries. Islam is alleged that it spreads through sword. Obviously it happens sometime. And in the context of India invaders are in most cases Muslims. But that Islam spreads only by swords cannot be generalised. Take the case of our state West Bengal with a population of almost 30% Muslims. Now it is proved that 98% of Bengali speaking Muslims is converted from lower caste Hindus, *shudras*. Who are responsible? Not Mohammed's ideology or so called barbaric Islamic force but the inhuman cruelty of upper caste Hindus. And accordingly Nirad Chaudhuri reiterates Vivekananda's stand on this polemic issue with utmost clarity, "The Mohammedan conquest of India came as salvation to the down-trodden, to the poor. That is why one-fifth of our people have become Mohammedans. It was not the sword that did it all, it would be the height of madness to think that it was all the work of sword or fire (qtd. in *Autobiography* 468)."[4] Swamiji affirms that there must be the recognition of one religion throughout the length and breadth of this land. What do I mean by one religion? Not in the sense of one religion as held by the Christians, or the Mohammedans, or the Buddhists. We know that our religion has some common grounds, common to all our sects, however varying their conclusions may be, however different their claims may be. So there are certain common grounds; and within their limitations this religion of ours admits of a marvellous variation, an infinite amount of liberty to think and live our own lives...[5]

According to Swamiji, religion is not just a talk on doctrines or theories, nor is it sectarianism. Religion does not live in sects and societies. It is a relationship between soul and god. He explained that religion does not consist in erecting temples or building churches or attending public worship. Also it cannot be found in the books or in words or in lectures or in organizations….Against the background of conflict among religions, he envisions the emergence of Universal Religion in modern times. It will liberate religions from the trammels of conflict and limitation….It has no location in space and time; its universal sunshine on all – on the Hindus and the Christians, on the

Buddhists and the Muslims, on the sinners and the saints (Islam and Sirswal 2013).

Vivekananda applauded the variety of religious traditions and pointed out that Vedanta had nothing against it. He said, "Whether you are a Christian, or a Buddhist, or a Jew, or a Hindu, whatever mythology you believe, whether you owe allegiance to the prophet of Nazareth, or of Mecca, or of India, or of anywhere else, whether you yourself are a prophet – it has nothing to say. It only preaches the principle which is the background of every religion and of which all the prophets and saints and seers are but illustrations and manifestations." He told his own followers: "Never judge the customs of other people by your own standards." Nor was he particularly enamoured of Hindu customs or rituals (Zakaria 166).

The Spiritual Hollowness

Forgetting the basic motto of religion we are all busy in throwing mud to one another. The religious issues which contemporary world is irking pathetically is all about the externalities of religion – whether one is wearing scanty dress, or burkha, or keeping beard or bearing other religious symbols. We are busy with symbols only, not on the inner soul of the man. Both the print and electronic media is flooded with the news of religious violence, communal clash, and sectarian violence. The world is witnessing a tremendous surge of religious violence. There is no need to cite examples. In India alone from 2005-2009, over 4000 religious violence occurred[6]. Is it Vivekananda's religious vision of India? Billions of dollars are being spent to maintain the externalities of religion by the fanatics. In India more than 50% people go to bed unfed. The scenes of child labourers, ragpickers, street children, and homeless beggars do not pain us. The destitutes are everywhere. If Vivekananda is to be followed, inhumanity is to be abolished first. Vivekananda cannot be confined to only a few intellectuals of Ram Krishna Maths and Missions who will go on conferencing on him availing all the luxury of life; he is more for the decrepitude subalterns. He is not for a particular religion. He is the man of the masses irrespective of her caste, creed and religion and country. Suniti Kumar Chatterjee wrote that Vivekananda, in the first instance, knocked off a lot of nonsense in our Hindu social life, and drew our attention to the Eternal Verities and not to the ephemeral accidental – social usages and such like – in our life. He was a sworn enemy of casteism. Untouchability was something which he abhorred both as a sannyasi and as a lay Hindu. He looked upon the poor and the humble, the suffering ones and the frustrated ones of society, as if they were deities incarnate or fragments of God, to serve whom was to serve God (Mukul Kantikar & Anoop A. J. 2019). He is an indomitable power who cannot be confined within a coterie of people with divisive and sectarian ourtlook. He denounced the upper classes as "walking carrions" and "walking corpses." He stressed time and again that the masses were the real foundations of Indian National life. It is through their physical labour only are possible, the influence of the Brahmans, the progress of the Kshatriyas, and the fortunes of the Vaishyas. He proclaimed, let India rise out of the peasants' cottage, grasping the plough, out of the huts of the fisherman, the grocer's shop, from beside the oven of the fritter-seller. Let her emanate from the factory, from marts and markets. Let her emerge from the groves and forests, from hills and mountains...They have suffered eternal misery, which has given them unflinching vitality…[7]

Vivekananda has a tendency to cite the name of a particular religion and criticise it, but then in the flow of the same speech clarify that he is referring the religion as it practised as negative, and in no way he is alluding to the religion in its doctrinal sense which was, in his opinion, positive. He is critical of Islamic invasion of India, and it is historically related fact. But he praises the concept of Islamic brotherhood, though he comments that it is not universal. Qur'an stresses on the casteless character of Muslims. Today Muslims are being divided into hundreds of castes by social scientists. But even today a zola, considered to be existing in the lower rung of society can pray with a sophisticated Muslim together. This immense strength of Islamic brotherhood and fellow feeling is recognised by Vivekananda himself. He praised Shahajahan for the love of his artistic sensibility, and he also pays esteem to Akbar for his liberal mind. Hindu-Muslim clash is a hindrance to the ethos of India, he knows that well. He has many Muslim friends and disciples. And he concludes that a new India can only be built with a Vaidantic heart and an Islamic body. (*Chintanayak* 280-281).[8]

Conclusion

In conclusion I want to emphasise that no religion is implacably pure and perfect. Each religion paves the way for a particular way of life as encapsulated in the saying of Vivekananda's guru Ramakrishna "*jato math tato path.*"And each religion leads to the God. The aim is the same, the ways are different. Vivekananda reiterates his guru:

> As different streams, having their sources in different places, all mingle their water in the sea, so, O Lord, the different paths which men take through different tendencies, various though they appear, crooked or straight, all lead Thee (Nikhilananda n. pag.).[9]

It is an altruistic vision of religion. 150th celebration of Vivekananda was observed worldwide with sheer enthusiasm. But the pitiable fact is that we have failed to understand him. If not, why is religious violence escalating day by day? Whether one accepts or denies the externals of religion, the rituals and customs linked with a particular religion, is a separate area of study. Devotion, or in other words, surrender to God is the most demanding task. And surprisingly and interestingly, religious violence primarily centres round the ways of performing externals of religion. There is a sense of unanimity in the basic concept of Allah, Brahma, God, or Iswar. The basic sprit of all religions is the same. If we admit it and practise it in our day to day lives, then I think, the misunderstanding and misconception of all religions will eradicate. And a new dawn will usher in the world. But is it possible, given the current nexus between politics and religion in contemporary world scenario?

To Vivekananda each race had its own greatness, and shone in the light of that central quality. As a religious teacher he made no attempt to popularise with strangers any single form or creed, whether of God or Guru. Rather, through him the might torrent of Hinduism poured forth its cooling waters upon the intellectual and spiritual worlds, fresh from its secret sources in Himalayan snows.[10] To him to think of India is to think of religious identity and religious belonging. He openly speaks of Hindu weakness, Hindu strength, and Hindu spiritualism. But He had not made his claims at the cost of other Indian communities, namely Muslims or Christians or Buddhists. His life was a quest for a 'common ground' where all religions in India can excel and flourish to its ultimate realisation of divine fruition.

To the Swami the Muslims were as good and human, and at heart as Indian, as the Hindus. There was affinity between Sufism and Advaita Vedanta. The distinction between them by reason of their different beliefs were subordinate to their identity as fellow countrymen. He was, no doubt, critical of some features of Islam but so was he of Hinduism. He was never dogmatic but a rationalist to the core. He always looked at the better side of every faith. He was a humanist to his fingertips believing in the eternal values which unite all sections of the human race, emphasizing that it will attain salvation only through love and compassion (Zakaria 169).

Notes

This article was orgnally titled "Vivekananda's Vision of Religion: A Brief Survey of Hinduism and Islam" and it was first published in *Research Chronicler: International Multidisciplinary Research Journal 2:3* (March 2014): 163-168. ISSN 2347-503X. Here it is modified and enlarged for the present work.

Work Cited

1. Basu, Prasun, and Sachindranath Bhattacharya, eds. *Vivekananda Rachana Samagra: Akhanda Bangla Sanskaran.* Kolkata: Nabapatra Prakashan, 1988. Print.
2. *The Qur'an.* Trans. M. A. S. Abdel Haleem. Oxford: Oxford University Press, 2010. Print.
3. Kidwai, Abdur Raheem. *The Quran: Essential Teachings.* Mumbai: Jaico Publishing House, 2007. Print.
4. Chaudhuri, Nirad C. *Autobiography of an Unknown Indian.* Ahmedabad: Jaico Publishing house, 2013. Print.
5. Majumdar, R C. "Swami Vivekananda: A Historical Review" in *Awakening Bharat Mata.* Ed. Swapan Dasgupta. Gurgaon: Viking, 2019.pp.169-70. Print.
6. "ASIA/INDIA – Statistics on communal violence: debate on the law for the protection of minorities. Available at < http://www.news.va/en/news/asiaindia-statistics-on-communal-violence-debate-o>. Accessed Feb 12, 2022.
7. Majumdar, R C. "Swami Vivekananda: A Historical Review" in *Awakening Bharat Mata.* Ed. Swapan Dasgupta. Gurgaon: Viking, 2019. pp. 162-63. Print.
8. Lokeswarananda, Swami, ed. *Chintanayak Vivekananda.* Kolkata: Ramakrishna Mission Institute of Culture, 1988. Print.
9. Nikhilananda, Swami. *Swami Vivekananda: A Biography.* 11th Dec. 2013. Web. Available at <http://www.vivekananda.net/PDFBooks/BiographybyNikhilananda.pdf >.
10. Sister Nivedita, "The National Significance of Swami Vivekananda's Life and Work" in *Awakening Bharat Mata.* Ed. Swapan Dasgupta. Gurgaon: Viking, 2019. p. 152. Print.
11. Banerjee, Partha. *Apni ki Deshadrohee?* Kolkata: R B Enterprises, 2021. Print.
12. Kantikar, Mukul & Anoop A.J. *Essential Vivekananda.* Rupa Publications, 2019. [Kindle Basic]. Retrieved from amazon.com.

13. Islam, Merina and Desh Raj Sirswal. *Philosophy of Swami Vivekananda.* Pehowa (Kurukshetra): Centre for Positive Philosophy and Interdisciplinary Studies (CPPIS), 2013. [Kindle Basic]. Retrieved from amazon.com. [Loc 307].

14. Zakaria, Rafiq. *Communal Rage in Secular India.* Mumbai: Popular Prakashan, 2002. pp. 162-169. Print.

CHAPTER 7

Nationalism, Patriotism & Rabindranath Tagore

> Whether India is to be yours or mine, whether it is to belong to the Hindu, or to the Moslem, or whether some other race is to assert a greater supremacy than either, that is not the problem with which Providence is exercised. It is not as if, at the bar of the judgment seat of the Almighty, different advocates are engaged in pleading the rival causes of Hindu, Moslem or Westerner, and that the party which wins the decree shall finally plant the standard of permanent possession. It is our vanity which makes us think that it is a battle between contending rights – the only battle between Truth and Untruth…
>
> Quoted in *Makers of Modern India* (2012),
> ed. Ramachandra Guha, pp. 187-188.

The Background

Much of twenty-first century nationalism, as Shashi Tharoor explains, is sahped by the current crisis of globalism. Kenichi Ohmae's classic *The Borderless World* argued persuasively in 1990 that national borders are less relevant than ever before in the new globally interlinked world economy. His certitude did not survive three decades. Globalisation was seen by much of the Western public as the ultimate project of the neoliberals, conceived by people in fancy boardrooms who made money out of tradingin money and shamelessly exploiting the privations of the poor. And the predictable backlash took two forms: economic and cultural. The economic backlash was straightforward. The poor and the unemployed in the developed world began to feel that they had no stake in the globalised system, and they demanded to know why their government's policies benefitted people in faraway lands like China and India with what used to be *their* jobs.They wanted to reduce the growing inequality in every 'developed' economy and go back to the security of older, more familiar economic ways, in which each generation would earn more and live better than their parents did.

The cultural backlash derived from the same resentment but expressed itself in a different arena: the political denunciation of global trade led to hostility towards foreigners, as more and more people sought the comfort of traditional identity and ways of life. Rage was expressed against the 'alchemical brew' served up in the name of progress – liberal politics, theologies of social emancipation, technocrats, trade agreements, multiculturalism. Out of the resentment of the global elites the masses easily adapted to their new narratives of victimhood. This translated into a rejection of the entire brew – cosmopolitanism, multiculturalism, and secularism in the name of cultural rootedness, religious or ethnic identity and nationalist authenticity. Political leaders were quick to seize the opportunity to tap into both kinds of backlash against globalisation (Tharoor, *The Battle of Belonging*). Today when we talk of patriotism or nationalism of varied hue, be it *ethnic nationalism, linguistic nationalism, cultural nationalism, religious nationalism, territorial nationalism, radical nationalism,* we need to put that in the said context. And Rabindranath Tagore, a universal man, a leading cultural icon of India, is beyond such narrow divisions of belligerent markers of human identity.

Rabindrik

Tagore was far away from what we popularly call patriotism. Our problem is that more we have been able to erase his ideals and ideas from our everyday life; more we have been able to be 'Rabindrik.' It is indeed sad to recognise this bitter truth. Our understanding of Rabindranath is confined to a mere recitation of his songs or keeping one or two copy from his vast literary oeuvre in our drawing room-book shelf. And we think we have entirely grasped his thoughts and ideas and we become extremely proud as a worshipper of this evergreen versatile thinker. Not that the very young people care or have the time or money to go through all his works. Rabindrasangeet is enough for them, and there is so much of it these days that one gets tired and smells something behind the propagation of Tagore culture through music.[1]

Tagore's Patriotism

Tagore was one of the greatest thinkers of the world of all ages. He was a 'karmayogi' – a tireless man of action. We need to go beyond his songs and poetry. And there we find the artist in multiple shades. He was a man of the entire world. He was beyond the periphery of national borders. He was never touched by the narrowness of caste, creed, religion or region. That is why Tagore is ever relevant to us and to the world. And he was ever ready to supply us food for thought in rain, summer or winter.

Rabindranath was never a blind patriot. Rather we can say he was a worshipper of truth, reason and justice. Unlike our present day clay-footed intellectuals he was always outspoken to uphold the sanctity of truth and justice. He fought against thousand ills and odds and championed the cause of humanity in his life-long struggle. He criticized the blind form of patriotism which is now enjoying a hay day across our country. Tagore's criticism of patriotism is a persistent theme in his writings. As early as 1908, he put his position succinctly in a letter replying to the criticism of Abala Bose, the wife of a great Indian scientist, Jagadish Chandra Bose: 'Patriotism cannot be our final spiritual shelter; my refuge is humanity. I will not buy glass for the price of diamonds, and I will never allow patriotism to triumph over humanity as long as I live.'[2]

What he meant by patriotism was finely manifested in his novel *Home and the World.* Nikhil is a social reformer and he works for the emancipation of women. But he finds no enthusiasm to work against the British. Consequently day by day his nationalist wife Bimala loses interest in him. She becomes more attracted to her husband's friend Sandip who talks big and acts with patriotic militancy. And in the end she falls in love with Sandip. Nikhil, however, refuses to change his views: "I am willing to serve my country ; but my worship I reserve for the Right which is far greater than my country. To worship my country as a god is to bring a curse upon it."

Tagore was not much enthusiastic about the glory of India's past. He condemned romantic over-attachment to past, what he called the tying of India to the past 'like a sacrificial goat tethered to a post', and he accused men who displayed it – they seemed to him reactionary of not knowing what true political freedom was, pointing out that it is from the English thinkers and English books that the very notion of political liberty was derived. (qtd. in *Argumentative Indian*, p. 105). He emphatically reiterated this argument in his book *Nationalism.*

Tagore's Nationalism

Nationalism refers to a set of beliefs about the nation. Any particular nation will contain different views about its character; thus for any nation there will be "different and competing beliefs" about it that often manifest themselves as political differences. Some may view their nation standing for individual liberty, while others may be willing to sacrifice that liberty for security. Some may welcome immigrants, and support policies that make it easy for them to become citizens; while others may be hostile to immigration. To take another example, consider disputes today in India. Some members of that nation have a narrow and intolerant view of their country by insisting that it should have only one religion, Hinduism; while others think that there should be freedom of all religions, namely, Islam, Christianity, Buddhism, Sikhism, and so on. Distinctive of nationalism is "the belief that the nation is the only goal worthy of pursuit" – an assertion that often leads to the belief that the nation demands "unquestioned and uncompromising loyalty." When such a belief about the nation becomes predominanat, it can threaten individual liberty. Moreover, nationalism often asserts that other nations are implacable enemies to one's own nation, an immigrant, or a person who may practise another religion or a different language (Steven Grosby 2005).

Rabindranath opined that India has never had a real sense of nationalism. Even though from childhood I had been taught that idolatry of the Nation is almost better than reverence for God and humanity, I believe I have outgrown that teaching, and it is my conviction that my countrymen will truly gain their India by fighting against the education which teaches them that a country is greater than the ideals of humanity.[3]

Tagore was much pleased with the diversity and broad base India boasted of: What is more, we have to recognise that the history of India does not belong to one particular race but to a process of creation to which various races of the world contributed – the Dravidians and the Aryans, the ancient Greeks and the Persians, the Mohammedans of the West and those of central Asia. Now at last has come the turn of the English…and we neither have the right nor the power to exclude this people from the building of the destiny of India. Therefore what I say about the Nation has more to do with the history of Man than specially that of India.

The history has come to a stage when the moral man, the complete man, is more and more giving way, almost without knowing it, to make room for the political and the commercial man, the man of the limited purpose. The process, aided by the wonderful progress of science, is assuming gigantic proportion and power, causing the upset of Man's moral balance, obscuring his human side under the shadow of soulless organisation. We have felt its iron grip at the root of our life, and for the sake of humanity we must stand up and give warning to all, this nationalism is a cruel epidemic of evil that is sweeping over the human world of the present age, and eating into its moral vitality (*Nationalism*, 58-59)

For example he highlighted the case of Japan. He was pained to see people's freedom being directly or indirectly curbed by Government's plural agencies. Japanese people, he lectured, were just robots or automated machines. They sacrificed their individuality and souls to the profit making monotonous machines.

I have seen in Japan, the *biswakabi* (poet of the whole world) says, the voluntary submission of the whole people to the trimming of their minds and clipping of their freedom by their government, which through educational agencies regulates their thoughts, manufactures their feelings, becomes suspiciously watchful when they show signs of inclining toward the spiritual, leading them through a narrow path not toward what is true but what is necessary for the complete welding of them into one uniform mass according to its own recipe. The people accept this all-pervading mental slavery with cheerfulness and pride… (*Nationalism*, 68). Tagore is confused with the form of Japanese materialistic progress. He is very much critical of such deathly, soulless progressive march.

Tagore's Broadness

There was no narrowness in his patriotism and Hinduism. (*O, amar desher mati tomar pore thekai matha/ tomate biswamoyeer tomate biswamayer aanchal pata.*) From this angle he does not wear the shoes the Bengalis of the past or present wear. To a Bengali Hindu his patriotism emanates not from the love of his country but from the hatred of the British. Likewise to him his Hinduism emanates not from his love of his religion but from his hatred of the Muslims. Both are false pride.[4] And Tagore cannot have any affinity or proximity to such lowly cultural Bengalis.

A Karmayogi

To Tagore a nation is not merely a piece of land. He sees it with the eyes of the universe. He wants to see his land fulfilled in all aspects. That is why he builds Shantineketan and Sriniketan for multiple developmental activities – modern agriculture, cattle rearing, fishery, handicrafts, development of Gram Panchayet, economic development of his subjects, removal of the curse of untouchability, health care facilities for the poor villagers, child and women education, vocational education, alleviation of poverty, maintenance of environment, greenery and ecosystem, sculpture and architecture. In pre-independence India such a versatile man of action was indeed rare. He had deep respect for the freedom fighters. His renouncement of Knighthood in solidarity of the people massacred in Jaliwanwalla Bagh, his patriotic songs against Lord Curzon's proposed division of Bengal touched millions of hearts. His independent and self-relient India was freed from the blemishes of narrow boundaries of caste, creed, religion or region or language, and such other numerous social divisive parameters.

Worshipper of Freedom and Rationality

Let us now concentrate on Tagore's poem 35 in *Gitanjali.* His attitudes towards politics and culture, nationalism and internationalism, tradition and modernity are adroitly captured here.

> Where the mind is without fear and the head is held high;
> Where knowledge is free;
> Where the world has not been broken up into fragments by narrow domestic walls;
> Where words come out from the depth of truth;
> Where tireless striving stretches its arms towards perfection;
> Where the clear stream of reason has not lost its way into the dreary desert sand of dead habit;
> Where the mind is led forward by thee into ever-widening thought and action
> Into that heaven of freedom, my Father, let my country awake.

I think this single poem encompasses what Tagore essentially is. To him to live is to live in freedom and with reason. He is dead against 'narrow domestic walls,' 'dreary desert sand of dead habit.' He is for 'clear stream of reason.' He aspires for a land 'where knowledge is free, where words come out from the depths of truth.' This poem demonstrates much of his idea of India, a land where the mind is led forward into 'ever-widening thought and action.'

Tagore's Cosmopolitanism

Tagore underlined: To feel unity in diversity, to establish unity amidst variety – this the underlying religion of India. India does not regard difference as hostility, she does not regard the other as enemy. That is why without sacrifice or destruction she wants to accommodate everybody within the great system. That is why she accepts all ways and sees the greatness of each in his own sphere.[5] Tagore, as Amartya Sen opined, wanted Indians to learn what is going on elsewhere, how others lived, what they valued, and so on, while remaining interested and involved in their own culture and heritage. Indeed, in his educational writings the need for synthesis is strongly stressed. It can also be found in his advice to Indian students abroad. In 1907 he wrote to his son-in-law Nagendranath Gangulee, who had gone to America to study agriculture:

> To get on familiar terms with the local people is a part of your education. To know only agriculture is not enough; you must know America too. Of course if, in the process of knowing America, one begins to lose one's identity and falls into the trap of becoming an Americanised person contemptuous of everything Indian, it is preferable to stay in a locked room (Qtd. in "Tagore and his India")

Tagore was a patriot without quite being a nationalist. He was no apologist for colonial rule; after British soldiers fired on an unarmed crowd in Amritsar in 1919, he returned his Knighthood to the King. At the same time, he was dismayed by the xenophobic tendencies of the populist edge of the Indian national movement. He thought that India had much to learn from other cultures, including (but not restricted to) the West…Tagore was the most widely travelled Indian of his generation. From what he saw at home and abroad, he arrived at an understanding of India's place in the world that was more nuanced, more layered, more complex and more profound than that articulated by any of his compatriots.[6]

Tagore's Reception by Bengali Bhadraloks

The Bengalis of West Bengal, I think, have been ruthlessly able to act against Rabindranath in all major ways – his views of patriotism, nationalism, and internationalism; his ideals of humanity; his ideas of freedom and reason. They have forgotten his contribution to the enrichment of Indian culture and spiritualism. We have been cut off from the skies Tagore loves to swim across with intrepidity. The killers of Gandhi are now our rulers, and we are happy to wash their murky feet with rose water. To remember Tagore in his birthday or death day has been just a facial show to the Bengalis. They miserably fail to imbibe a single thought or idea of him into their daily life. Tagore is for everyday. He is not for his birthday or death day celebration only. Quickly we learn, quickly we will be better human beings, better Bengalis too. It is a pity that the thoughts of a versatile Bengali genius like Tagore seem to lose steam in the hot weather of Hindutva militant nationalism. And Bengalis, it is sad to acknowledge, take pride in paying lip service to one of the greatest modern thinkers of India.

A Weapon against Hindu Militant Nationalism

Tagore can be a weapon against the Hindu militant nationalism, successfully espouched by current ruling dispensation. For example, we need to understand why has not been a Bengali intellectual Swapan Dasgupta able to include Tagore in his recent work *Awakening Bharat Mata: The Political Beliefs of the Indian Right* (2019). Chapters on Hindu political beliefs are carefully selected from such Bengali intellectual lumanaries as Bankimchandra Chattopadhyay, Sri Aurobindo, R C Majumdar, Jadunath Sarkar, Nirad C Chaudhuri and N C Chatterjee. A couple of chapters are devoted to Swami Vivekananda. In the entire scheme of things Tagore is absent, not as a writer or as part of the writing. Why? Over 400-page book R C Majumdar in his article, however, liberally gives Tagore six or seven lines, and they are limited to only how Vivekananda influenced the great poet:

> Some of the poems of Rabindranath indicate that he was also influenced by Swamiji's ideas of living; and working among men, and serving the God in man. In one of his poems, the great poet denounces the attitude of Hindus towards the low castes almost in the same vigorous language as Swamiji used, and he actually uses the word manusher narayana, corresponding to daridra narayana of Swamiji (163-64).

Can a humongous tree like Tagore be stunted this way? This is what generally called knowledge production mechanism. Preach only what we believe, and discard what is indigestible. Rewriting of history! What a mockery of intellectual exercise! What a waste of energy! Bengalis like Guptas are acting against the principles and ideologies of the great poet who is revered throughout the globe as a supreme humanist. He is a resilient icon of a distinct Bengali culture and he is abhorred even in the land of its origin. In today's India he is the declared enemy to the violently muscular Hindu nationalism enthusiasts. To save Tagore we need to spread his thoughts among the masses. He cannot be confined to a drawing room shelf; he cannot be confined to the Rabindriks only. Tagore is an assest for all. We should not worship him going by the calendar. We must understand the man and his mind and his karma with logic and rationality. This can be one of the best ways to pay tribute to the great man and keep him ever relevant to the discourses of Indian culture and philosophy.

Works Cited

1. Samar Sen. *Babubritanto O Prasonghik*. Kolkata: Deys, Fourth Revised Edition, Baisakh 1411, p. 227. Print.
2. Amartya Sen. "Tagore and his India" in *The Argumentative Indian*. London: Penguin Books, 2005, p. 108. Print.
3. Rabindranath Tagore. *Nationalism*. Fingerprint Edition, 2020, p. 95. Print.
4. Nirad C Chaudhuri. *Atmaghati Rabindranath*. Akhanda Sanskaran. Kolkata: Mitra & Ghosh, 1421, p. 101. Print.
5. https://theprint.in/india/why-bengal-needs-to-learn-from-tagores-words-on-resolving-conflicts-though-hindu-viewpoint/653843/. Web.
6. Guha, Ramachandra, ed. *Makers of Modern India*. New Delhi: Penguin Books, 2012. p.186.

   Print.
7. Dasgupta, Swapan, ed. *Awakening Bharat Mata: The Political Beliefs of the Indian Right*. Gurgaon: Viking, 2019. Print.
8. Tharoor, Shashi. *The Battle of Belonging: On Nationalism, Patriotism, and what it Means to be Indian*. Aleph Book Company, 2020. [Kidle Basic] Retrieved from amazon.com. [Loc 70].
9. Sen, Amartya. "Tagore and his India." Available at https://www.nobelprize.org/prizes/literature/1913/tagore/article/

   Accessed, June 3, 2022.
10. Grosby, Steven. *Nationalism: A Very Short Introduction*. Oxford University Press, 2005. [Kindle Basic]. Retrieved from amazon.com. [Loc 231].

CHAPTER 8

Advocacy of Gikuyu: Ngugi wa Thiong'o's Exemplary Resistance to Cultural Imperialism

> If you know all the languages of the world and you do not know your mother tongue, that is enslavement. Knowing your mother tongue and all other languages too is empowerment.
>
> Ngugi wa Thiong'o

Bare Words

In this article titled "Advocacy of Gikuyu: Ngugi wa Thiong'o's Exemplary Resistance to Cultural Imperialism" I try to argue the key role one's mother tongue plays in sustaining and rejuvenating one's innate literature, culture and heritage. Each language has its unique rhythm, essence and nuances. Language may be a bare medium of communication in the fields of science, commerce and technology. But in literature it is a demonstration and reflection of one's cultural ethos, one's self. A language because of its poor global reach, limited scope as a bearer of cultural legacy, and other such alleged hindrances cannot be simply rejected by its native tongues. For Thiong'o, Gikuyu, his mother tongue, is a weapon of resistance to the cultural hegemony of English. His desertion of English and espousal of Gikuyu is a giant step to claim his cultural root, racial identity and kind of freedom he urges for his peasantry and working class countrymen. It culminates in his anti-colonial belligerent stand as well as reclaiming his sacred African self.

What Colours Ngugi's Stand?

Ngugi wa Thiong'o, born in 1938 in Kamirithu, a village in the north of Nairobi, is one of 28 children of a mercurial father with four wives. In the 1950s, his older brother, Good Wallace, joined the Mau Mau uprising against a ruthless British occupation whose prison camps were described by the then-solicitor general as having been "distressingly reminiscent of conditions in Nazi Germany or Communist Russia," according to secret documents released by the Foreign Office in 2012. Ngugi's half-brother Gitogo was shot in the back and killed for refusing to obey a British soldier's command. He hadn't heard it because he was deaf. His mother, who is the driving force behind his work, was detained in solitary confinement for three months.[1] Edward Said affirms that Europe's Orientalist stereotypical descriptions of Africa, India, Middle East and the Far East, Australia and the Caribbean bear its imperialistic designs. These Africanist and Indianist discourses are integral parts of the "general European effort to rule distant lands and peoples," to bring "civilization to primitive or barbaric peoples." And the ideas about "flogging or death or extended punishment" are required when *they* misbehave or became rebellious, because *they* mainly understand force or violence best. "*They* are not like *us*, and for that reason deserved to be ruled (*Culture and Imperialism*)." Ngugi has been fighting against this stereotypical racial division of so called colonial superiority self and colonized inferiority self. He knows well what Said emphasizes; culture is a sort of theatre where various political and ideological causes engage one another. Far from being a placid realm of Apollonian gentility, culture can even be a battle ground on which causes expose themselves to the light of the day and contend with one another (*Culture and Imperialism* Loc 129).

Ngugi's Cause

Said has asserted that stories are at the heart of the colonial history and the world of empire. They also can become the method of colonized people's assertion for self identity. The main battle in imperialism is over land, but when it came to who owned the land, who had the right to settle and work on it, who kept it going, who won it back, and who now plans its future – these issues were reflected, contested in narrative....The power to narrate, or to block other narratives from forming and emerging, is very important to culture and imperialism, and constitutes one of the main connections between them. The grand narrative of emancipation and enlightenment mobilized people in the colonial world to rise up and throw off imperial subjection (*Culture and Imperialism* Loc 117). Ngugi's narrative is the assertion of the native culture of Kenyan mass. His works include novels, plays, short stories, and essays, ranging from literary and social criticism to children's literature. His short story collection *The Upright Revolution: Or Why Humans Walk Upright* is translated into 90 languages around the world. He is one of the cult figures who has revolutionised African literature and peeled its colonial umbrage. What was working on his mind when he took pen to write novels was categorically stated in his famous essay 'Moving the Centre' (1992):

> The very choice of writing a novel in 1960s that examined the lives of ordinary Kenyans was part of a wider 'struggle for the right to name the world for ourselves.'[2]

"His narrative constitutes a vital attempt to give voice to the people's collective identity and history."[3] Novels and plays are also his accepted medium of expression of human condition. But he believes that to express immediate African reality one should write in one's mother tongue. And why is colonial language English not suited for the cause of his Kenyan men and women? His answer is simple. If one accepts English he must suffer from a sense of 'derivativeness.' That is a hindrance to revitalise one's culture. It mutilates one's self. Self-image is a serious area of postcolonial exploration. Ngugi's search for a pristine African self finds its way to his advocacy of Gikuyu. It is risky but it is immensely rewarding too. So he takes the risk with a broad smile on his resolute face. African literature and orature (oral literature) is written in varied languages such as Igbo, Gikuyu or Kikuyu, Hausa, Somali, Swahili, Arab and French. Ngugi felt that if things were to be seen from African perspective, literary representations must be primarily in an African language and not that of the former coloniser.[4] Ngugi believed that even well meaning anti-colonial nationalist leaders were limited in their authenticity because their thought and action remained imprisoned within European language (Tharoor, *The Battle of Belonging*).

Exploration with Kikuyu or Gikuyu

Ngugi's embrace of Kikuyu began in earnest with his 1977 play *Ngaahika Ndeenda* or, *I Will Marry When I Want*. The story of a farmer swindled out of his land by corrupt elites, it dealt directly with the plight of ordinary Kenyans and cast untrained villagers in starring roles. The play was a hit for six weeks before the authorities shut it down. On New Year's Eve, then vice-president and later dictator Daniel arap Moi sent Ngugi to the notorious Kamiti Maximum

Security Prison. There he wrote *Devil on the Cross* (1980) – in secret, on prison-issued toilet paper – and followed it with *Detained: A Writer's Prison Diary* (1981). An Amnesty International campaign helped to free him after one year of detention. It was in prison, he tells me, that he became determined to write only in Kikuyu.[5]

His decisive aim is to usher in a novel form of theatre in his native Kenya that sought to liberate the theatrical process from what he held to be "the general bourgeois education system," by encouraging spontaneity and audience participation in the performances. His project sought to "demystify" the theatrical process, and to avoid the "process of alienation [that] produces a gallery of active stars and an undifferentiated mass of grateful admirers" which, according to Ngugi, encourages passivity in "ordinary people."

In *Caitaani Mutharaba-ini* (1980; *Devil on the Cross*), a novel written in Gikuyu and English versions Ngugi presented these ideas in an allegorical form. Written in a manner meant to recall traditional ballad singers, the novel is a partly realistic, partly fantastical account of a meeting between the Devil and various villains who exploit the poor. *Murogi wa Kagogo* (2004; *Wizard of the Crow*) brings the dual lenses of fantasy and satire to bear upon the legacy of colonialism not only as it is perpetuated by a native dictatorship but also as it is ingrained in an ostensibly decolonised culture itself.

Opposed Forces Reigning African Reality

In opinion of Ngugi there are two mutually opposed forces governing African realities: an imperialist tradition in one hand, and a resistance tradition on the other. Imperialist tradition is maintained by the international bourgeoisie using the multinational and of course the flag-waving native ruling classes. The economic and political dependence of the native ruling classes is reflected in its culture of apemanship and parrotry enforced on a restive population through police boots, barbed wire, a gowned clergy and a judiciary. Ideas of the neo-colonialists are supported and spread by a corpus of state intellectuals, the academic and journalistic laureates.

The resistance tradition is being carried out by working people, mainly peasants and proletariat. They are also aided by the patriotic students, intellectuals, soldiers and other progressive elements of the middle class. This resistance is reflected in their advocacy of peasant/worker roots of their national culture.

The classes fighting against imperialism even in its neo-colonial stage and form have to confront this threat with the higher and more creative culture of resolute struggle. These classes have to wield even more firmly the weapons of the struggle contained in their cultures. They have to speak the united language of struggle contained in each of their languages. They must discover their various tongues to sing the song: 'A people united can never be defeated.'[6]

Already Ngugi is a celebrated name by publishing four novels in English: *Weep Not, Child* (1964), *The River Between* (1965), *A Grain of Wheat* (1967), *Petals of Blood* (1977). Consequently it leads him to the door of the English Department at Makerere University. So he is quite successful. But what makes him forsake English and its inherent imperial impositions? Answer he offers thus:

> But I was becoming increasingly uneasy about the English language. After I had written *A Grain of Wheat* I underwent a crisis. I knew whom I was writing about but whom was I writing for? The peasant whose struggle fed the novel would never read it.[7]

He elaborated on his rationale: "the bullet was the means of the physical subjugation; language was the means of the spiritual subjugation." He famously opined, "'To starve or kill a language is to starve and kill a people's memory bank.'"[8]

Greater Cause

In *Homecoming: essays on African and Caribbean literature, culture and politics* (1972) he was quite emphatic about the language issue:

> Equally important for our cultural renaissance is the teaching and study of the African languages. We have already seen what any colonial system does: impose its tongue on the subject races, and then downgrade the vernacular tongues of the people. By so doing they make the acquisition of their tongue a status symbol; anyone who learns it begins to despise the peasant majority and their barbaric tongues. By acquiring the thought-processes and values of his adopted tongue, he becomes alienated from the values of his mother tongue, or from the language of the masses. Language after all is a carrier of values fashioned by a people over a period of time. It seems to me that in a country where ninety percent speak African languages, it is very unwise not to teach these in schools and colleges. We need to develop a national language, but not at the dire expense of the regional languages. In a socialist economic and political context, the development of ethnic languages would not be inimical to national unity and consciousness. It is only in a competitive capitalist set-up that the warring interests exploit ethnic and regional language differences to the detriment of the common cause of peasantry and the workers (*Decolonising the Mind,* 72).

Language as Carrier of Culture

Ngugi's repetitive assertion of the relevance and usability of language as a supreme carrier of one's culture is emphatically reflected thus:

> Language carries culture, and culture carries, particularly through orature and literature, the entire body of values by which we come to perceive ourselves and our place in the world. How people perceive themselves affects how they look at their culture, at their politics and at their social production of wealth, at their entire relationship to nature and their beings. Language is thus inseparable from ourselves as a community of human beings with a specific form and character, a specific history, a specific relationship to the world. (*Decolonising the Mind,* 16)

The same perspective is shared by one of the renowned and versatile literary gems of West Bengal, Buddhadeva Bose:

> *Manush parovashai prai je kono kaj e chalate pare, pare na shudhu kabbo, natok,uponaas likhte, sristhishil sahitto rochona korte. Keno pare na? Jehutu sahityo jekhane sristishil sekhane manusher somogro ontoratma sokriyo hoye othe – shudhu tar buddhi, indriybodh o hridoybritti noy, tar nirjjan mon, tar atmay odhisthit norok o sorgo, tar purbo purusher dhusor smritipunjo.* (A man can do anything in foreign language. But he cannot write poetry, drama, novel, or creative literature. Why cannot he write? As in creative literature a writer's inmost soul becomes active – not only his intellect, sense-perception or heart's workings alone. Here his altruistic mind, concept of hell and heaven embedded to his soul, his ancestors' grey memories come into play.) [9]

Ngugi's Urge to Fellow Writers

In a challenge to the imprisoning authorities through *The Detainees Review Tribunal*, dated 23 June 1978 he concluded:

> Kenyan writers have no alternative but to return to the roots, return to the source of their being in the rhythms of life and speech and languages of the Kenyan masses if they are to rise to the great challenge of recreating, in their poems, plays, and novels, the epic grandeur of that history.
>
> Instead of being suppressed and being sent to maximum security prisons and detention camps, they should be accorded all the encouragement to write a literature that will be the pride of Kenya and the envy of the world (*Decolonising the Mind,* 72).

Thus he comes out of what Chinua Achebe called, 'a dreadful betrayal' in his speech entitled 'The African Writer and the English Language in 1964:

> Is it right that a man should abandon his mother tongue for someone else's? It looks like a dreadful betrayal and produces a guilty feeling. But for me there is no other choice. I have been given the language and I intend to use it (qtd. *Decolonising the Mind* , 7)…. The dissociation, divorce,

> or alienation from the immediate environment becomes clearer when you look at colonial language as a carrier of culture (*Decolonising the Mind,* 17).

Ngugi's Frustration

Ngugi elaborates his frustration about teaching activities done in his department:

> The syllabus of the English Department for instance meant a study of the history of English literature from Shakespeare, Spencer and Milton to James Joyce and T. S. Eliot, I. A. Richards and the inevitable F. R. Leavis. Matthew Arnold's quest for the sweetness and light of a Hellenized English middle class; T. S. Eliot's high culture of an Anglo-Catholic feudal tradition, suspiciously close to the culture of the 'high table' and to the racial doctrines of those born to rule; the Leavisite selected 'Great Tradition of English Literature' and his insistence on the moral significance of English literature; these great three dominated our daily essays. How many seminars we spent on detecting this moral significance in every paragraph, in every word, even in Shakespeare's commas and full stops? (*Decolonising the Mind,* 90)

English colonial language education not only responds to the demands of access to European knowledge, but also it is way of effective governance over the colonized people. Under the mask of the moral duty to enlighten uncultivated subjects, the established discourses of Anglicism and Orientalism aim at fashioning the tastes, opinions, and morals of the ntaives after the British imperial style, making them deny their origins in an attempt to become more English than the Englishman….The indigenous cultures and languages are regarded as unable either to contain or to convey any sort of valuable information, because of being primitive and rude as the natives themselves. This motion leads to the alienation of the aboriginal personality….Due to systematically destruction of the native languages and the imposition of the one of colonial power, a wide gap opens between the experience and reality….The motion of the supremacy of the English, established by the English colonial language policy, leads to the phenomenon that the colonized voluntary want to be absorbed, to become replications of the colonialists….The postcolonial personality suffers, because of its internal split between the adopted imperial culture and its colonial origins, being pressed and shown as unworthy. Te attitudes of racism of the superior whites and their attempts to position the postcolonial newcomers as inferior and backward make the search of a self even more difficult (Rositsa Kronast).

Present Stand

In an interview with Neil Munshi of *Financial Times* on 16th November 2016 his basic position he clearly states, "No matter how you are recognised in other countries [with awards or prizes], there is something special about home. There's no point being a prince elsewhere, when you are a pariah at home."

I wonder, commented Munshi, what he makes of the fact that today most well-known African writers publish in English, often from abroad. In 2013, Ngugi said that such writers – including his son Mukoma, a professor at Cornell University, and one of four published authors among his nine children – are part of a "metaphysical empire," contributing to the expansion of English. But now he seems to have softened his view.[10]

Languages of the imperialist imposition were favoured even by the most radicals and pro Africans. They held the view that renaissance of African cultures lay in the language of Europe, he ruled in *Decolonising the Mind.* And many global literary giants like W. B. Yeats, Salman Rushdie, Amitava Ghosh, to name only a few, have found no substance in Thiong'o's argument for championing afrocentricity through Gikuyu. Arundhati Roy airs the same view in the context of accepting English in relation to multilingual, multicultural, heterogeneous India:

> Guilt in this case is an unhelpful sentiment. India as a country, a nation-state, was a British idea. So, the idea of English is as good or bad as the idea of India itself. Writing or speaking in English is not a tribute to the British Empire, as the British imperial historian had tried to suggest; it is a practical solution to the circumstances created by it….It is the language of privilege and exclusion. It is also the language of emancipation, the language in which privilege has been eloquently denounced. *Annihilation of Caste* by Dr B. R. Ambedkar, the mostwidely read, widely translated, and devastating denunciation of the Hindu caste system, was written in English. It revolutionised the debate on perhaps the brutal system of institutionalised injustice that any society has even dreamt up. How different things would have been had the privileged castes managed to contain Ambedkar's writing in a language that only his own caste and community read.[11]

Resisting Cultural Bomb

But that is a different story for my argument. Whether Ngugi is a loser or winner matters least. What really matters is his love, zeal, sheer activism for his pesantary villagers and countrymen and his resilience and resistance to colonial and neocolonial masters' imposed cultural crudities, cruelties, assaults through the agency of the language hegemony of the white supremacists. The effects of a cultural bomb are multiple, as he analysed in his *Decolonising the Mind*:

1. It annihilates a people's belief in their names, in their languages, in their environment, in their heritage of struggle, in their unity, in their capacities and ultimately in themselves
2. It makes them see their past as one wasteland of non-achievement
3. It makes them want to distance themselves from that wasteland
4. It makes them want to identify with that which is furthest removed from themselves; for instance, with other people's languages rather their own
5. It makes them identify with that which is decadent and reactionary, all those forces which will stop their own springs of life
6. It even plants serious doubts about the moral rightness of the struggle
7. Possibilities of triumph or victory are seen as remote, ridiculous dreams
8. The intended results are despair, despondency, and a collective death-wish
9. Amidst this wasteland imperialism presents itself as the cure and demands that the dependent sing hymns of praise with the constant refrain: 'Theft is holy'

And for Ngugi, advocacy of Gikuyu and other African local languages, local cultures, is the best way to resist the imposition and progress of the imperialists' racist hegemonic agenda on indigenous people and native communities.

Works Cited

1. "It was defiance': an interview with Ngugi wa Thiong'o" <https://www.ft.com/content/5305acae-aa82-11e6-9cb3-bb8207902122> Accessed Feb 10, 2020.
2. Qtd. in John McLeod's *Beginning Postcolonialism*. New Delhi: Viva Books, 2015. p. 93.
3. Ibid.

4. Sarkar, Parama. *Postcolonial Literatures.* Hyderabad: Orient Blackswan, 2016. p. 137.
5. "It was defiance': an interview with Ngugi wa Thiong'o" <https://www.ft.com/content/5305acae-aa82-11e6-9cb3-bb8207902122> Accessed Feb 10, 2020.
6. Thiong'o, Ngugi wa. *Decolonising the Mind: The Politics of Language in African Literature.* New Delhi: Worldview Publications, 2007. p. 3.
7. Ibid. p. 72.
8. "It was defiance': an interview with Ngugi wa Thiong'o" <https://www.ft.com/content/5305acae-aa82-11e6-9cb3-bb8207902122> Accessed Feb. 10, 2020.
9. Bose, Buddhadeva. "Vasha, kobita o manushotto" in *Prabandha-Sankalan.* Kolkata: Dey's Publishing, 1982. p. 209.
10. "It was defiance': an interview with Ngugi wa Thiong'o" <https://www.ft.com/content/5305acae-aa82-11e6-9cb3-bb8207902122> Accessed Feb. 10, 2020.
11. Roy, Arundhati. "In What Language Does Rain Fall over Tormented Cities" in *Azadi: Freedom. Fascism. Fiction.* New Delhi: Hamish Hamilton, 2020, pp.10-11.
12. Tharoor, Shashi. *The Battle of Belonging: On Nationalism, Patriotism, and what it Means to be Indian.* Aleph Book Company, 2020. [Kidle Basic] Retrieved from amazon.com. [Loc 93].
13. Said, Edward. "Introduction." *Culture and Imperialism.* Vintage Books. [Kindle Basic] Retrieved from amazon.com. [Loc 92].
14. Kronast, Rositsa. "Introduction: The Impact of the English Colonial Language Policy on the Postcolonial Identity." *English Colonial Language Policy and Postcolonial Literature.* Bachelor Thesis, 2007. [Kindle Basic] Retrieved from amazon.com.

CHAPTER 9

Afzal's Religious Identity and the Question of Belonging in B. S. Tyagi's *Afzal*

> Who has done all this – Muslim or Christian or someone else? Are they less than terrorists? Why aren't they dubbed terrorists? Why aren't they detained under POTA? Why don't people shout –hang them? Or spit at them? Why aren't these rapists hanged publicly?
>
> *Afzal* (2019)

Choiceless Identity

Indeed, many of the conflicts and barbarities in the world are sustained through the illusion of a unique and choiceless identity. The art of constructing hatred takes the form of invoking the magical power of some allegedly predominant identity that drowns other affiliations and in a conveniently bellicose form can also overpower any human sympathy or natural kindness that we may normally have. The result can be homespun elemental violence, or globally artful violence and terrorism. In fact, a major source of potential conflict in the contemporary world is the presumption that people can be uniquely categorised based on religion or culture. The implicit belief in the overarching power of a singular classification can make the thoroughly inflammable…the world is frequently taken to be a collection of religions or civilisations or cultures, ignoring other identities of class, gender, profession, language, science, morals and politics. This unique divisiveness is much more confrontational than the universe of plural and diverse classifications that shape the world in which we actually live.[1]

A Brief Overview of *Afzal*

Tyagi's novel under review *Afzal* (2019) has three parts. It has a linear narrative. Introductory part 'Out of the Ashes' is a scintillating historical account of the town of Azampur situated in North Uttar

Pradesh and the heroic participation of its people in India's freedom struggle. The story comes alive through the mythic narrative of Kazi Sahab, the last courtier of Azam Khan after whom the town was named. The second part 'The Escapades' details Afzal's harrowing odyssey in post-independence India where he encounters myriad shoddy and humiliating experiences as a job seeker. His stays at Imran Pahalwan's City Garage as an apprentice mechanic, as an ashram member at Mukti Ashram, as a cab driver at professor Tripathi's house, as a domestic helper at a famous judge's house – are an eye opener to the easy, moneyed, unscrupulous, lusty, dishonest ways of postmodern Indian life. Disillusioned, he comes back home only to be picked up by the police as a mastermind in the Jaipur Triple Blast case. And the concluding part 'Hamam' engages us how Afzal is dragged into politics as a ploy. He quickly learns the techniques of earning and wielding power. He is now a leader of the masses. Universities are offering honorary doctorate on him. Azampur is proud with its son of the soil. Afzal, however, takes account of his whole life and validates his pure and sinful days and comes to terms with his real self.

Afzal Rechristened

Let me quote a poem titled "Distrust" from my anthology *Shadows of Mourning* (2022) to enumerate the complexity of Hindu-Muslim relation which in general lacks trust and belief, the most powerful cohesive qualities that can withstand the vagaries of time:

> You call me bhai
> And pat my back
> Flashing smiles
> That is fine.
>
> But I know
> You are the first
> Who will harm me
> At accursed hour.

In India and other non-Western and Western countries distrust has deepened among races, communities, cultures, or say, religions. The world is burning on the fuels of differences of caste, creed, culture, religion, language, nationality and locality. Across the globe authoritarian regimes are banking on the identity of the majority. In USA it is poor white Americans. In India it is the majority Hindus who are claiming a new Hindu identity. Had they been non-Hindus before BJP coming to power in 2014? Or had they been enslaved by the Muslim or Christian rulers after independence? Is Hinduism and Hindutva same? Questions are many and they lead people to endless arguments. If terror derived from religious fundamentalism has one headquarter in India, it is the RSS. Their younger siblings, the Islamic, Sikh or Christian fundamentalists, though dangerous in their own ways, cannot match the organisational network, financial muscle or political legitimacy that the RSS owns("Unravelling Hindutva Terrorism")

One of my good friends one day shared a lovely story. A Muslim boy wanted to change his name. They boy blamed his parents for giving his name Sabir. He wanted to change it into Suman. Sabir is a pass graduate Bengali Muslim youth who does a dozen casual jobs. He can read paper, understand the issues debated on TVs, or in trains and buses and clubs or neighbourhood tea shops. Sabir is unlucky and he feels sad. He has not yet changed his name. He is merely thinking of doing so. He is confessing his wish to one of his bosses and the boss happens to be my friend. Many of our Muslim boys and girls during their student life have to change their names, (verbally not officially) in order to be accommodated in different messes and hostels owned by Hindu landlords or landladies. Little sacrifice they have to make for being minority in Bengal. For instance, Samiruddin has to be suitably renamed as Samir, Mamtaj as Mamata, Hilaluddin as Hillol, from Aeyasha to Asha etc. What I want to stress is that mutilation of Muslim names is so common that it hardly matters in today's *atmanirvor bharat*. Afzal in Tyagi's novel is not a singular case. Such cases are rising and abound even at the remotest villages of our country.

Changing Muslim Names into Hindu Ones

Changing one's name equals to sacrificing one's identity, one's culture, one's beliefs, and one's immediate sense of belonging. Name is an asset lovingly given by the elder members of the family. Name is akin to one's entire being; one's mooring to existential habitation. So under what circumstances one has to change or hide one's name is an alarming issue and more and more researches need be directed to this neglected field. One can collect million data related to the name changing issue of the Indian Muslims from field study. One may also collect inexhaustive data of empirical evidences from the internet. Circumstances may vary, methodologies can vary, ethnographic details may vary, but the victims of this forced cultural onslaughts are the minority, especially the Muslims. They are openly abused, lynched, killed, and murdered in broad daylight. Their houses are being burnt, their women raped. Visit a virtual platform and you will be appalled to see the battles Modi's digital army fighting against the arch enemy Muslims. Apart from riots, threats of genocide, regular hate speeches, cases of humiliation and denigration and dehumanisation, there are other misogynistic cyber strategies like 'Bulli Bai' and 'Sulli Deals' , specifically targeted to tarnish the image and respect of the high profile Indian Muslim women. When the women are being openly auctioned in online market, changing name seems to be a trivia.

One day Maharajji inducted Afzal into the fold of his disciples by blessing him with a new name-Vedant and gave him a set of saffron clothes. Now he was happy to be the inmate of the Mukti Ashram. Before joining the judge's house as a domestic helper Afzal's name is again changed by his introducer. Afzal, the idealistic boy, gets confused. He wanted to know why Satish had changed his name. He was a bit fearful about his identity. If the judge learnt about his Muslim identity, it could land him in some serious trouble. He didn't want to hide anything. He was proud of his name. He wanted to live and work with his real name. He had done nothing wrong or shameful. He had been honest and hardworking in life…

> 'Why did you change my name?' asked he [Afzal]
> 'Because I didn't want you to lose this job?' [said Satish]

Afzal's pride in his family name is mowed down. 'Today he buried deep Afzal-*straightforward Afzal.* He was Narayan-a new man working in a judge's house.' Changing Muslim names into Hindu ones to save a job or a life is not at all an unprecedented phenomenon in contemporary India. Muslims are stereotypically represented in cultural or daily living space as villains, betrayers, terrorists, rapists, and what not. They are systematically denied entry into posh housing areas and many decision making bodies and opinion making platforms. The novelist through the mutilation of Afzal's name and its resultant humiliation has effectively punctured the myth what Khushwant Singh called *hindu-muslim bhai bhaism* or our revolutionary poet Nazrul Islam's *Eke brinte duti kusum hindu musolman* or India's syncretic cultural legacy so dearly upheld by the so called liberals. Animosity, hatred, intolerance is deeply entrenched in the blood of both the communities. The gap between the two cultures is widening day by day. Media is agog with the stories of communal animosity, hatred, violence and so on and forth. Spiritual, tolerant image of India is getting tarnished at each minute. New India is rising on the persecutions of the minorities, women and dalits. The story is the emergence of ethnic identity or majoritarian identity. Christophe Jaffrelot, for instance, in his *Modi's India* shows how Modi government has moved India towards a new form of democracy, an ethnic democracy that equates the majoritarian community with the nation and relegated Muslims and Christians to second-class citizens who are daily harassed by Hindu vigilante groups. He also shows the promotion of Hindu nationalism has resulted in attacks against secularists, intellectuals, universities and NGOs.

Bigotry of Religious Identity

Afzal also lays bare the ugly tentacles of religious bigotry. Mukti Ashram has the luxury of a five star hotel. The maharajas and the VIP guests enjoy the pleasure of flesh by sleeping with foreign pretty girls. Yes. At the Mukti Ashram! Here the author scathingly attacked the modern day religious hypocrisy. Here is no 'mukti' or salvation of the soul; Ashram's walls are draped with carnal desire. Afzal himself is a witness to the immorality and sexual laxity of the inmates of the famed ashram:

> He stopped holding his breath near the window of Veetraji's room. He strained to listen but there was no voice. The door opened silently. He retreated and stood aside. A woman slipped out of the room, tiptoed. It was Ma Sadhana! She hurried down the stairs bare feet and disappeared into her room (Loc 1510).

Layered Corruption

The concluding chapter 'I am Afzal' is a stunning attempt to claim his real identity – an honest, hardworking, loyal Muslim boy. In a trance he murmurs the checkered happenings of his life. He had seen and known much of the world. He comes to realise the bitter truths he experiences through his odd journey – Mukti Ashram is much like a harem, professor Tripathi is a cheater and morally degradable, Chhote Masterji is a fraud, criminal and seasoned politician whose farm house is flooded with the flow of wine and women, corrupt uniformwallahas and their rotten bosses, corrupt judge and his twin wayward daughters' night revelries, at City Garage Ustad's shoddy night dealings and his bonhomie with the police, media and lawyers can be easily bought and the peoples who spat on him as mastermind are now ready to lick his boots. Charisma of power! Corruption both in private and public life; religious bigotry; lust for unaccounted wealth wine, women; paid media, paid judges, moral degeneration and ethical devaluation both in private and public life, police brutality, jingoism, hatred have painted Afzal, who was once honest, hardworking and loyal, black from head to toe.

Afzal's Reclaimed Self

Afzal's transformation, however, from a poor village boy to a powerful political leader does not steal the aura of his pure and pristine soul. He has done many wrongs. Yes, he is a sinner. But is he singularly culpable for his fall from grace? The novel is a befitting answer.

Afzal, however, takes all ills on his shoulder and frantically calls for his punishment, 'Hang me…hang me…hang… hang…ha…h…h…. 'Here lies his greatness and magnanimity. In the words of the narrator, 'Afzal the protagonist proves himself to be the guru of all that had taken him so lightly. He is culturally 'other', poor, not qualified enough for white collar work. But his honesty, his openness, his politeness is conspicuously absent among his highly qualified, socially sophisticated Indian babus and bosses.

A Commentary on Contemporaray India

Afzal is a must read for its heterogeneous structural threads, ranging from Azampur's past glory to present penury and allegedly 'a terror hub', from political corruption to spiritual hollowness, from moral degeneration in public life to private debauchery and dishonesty, from money power to lust for wine and women, from sectarian and communal turpitudes to ghettoisation of post-independence Indian Muslims and its corrosive effects on syncretic socio-cultural edifices. I love this book because it demystifies the myth of communal harmony, myth of vibrant Indian democracy, myth of India as an oasis of spiritual bliss, myth of accountability of public servants. *Afzal* is a tight slap on our face! The ugly fact is that corruption, hatred, lust for power, wine, women rule the roost. The novel is a brilliant commentary on the disturbing images of contemporary India.

Hindu-Muslim Identity Issue

Afzal can also be read through the age-old story of Hindu-Muslim identities that take different hues depending upon the colour of the ideological lenses, basically from the avowed secularists and the liberals in one hand and the conservative Hindu nationalists on the other. For the liberals with leftist leanings, the story is bathed in a roseate glow of the pre-colonial golden age of Hindu-Muslim amity. The tale is of a commingling and flowering of a composite, symbiotic cultural tradition, especially in art, music and architecture. The tale is of gradual drawing closer of Hindus and Muslims in the forms of their daily lives and of an enthusiastic participation in each other's festivals. From this angle there is little room of conflict between the communities. Sporadic outbreaks of violence are considered to have some issues of economic interests and political compulsions. To the Hindu nationalist, on the other hand, for whom the Hindu saffron and Muslim green do not mix to create a pale pink, the rift between the communities is a fundamental fact of Indian history. They see Hindu-Muslim relations framed by a thousand – year-old 'civilisational' conflict in which the Muslims, militarily victorious and politically ascendant for the centuries, tried to impose Islamic civilisation on their Hindu subjects through all means, from coercion to bribery and cajolery, and yet had only limited success. The composite civilisation, according to this view, was limited to small sections of the population around the Muslim courts and court-patronised arts like music and architecture. Of course some Hindus adopted the Persian-inspired language and the ways of life of the rulers, but the vast majority of Hindus kept their civilisational core intact while they resentfully tolerated the Muslim onslaught. In this view the outbreaks of violence between the two communities were inevitable. The rage of the denigrated Hindus was stored up over a long period of time, and it was to explode once historical circumstances sanctioned such eruptions.[2] The novel has merits from both the perspectives – the unity and shared life of the two communities and the rift that has been steadily encroaching into their individual and collective spaces. The fissures are too many and they are constantly being filled with ever increasing doubts, denials, distrusts, treacheries, and betrayals. The novel raised questions that went unanswered,

> Why is Azampur targeted? Who'll do justice to Afzal and many others like him languishing in the jails? Who'll bring the real culprits to book? Is there anyone listen to the poor in this country? Where should they go? How long will the poor be victimised? When will this end?

Doubly Marginalised

To be poor and to be Muslim in our country has huge double benefits. She can be easily arrested, can be labeled as terrorist, can be declared anti-national, can be made people's enemy in a second with the help of virtual platform, can be lynched or killed. It is happening all before our eyes. Who can deny it? Who are targeted in the name of NRC? Against whom are hate speeches being hurled? Against whom are the intimidations of pogroms and riots targeted? Muslims. I am not going to substantiate my arguments with newspaper articles which are available in public domain and can be checked at the click of a mouse. What I am claiming is that to be born as 'Afzal' is a huge burden in today's India. Name is enough. It tells the real story. His identity is his challenge. Either he has to change his name to be accommodated in 'Hindu' public spheres with ease or he should be ready to live in ghetto and even be ready to sacrifice his life if he wants to keep his identity intact. Identity is a huge marker in developed and developing countries. Wearing veil or keeping beard may cost her/his job. Her culture is a doorway to hundred denials and disadvantages. Muslims are in constant fear of being jailed for one reason or other. The novel read thus:

> People gathered in the Hall of Azampur College. There were elderly men who had seen good times and the next generation which felt hurt at 'terror tag' and the young boys who could be picked up on suspicion…they suffered from the crisis of faith. Iqbal stood up and began: 'If things go on like this, many of our boys will be picked up. All our life we wait for the boys to grow up and earn their living, and when they grow up, they are branded as terrorists and thrown into the prison. Whenever there is such incident, the police are under pressure. Their teams start watching 'Muslims hubs' and pick up some young boys and later dub them as 'terrorists (Loc 3189).

Burden of Muslim Identity

Religious identity proves to a liability for a Muslim boy or girl. She may have multiple identities, but her singular religious identity is the defining factor in his life. Of course dirty politics is playing its game so well. But what is about our civil society at large? They, the majoritarians, are also thumping breasts leveraging on their singular Hindu identity. Afzal's harrowing odysseys, his sagacity and honesty in varied jobs, his ascent and descent in politics, his outlooks and thoughts, his defeats and victories, his individual self and his collective self, his loss of identity and his reclaiming of that identity –

all interlinked with his primal identity, that is, his religious or ethnic identity. Afzal is an honest boy who loves to work and earn with integrity. But the world around him has stolen his nobility, honesty and generosity and pushed him to his bewildering sense of belonging. He is seen murmuring towards the end of the text:

> *Mukti Ashram! …good place…food…meditation…pranayam…path to salvation…see God. I read holy books…failed to get…jiva, jagat…Brahman…many big men…women flocked there. Pretty girls…other countries…stayed there…favourite with young sanyasis…professor…crush on her…she too. Both in the room…hoursas…a chet…fraud…astrologer. Men…women came…charmed…trapped them. Tantra…a great attraction for…came in Farm House with Chhote masterji…learnt…call him sir. I was happy…passed time…joyfully. Many men…women came…enjoyed parties…officials…Horrible!...was thrown…freezing cold canal. Biting winter…lay on …bare bank=enervated, numb…was dawn…blowing icy…followed…They turned but…kept trudging…reached…small station…Not crowded…She…nubile…feisty…kept screaming…hissing and embraced…tightly as I pumped…her fiercely…tongued her full…breasts…then lay still…uniformwallah came and …abused and slapped…I helpless, weepy…was beaten, tortured, starved, insulted…humiliated…Two years…dingy cell. Ho..rrible…Abba cried his eyes out. Ammi wailed…Town moaned…Days passed…at last prepared myself for…noose. All swept away. I relaxed. No fear or tear…tranquility…Judge! Fie…! Fie!...daughters…pleasure…enjoyed…night revelries…lavish in style…She …disheveled and drunk…she happy, satisfied…was in a green nightie…loose hair…pert breasts…they were item. I left the Farm…police raided…Judge was pounced…living room. They ransacked…whole place…City Garage! Ustad! Looked polite…Ustad got well with police. He…me to do as other lads…Brat! I left the place…not know why Chhote masterji dragged…into…and fielded me…I…not know ABC of…I was cheered, patted…congratulated…Hope flicker…Townsfol campaigned…wind blew…favor. And I won. Chhote delighted. Abba …glad. Ammi…overjoy…She…tears…They celebrated…home coming…victory and became…great man overnight! Afzal Zindabad…I came and stayed in the Farm House…then sarkari niwas…big house…good…Netaji!...fraud…corrupt…criminal…extortionist…womanizer. Travellled abroard…other girls. Pooh!...change leadership. CM…unwilling…quit…wanted to see…son…hired goons…they…him. …son frightened…cronies fled…townsfolk admire…adore…Abba…proud. Uncle Shamshad, Abba, Faiyyaz, Munshiji…call… worthy son. And maulvi…pats…proudly…media call…leader of stature…Mr. Clean. BL university…confer…degree… (Loc 3207 onwards)*

In the end Afzal asked the most pertinent question. He rued for the loss of his unblemished self. But he knew there was no way to return home:

> *…Am I Afzal? Where…Afzal-Azamurwallah (sick) gone? Where…? When…? How…? Why…? I even…not know! …forgot…nice things! Completely clean! I've fallen…low abysmal!*

Question of Afzal's Belonging

The dichotomy and duality of Afzal's public appearance and his inner self was well expressed throughout the pages of the novel. He had lost his pristine identity and his sense of belonging as *Azampurwallah*. But he could compensate the loss with his achievements as a 'clean' leader, 'a leader of stature', being showered with honorary degrees from universities. Thus question of religious identity is interlinked to understanding of the nuanced shades of belonging and un-belonging of Afzal in an increasingly anti-Muslim Indian air.

Notes

Tyagi, B S. *Afzal.* Lucknow: Lokoday Prakashan, 2019. [Kindle Basic]. Retrieved from amazon.com. All the textual references are taken from this edition.

Works Cited

1. Sen, Amartya. "Preface." *Identity and Violence: The Illusion of Destiny.* [Kindle Basic]. Retrieved from amazon.com.
2. Kakar, Sudhir. *The Colours of Violence.* New Delhi: Penguin Books, 1996. pp. 19-20. Print.
3. "Unravelling Hindutva Terrorism," Editorials. *EPW.* (Vol. 45, Issue No. 21, 22 May, 2010). <http://www.epw.in.iproxy.inflibnet.ac.in:2048/journal/2010/21/editorials/unravelling-hindutva-terrorism.html >, Accessed July 14, 2017. Web.
4. Jaffrelot, Christophe and Cynthia Schoch. Modi's *India: Hindu Nationalism and the Rise of Ethnic Democracy*, Princeton University Press, 2021. [Kindle Basic] Retrieved from amazon.com.
5. Biswas, Soutik. "Is India waging a 'war' on Islamic Names?" Available at https://www.bbc.com/news/world-asia-india-46191239 Accessed June 9, 2022.
6. https://www.globalvillagespace.com/indian-muslim-police-officer-plans-to-change-name-in-fear-of-his-life/ Accessed June 9, 2022.
7. Ara, Ismat. "Delhi violence aftermath: Muslims change their names, avoid Islamic greetings, do away with hijab to stay safe." *Firstpost.* Available at https://www.firstpost.com/india/delhi-violence-aftermath-muslims-change-their-names-avoid-islamic-greetings-do-away-with-hijab-to-stay-safe-8113951.html Accessed June 9, 2022.

CHAPTER 10

Invisible Woman in Syed Waliullah's "Ekti Tulsi Gacher Kahini"

> Places inhabit us, as much as we inhabit them. They form the myths and lore of who we are. Landscapes with edges softened by memory, imagined homes, burnished light – dream-soaked remnants of loves and lives, stubborn in how they bind us to the past even as we are propelled into the future.
>
> Mara Ahmed, *A Thin Wall* (2017)

Bare Words

Partition stories are ripe with stories of suffering, indecency, rape and sexual violence, loot, murder, torching of houses, decay and deaths. Multiple sources find over 75000 women were abducted, raped, mutilated during partition. But Bangladeshi writer Syed Waliullah's (1922-1971) *Ekti Tulsi Gacher Kahini* or *Story of a Tulsi Plant* is a clear departure from this mainstream narrative of gory details of violence and fears and killings linked with the greatest tragedy of the subcontinent. While in stories such as Banaful's *Dangar Samoy* or Samaresh Basu's *Aadab* we are shuddered with the horrific, gory details of partition-tragedy and its inherent cruelties, in Syed Waliullah's *Story of a Tulsi Plant* only some bare hints of the tragedy are offered. Subtlety of thoughts interwoven and intertwined with emotional threads of the narrative and omissions of cruel details invite readers to fill in the textual lacunae with individual resources. In this article I try to argue that *Story of a Tulsi Plant* is a story of the unsaid Hindu woman. Invisible woman of the house is visible in each turn and twist of Waliullah's narrative. Colours of partition violence can be unearthed in the story of the dying tulsi plant or in the invisible lady's glossy black sari with red border dangling from a pole in a slum in Asansol, Baidhyabathi, Lilua or Howrah.

Kaur's Widow Colony and Waliullah's Empty House

Two and half meters high surface painted in bright yellow paint – peeling off at some places and spotted randomly with green fungus at others acts as a protective boundary within which widows of India's Partition violence were "rehabilitated." The signs of despair, damage, and neglect are apparent. After a gap of a decade broken bricks, concrete slabs dust, shreds of green plastic sheets, empty bottles, and rubble outline the area which once popularly known as "widow colony" where young widows and their children were to live their everyday life.[1] This is how the historian Ravinder Kaur painted the partition violence.

Waliullah's partition story *Ekti Tulsi Gacher Kahini* published in 1965 collection, *Dui Teer O Onnanno Golpo* begins with the description of an empty, abandoned house whose members have fled for life:

> Just over the bow-shaped concrete pool the house stood. It was two-storied, big, building. It seemed the house stood on the street as it had not spared an inch front space for footpath. However, inside, it had a huge backyard, a broad yard too. Just after the toilet, bathroom the backyard was full of trees – mango, rose apple, jackfruit, etc. It looked like a jungle where even at noon the sun looked shy and there was a fusty smell in the weed-carpeted shadowy soil.[2]

The house is unnamed. Here is no question of Kaur's rehabilitation of widows. We have not been offered details of the owners of the house. Only we know it has been usurped by a group of men, Motin, Amzad and their friends, who have fled from Kolkata. They are badly in search of a shelter. They find the house empty and locked. They break the gate and occupy it.

Now why I am referring this house where the tulsi plant is slowly dying to the boundary of Kaur's "widow colony." Apparently there is a mismatch. Here are no broken bricks or empty bottles. But an air of emptiness, desolation, despair links Waliullah's story to the trajectory of Kaur's widow colony:

> They did not know well the ways of Hindu culture. However they all know that in evening Hindu women light a wick under the basil-stand, bow head wrapping neck with the end of sari. Under this abandoned weed-covered basil plant once every evening someone would light a wick. That lonely wick, when the evening star alone brightened the sky, was lit by a vermilion-worn quiet woman. Both in wedding and funeral, in sun and shower the wick under the basil plant has spread its light without a miss.

Basically it is a story of a 'vermilion worn quiet woman' who nurtures the basil plant in sun and shower, who along with other male and female members of the family has to desert the white house. *Story of a Tulsi Plant* is mainly the story of the invisible 'vermilion-worn quiet woman.' 'Invisiblity' suggests the situation of a group stripped of its native culture and forced to adhere to alien standards and values while its own cultural qualities were ignored. Socially it reflects the conditions of a group whose basic plight was long overlooked or pushed into obscure shadows. Most significantly it embodies the complex psychological dilemmas of men without a sense of vital group identity, whose sense of human identity is often denied by the dominant society (Todd M. Lieber). Here, my discussion of the metaphor of invisibility is, however, limited to the physical space only. The lady in question in Waliullah's story is physically absent, but her moral and cultural presence unlike Ralph Ellison's underpinnings of it in his much acclaimed 1952 novel *Invisible Man* is felt in each nook and corner of the empty house.

Violence in Partition Stories

Partition stories are in general choked with an air of gruesome, cruel incidents of rapes, riots, torching houses, kidnapping, communal killings, murders, deaths. Banaful's *Dangar Samoy* opens thus:

> *Hindu-musolman danghar atonkhe akash batash thom thom korche. Diner belata tobuo konorokome kathe kintu ratta arr kat teh chaina. Oi bujhi shankho banjlo, oi bujhi 'bondeh matarom...ginni kebol todarok kore beran prottek kopater prottek khil, prottek janalar prottek chitkani thik ache kina'"* (Air is heavy with fear of Hindu-Muslim riot. Days pass somehow, but nights seem too long. Ears are ever awake for blowing of conches or slogans of 'bandhe matarom'...Lady of the house is checking times and again each door and each window if they are securely shut or not.)[3]

In Samaresh Basu's *Aadab* we are chilled with the scene of bloody communal violence:

> *Dangha bedheche hindu arr musolmane. Mukhomukhi lorai, dah, sorki, churi, lathi niye. Tachara choturdikhe choriye poreche guptghatoker dol – choragopta haanche ondhokarke ashroy kore. Lutherera beriyeche tader ovijhane ...bostite bostite agun jolche. Mritukator nari-shishur chitkar sthane sthane abhaoke bishakto kore tulcche.* (Riot among Hindus and Muslims has started. Face to face fight with knife, lathi, scythe, axe, etc. Moreover assassins have hay days. Looters are prowling in the streets...slums are being torched. Children and women are tearing the skies with their death-wails.)[4]

The cruelty of partition is delineated by Khushwant Singh thus: The fact is, both sides [Hindus and Muslims] killed. Both shot and stabbed and speared and clubbed. Both tortured. Both raped...the riots had become a route. By the summer of 1947 ten million people – Muslims and Hindus and Sikhs – were in flight. By the time the monsoon broke, almost a million of them were dead.[5]

In order to grasp the immensity of partition violence particularly against women, one may begin by searching available facts and numbers. Ritu Menon and Kamla Bhasin in their book *Borders and Boundaries: Women in India's Partition*(1998) claim that the official number of abducted women stood at 50,000 for Muslim women kidnapped by Hindu and Sikh men on their way to Pakistan, while 33,000 Hindu and Sikh women were abducted as they attempted to migrate to India (1998, p. 70). Urvashi Butalia in her seminal book *The Other Side of Silence* gives similar numbers; she claims that a total of 75,000 women were abducted from both sides of the border (1998, p. 3). It is also very likely that the actual numbers might be a lot higher than the official estimate found in books and archives.[6]

Waliullah's Invisible Woman

In Waliullah's story we get, however, a sense of uneasy respite from the harrowing, chilling details of partition violence. No story of women jumping into wells, no forcible killings or rapes or pillage or any other forms of violence. What remains is the residue of historical wounds, signs of loss and mourning – a dying tulsi plant, an abandoned back garden, some casually hand-written names on the stair wall of the empty house.

"Can't you see the tulsi plant standing awkwardly there? It has to be uprooted. No trace of Hindu culture will be put up with." Modabber heatedly argued.

They in disappointment looked at the basil plant. It seemed to have died. The green leaves had turned into yellow. Weeds had covered its root. It might not be watered for days.

"What are you watching? Root it out!" boomed Modabber.

They stood petrified. With this sudden discovery they were puzzled. The house seemed to be empty and abandoned though it had on its stair-wall some casually hand-written names. Now it changed its colour. Caught abruptly by the visitors the dry, dying basil plant, it seemed, was unfolding the hidden story of the house.[7]

Modabber impatiently yelled again, "What are you thinking still? Uproot it!"

None of them, however, moved. They did not know well the ways of Hindu culture. However they all know that in evening Hindu women light a wick under the basil-stand, bow head wrapping neck with the end of sari. Under this abandoned weed-covered basil plant once every evening someone would light a wick. That lonely wick, when the evening star alone brightened the sky, was lit by a vermilion-worn quiet woman. Both in wedding and funeral, in sun and shower the wick under the basil plant has spread its light without a miss.[8] The climax of the story culminates in Walliullah's hand thus:

> Where is the woman of the house who years after years lighted the wick under this basil plant? Motin once worked in the railway. Without a reason pictures of varied railway-goomties (sheds) surfaced before his eyes. Perhaps that woman had found a shelter in one of her relation's shanty in Asansol, Baidhyabathi, Lilua or Howrah. He once saw in one railway-shed a sun-baked glossy black sari with red border. It might be hers. It sadly danced in the mild air. Or she might be sitting at window side in a running train. She looked out of the window. Her eyes searched something beyond the horizon. Her journey might have not ended yet. But wherever she stayed at the end of the day her eyes turned teary for her beloved basil plant.[9]

Waliullah's Departure from the Mainstream Partion Narrative

If the quiet lady of the deserted white house, we still don't have a clue, will have to share or not, the lot of Manik Bandhopadhyay's Mallika in *Upaye* or *The Final Solution* who has to sell her body to her supposed protectors to feed her dying child. Partition stories are filled with stories of suffering, indecency, rape and sexual violence, loot, murder, torching of houses, deaths. Waliullah's *Story of a Tulsi Plant* is a clear departure from the mainstream narrative of gory details of violence and its induced fears and phobias. Subtlety of thoughts and omission of cruel details make the story an immaculate achievement in the field of partition literature. "Note that *omissions* are important here, that is, when a text doesn't tell us things we would expect to be told."[10] I mean what is said in the text is important but what is unsaid is more and more important. Waliullah does not offer even the name of the house or its inhabitants. Only some hints are dispersed here and there. Readers are left with the resources of their fertile imagination. *Ekti Tulsi Gacher Kahini* or *Story of a Tulsi Plant* is, thus, a story of the unsaid. Invisible woman of the house is visible in each turn and twist of the narrative. Her absence is her presence.

And when the occupiers leave the house, "The empty house bore the signs of the usurpers' temporary stay – torn pieces of newspaper littered here and there, an old rope used as clothesline, butts of biri and cigarette, heel of a torn shoe." This scene reminds me of the broken bricks, dust, and such residue of Kaur's "widow colony." The house is a site of residue of despair, decay, and darkness. Darkness of the partition is attested thorough omissions and absences. Hints are more powerful than detailed description of a colossal human tragedy. The weight of the story lies on the tales of the absentees – the inmates of the house, particularly the invisible lady of the house who takes care of the tulsi plant. Why have they fled from their house? What fears have gripped them? Have they found a shade or a roof after reaching West Bengal? Could they forget their house, their garden, fields and village and neighbours and neighbourhoods? Have they lost their relatives and dear ones during the exodus? So many particulars! So many questions! Waliullah remains silent to all such apparent queries. Rather he touches us with the tale of a dying tulsi plant. Tulsi plant and the nameless woman of the house who used to regularly water it have a symbiotic relationship. Now the chord between the tulsi plant and the woman who nourished it has been cut off. And the desolation and decay is before us. Dying tulsi plant is a syombol of a dying culture, a dying communal legacy life of their native land:

> The tulsi plant at the edge of the yard looked dry. Its leaves became brown again. After the arrival of the police nobody watered it. Nobody recollected the teary eyes of the woman of the house.

Conclusion

The teary eyes of the homeless Hindu woman reminds me of the the heart-wrenching ending of Kenyan author Grace Ogot's (1930-2015) short story "The Green Leaves" where Nyamundhe, the protagonist's wife, weeps wildly upon the death of her husband:

> My lover the son of Ochieng
> The son of Omolo
> The rains are coming down
> Yes, the rains are coming down
> The nights will be dark
> The nights will be cold and long
> Oh! The son-in-law of my mother

I have no heart to forgive,
I have no heart to pardon
All these mourners cheat me now
Yes, they cheat me
But when the sun goes to his home and
Darkness falls, they desert me.
In the cold hours of night
Each woman clings to her man
There is no-one among them
There is none
There is no woman who will lend me a
Husband for the night.

Nyamundhe has lost her husband; the invisible woman of Waliullah has lost her home and family and her sense of belonging, her rootedness, her place of birth and growth, her life's mooring. She is rootless, a refugee in search of a shelter in one of her relation's shanty in alien Asansol, Baidhyabathi, Lilua or Howrah. The poignancy and keenness of her tragedy is appalling, and it is calmly but keenly, somewhat resignedly, dealt with by the master storyteller Syed Waliullah.

Notes

I have used the story from Syed Waliullah's. "Ekti Tulsi Gaccher Kahini" in *Galpo Samagra* (Collected Stories). Dhaka: Protikbooks, 2017, Sixth Edition. Print. I have translated original Bangla story "Ekti Tulsi Gaaacher Kahini" into English. It is titled "Story of a Tulsi Plant" and available at https://www.backgroundenglish.com/books-culture/short-fiction-books-culture/story-of-a-tulsi-plant/ All the references are from this particular translation, if not otherwise mentioned.

Works Cited

1. Kaur, Ravinder. "Bodies of Partition: Of Widows, Residue, and Other Historical Waste" in S. Jensen & H. Ronsbo (Eds.), *Histories of Victimhood.* Philadelphia: University Press of Pennsylvania, 2014. pp.44-63. Print.
2. Waliullah, Syed. *Ekti Tulsi Gacher Kahini* in *Galpo Samagra* (Collected Stories). Dhaka: Protikbooks, 2017, Sixth Edition. Print.
3. Banaful. "Danghar Somoy" in *Dui Banglar Deshbhager Akshan*, Ed. Sushil Saha. Kolkata: Sopan, 2019. p. 19. Print.
4. Basu, Samaresh. "Aadab" in *Dui Banglar Deshbhager Akshan*, Ed. Sushil Saha. Kolkata: Sopan, 2019. p. 55. Print.
5. Singh, Khushwant. *Train to Pakistan.* New Delhi Penguin Books, 2009. pp.1-2. Print.

6. Dey, Arunima. "Violence Against Women During the Partition of India: Interpreting Women and their Bodies in the Context of Ethnic Genocide." *ES. Revista de Filología Inglesa* 37 (2016). Retrieved from https://dialnet.unirioja.es/ accessed Aug 13, 2021. Web.
7. https://www.backgroundenglish.com/books-culture/short-fiction-books-culture/story-of-a-tulsi-plant/. Web.
8. Ibid.
9. Ibid.
10. Barry, Peter. *Beginning Theory: An Introduction to Literary and Cultural Theory.* 2nd Edition. Manchester: Manchester University Press, 2002. p. 75. Print.
11. Lieber. Todd M. "Ralph Ellison and the Metaphor of Invisiblity in Black Literary Tradition." *American Quarterly* Vol. 24, No. 1 (Mar., 1972), pp. 86-100. Available at https://www.jstor.org/stable/2711916 Accessed June 8, 2022.

CHAPTER 11

William Faulkner's "Dry September": A Tale of Lynching

"Shoot the Traitors/ Goli Maro"

(a popular hate slogan of the saffron fascists during anti-NRC protests in India)

Racial Hatred and Lynching in America

Within the intertwined criticism of the politics of race and gender, is also embedded a critique of lynching in the racist America. It would be worthwhile to remember that lynching in America was a spectacle; a carnival like event which had people flocking to the site to witness the drama of lynching. A quick glance at the photographic archive of images and photographs of the time, document the terrible drama that would unfold in a manner of public event. That the hanging lynched black bodies had people jeering and kind-of-celebrating the white supremacy is telling not only of the white brutality of it but the spiritual, moral and ethical emptiness of the white folk. It is a terrible fact that racism continued long into the twentieth century despite the constitutional abolition of slavery. The disregard for the freedom guaranteed under the law, and the concomitant Jim Crow laws that enforced a 'racialised code of behaviour' along with racial segregation in public places speaks volumes about the position of the blacks and the African American or mixed race people in the America. It is reflective of the various forms in which violence and racial hatred would manifest itself in both obvious and insidious ways.[1]

Southern Myth of White Goddess

"Dry September" was one of William Faulkner's (1857-1962) best short stories. It is a tale of 'lynching.' The story weaves the theme of lynching, rumour, gossip, prejudice, repression, justice, hypocrisy, racial identity into an artistic piece through the killing of an innocent Negro Will Mayes by a war-veteran despot McLendon. It also takes resort to the paranoid theme of White Goddess concept of a Southern Belle. There is no question of justice or a chance of trial. In spite of a few past evidences to Minnie Cooper's susceptibility to flirtation and coquetry McLendon and his cohorts never nourish an iota of doubt.

The rumour is a chance to take revenge on the black male. Will is guilty simply because Minnie Cooper has suggested that he raped her. And like other black people at the time the story was written, he was considered to be at the bottom of the hierarchical system that was predominant in the South. Minnie Coopers can't lie, as she is a Southern White woman. This prejudice is so deeply entrenched into the veins of the white Southern males that a neutral reasoning finds no avenues to their heated heads. White myths of black male sexuality created images of a savage beast consumed by lust for white women. In this fantasy whites were civilised, blacks were uncivilised. White women were the "purest" form of civilisation, black men the most savage and "unclean." Sex between a black man and a white woman was a defilement of the ultimate sort. Sexual attraction opened up the possibility of a genuine human relationship, with the potential even of equality between a black man and a white woman expressed in sex and even love. Part of this story included the fear of some white men that white women were sexually attracted to black men. Moreover, such a relationship was liable to produce "mixed" and therefore "unclean" offspring. White women, so white men wanted to believe, would never willingly engage in sexual relations with a black man. Only rape, in opinion of Iulia Andreea Milica, provided lustful black men with sexual access to white women. In such tangled webs of race and gender, white men were obliged to protect white women. Men who protected white female purity were also protectors of community values and of civilisation itself (qtd. in Milica).[2] From the depth of the painfully raw experiences Faulkner builds this lynching story with some bare but subtle touches. And his language, rough, coarse, is attuned to the black theme in its marvellous exactitude.

Historical Background of Lynching

Milica persuasively pointed out that lynching was not a post-Reconstruction invention, it had existed since the foundation of the American colonies, but it referred, then, to many other forms of punishment, such as beating, whipping, tar-and-feathering, and, only occasionally killing, and was directed less against the black slaves and more against whites who disobeyed different rules of the community. Most of the times, the slaveowner was in charge of choosing the punishment for his own slave, the community rarely interfering with affairs on the plantation, which was, more or less, a closed system. Mob violence against the black people in the form of what is now known as lynching started to be put into wider practice after the emancipation of the slaves, when the white people attempted to find new forms of controlling the masses of people who wanted more rights and aspired to equality to the white population. The number of lynchings, as mob violence against the black, grew after the Reconstruction, and coincided with the adoption of the "Jim Crow" laws, which legalised the segregation between the whites and the blacks. Lynching, therefore, became a rather widely-employed form of control of the black population by intimidating and constantly threatening them, and, in this way, promoting the idea of white power and superiority.

Lynching was always intended as a metaphor for, or a way to understand, race relations. While there were many different types of lynchings, lynch mobs typically worked to ensure that black audiences were aware of the strength of white supremacy and the costs of violating the boundaries of the racial order; at the same time, they wanted to reinforce images of white men as chivalrous protectors of white women. In other words, lynching is nowadays considered as a means of keeping the black population in terror and submission by proclaiming white superiority. According to James H. Madison, from 1880 to 1930, angry mobs lynched 4, 697 Americans. Of these victims 3,344 were African Americans. Race was a central factor in this tragedy, as in many of America's tragedies (p. 13). Since the South was more closely affected by racial problems than the rest of the Union, due to its past of slavery, it is widely considered that lynching was a Southern problem, though there were such actions recorded in other parts of the country, targeting Native Americans, Mexicans or Asians. Jonathan Markovitz, for instance, in analysing the figures related to lynchings given by different authors, appreciated that lynchings became a Southern problem especially in the twentieth century when, from the number of lynchings in the United States, 95 percent occurred in the South, and the victims were primarily African American.

Miss Minnie Cooper – a White Goddess

Under this socio-cultural setting we need to put Faulkner's story. The story was originally published in *Scribner's magazine* in 1931, and later included in collections of his short stories. The story weaves the theme of rumour, gossip, prejudice, repression, justice, hypocrisy, racial identity into an artistic piece. The story is unfurled through an unnamed third person narrator. And it explores the paranoid theme of White Goddess whereby the Southern male believes that a woman, particularly a white Southern woman cannot tell a lie. In essence they are to be held up on a pedestal and everything they say is to be believed, without any need for proof. It is through this concept that the story develops, Faulkner highlighting to the reader the willingness of the men of Jefferson, particularly John McLendon, to believe Minnie Cooper and form a lynch mob to kill Will Mayes.[3]

Rumour and gossip spread like flames and burns Will Mayes, the innocent Negro man in the end by a despot McLendon. He takes the leading role, and whets others to kill Will Mayes. They are on a sacred mission to save the honour of a white woman Minnie Cooper, a typical Southern Belle. People are mad to pursue the blacks and kill them at the drop of a coin. Henry Hawkshaw, the barber, is a sensible man who takes risk even of his life to save Will Mayes. His repetitive clarifications, 'I don't believe Will Mayes did it. I know Will Mayes' fall flat to the self-proclaimed moral guardians and the protectors of the purity of race, who summarily abuses him as a 'damn nigger-loving.' Hawkshaw reasonably argues:

> Will Mayes never done it, boys...Why, you all know well as I do there ain't any town where they got better niggers than us. And you know how a lady will kind of think things about men when they ain't any reason to, and Miss Minnie any way...

But he fails to convince the rowdy boys who pay no heed to his sound words. He runs after the boys. McLendon, Butch and others rummage the 'dark bulk of the ice plant where the Negro was a night watchman,' drag the Negro to the car, and shout 'Kill him, kill the black son.' The barber sweats, and is 'sick at the stomach.' Will Mayes is manacled and bruised, and hurled torrents of abuse. The Negro is cowered, and he knows his day will end soon. He appeals to their better sense for his life:

> "What you all going to do with me, Mr John? I ain't done anything. White folks, captains, I ain't done anything: I swear 'fore God."

McLendon – Self-Appointed Moral Guardian of Racial Purity

There is no question of justice or a chance of trial. McLendon together with other speakers at barber's shop takes law into their own hands, and punishes the alleged culprit. In spite of a few past evidences to Minnie Cooper's susceptibility to flirtation and coquetry McLendon and his cohorts never nourish an iota of doubt. The rumour is a chance to take revenge on the black male. And it is interesting to note that even a man who is not form Jefferson also supports McLendon's cause: 'I'm with him [McLendon]. I don't live here, but by God, if our mothers and wives and sisters….' This twist adds to McLendon's cause a kind of universal dimension, and bolsters their argument in favour of racial purification. Will is guilty simply because Minnie Cooper has suggested that he raped her and like other black people he would be considered to be at the bottom of the racialised hierarchical system .

Minnie Coopers can't lie, as she is a Southern White woman. This fallacy is so deeply rooted in the veins of the white Southern males that clear and neutral reasoning finds no avenues to their tormented heads. McManus lucidly points out Minnie's cause of frustration:

> It is also interesting that Minnie appears to suffer a breakdown while she is in the movie theatre. Perhaps the reality of what she has done (lied about Will Mayes) has become too much for her. It would appear that Minnie's main difficulty is that she is sexually repressed and by lying about Will Mayes raping her she has succeeded in people showing an interest in her again, however it is at the expense of Will Mayes's life. It would also appear that none of Minnie's friends really believe that she has been raped. Just as Henry Hawkshaw doubted it, so too do Minnie's friends.

Faulkner's Usage of Evocative Images

Faulkner heavily takes resort to symbolism in the story, particularly the weather. In the first section of the story, Faulkner uses such words and phrases as words 'bloody September', 'rainless days', 'dry grass', 'dead', 'stale', etc. to set the tenor of the story. These images foreshadow to what will happen to Will Mayes later. The opening line of the story also acts as foreshadowing to the eventual killing of Will Mayes, Faulkner using the word 'bloody' to describe the September twilight. Also in section three of the story Faulkner again describes the air, though this time uses the word 'lifeless.' He also describes the day as having 'died in a pall of dust.' This may be significant as Faulkner could be suggesting that the residents of Jefferson, particularly McLendon and the lynch mob are morally dead, by taking the law into their own hands.

Other notable symbolism in the story includes McLendon's gun. It not only can be seen as a symbol of violence but it can be seen to represent violence in the past, present (possibly) and future. It is first introduced when McLendon walks into the barber shop, the reader learning that McLendon was a soldier in WWI (past violence). It is assumed the McLendon uses the gun to kill Will Mayes in section three of the story, which would suggest violence in the present and at the end of the story, McLendon puts the gun down on the table in his bedroom, which would suggest that it is to be used again, sometime in the future.

McLendon's Proven Hypocrisy

The story ends with a significant subplot subtly woven through McLendon's interaction with his wife, and by which Faulkner appears to be injecting irony into the body of the story. Will Mayes has been killed by McLendon in order to preserve Minnie Cooper's integrity and honour. And the same McLendon strikes out at his own wife when he returns home from the killing. Follow the attitude of the killer to his wife. After killing Will Mayes at midnight he returns home and locks it. Faulkner uses the word 'birdcage' to refer to his neat, clean, trim and fresh green-and-white paint house. And McLendon's wife is a caged bird, whose wings flutter for freedom but she cannot fly.

Faulkner is a master storyteller. He with some bare words marvelously paint the scene of domestic violence toward the end of the story:

> He locked the car and mounted the porch and entered. His wife rose from the chair beside the reading lamp. McLendon stopped in the floor and stared at her until she looked down….
>
> "Haven't I told you to about sitting up like this, waiting to see when I come in?"
>
> "John" she said. She laid the magazine down. Poised on the balls of his feet, he glared at her with his hot eyes, his sweating face.
>
> "Didn't I tell you?" he went toward her. She looked up then. He caught her shoulder. She stood passive looking at him.
>
> "Don't John. I couldn't sleep…The heat; something. Please, John. You're hurting me."

> "Didn't I tell you?" He released her and half struck, half-flung her across the chair, and she lay there…

It would appear that there is one rule for McLendon and one for Will Mayes (and other black people). At no stage does the reader suspect that McLendon respects his wife in any way, if anything there is a sense that McLendon's violence against his wife may be a daily occurrence. Unlike Minnie Cooper who McLendon has held up on a pedestal, even though she has lied about what has happened to her, McLendon's wife is not afforded to the same luxury. In many ways McLendon, who has acted as the figure of moral authority throughout the story, is a hypocrite par excellence.

Faulkner – the Master Storyteller

Narrated in five parts the story has presented the picture of Jefferson life of Faulkner's time. The race problem engulfed the South. From the depth of the raw experience he builds this lynching story in immaculate precision. No more, no less. No trash. The setting, the beginning paragraph, the end part, the symbolism, the bare words, repetitive use of his favourite epithets – all pave the way for his 'doomed' world.

Relevance of the Story to India's Rising Hate Crimes

If we replace John Mclendon to Shambhulal Regar, Will Mayes to Afrazul Khan, And Miss Minni Cooper to a Hindu girl, then a fitting relevant commentary on our present Indian race scene can be easily grasped. If we extend the story to adapt to our land, and read it again, and we will be amazed with the irony and sordidness of human predicaments of South America Faulkner presents so immaculately years ago. A cursory glance to this site https://www.thequint.com/quintlab/lynching-in-india/ is immensely helpful in studying the rising cases of lynching in 'new' India. What I stress here is that racial purity was not the sole privilege of the Southern white Americans. It was the same ideology Germans took against the Jews and the Jews are using against the Palestinians. Racial hatred and violence is not a segregated topic. It is a very much living reality of contemporary world. Racial identity is an entitlement to the majority and it is a burden to the minority and the underdogs. Poor economic condition together with lower caste or race status in India is a serious hindrance to the promotion of a just society. Faulkner's story is an eye opener to the deeply entrenched racial divisions and differences that the Left often tends to ignore for pursuing their own ideological ambitions. Faulkner's story is a tale of lynching, and India has of late been arguably turned into a lynchistan. So the story, though background is different, has an immense resemblance to the disturbing happenings of new India.

Lynching of Muslims and Dalits in India

The lynching stories have been severely undermining the fundamental rights to life of minorities and the Dalits. It, consequently, challenges identity of Indian Muslims and their sense of belonging. Harassing the Muslims, and even killing them in the name of cattle thieves or anti-national activitiers or keeping beef at home or wearing hijab, and so on and forth has been a daily entertainment. Dalits in India are facing the same racial violence. Both the communities have been targeted by Hindu ultranationalists and Hindu terrorists. One is appalled to listen to heart-wrenching tales of lynching across the country. Now the two communities have become easy target by Hindu terrorists who under various pretexts create conditions for an agitated mob to lynch them. The police, representing the ethos of terrorists, record only those incidents captured by someone on cameras. Otherwise, hundreds of such incidents go unreported and often publicly unheard. The lynching of Dalit is a simple act. Some people belonging to upper caste catch a Dalit under any pretext, false or real, and beat her until she is dead. But in the case of a Muslim lynching, they add a religious element to it. They catch a Muslim, accuse him of stealing or keeping beef at home, and forcibly make him utter Jai Shri Ram and keep on hitting him or her with sticks, stones and knives until death (Aslam Abdullah).

Concluding Comment

Thus, Faulkner's "Dry September" can be read by Indian readers referring to Indian context of rising cases of mob violence, mob lynching and other hate crimes. Then the potential of the story will have a transnational reach in its cultural identity and belonging space. Identity of one's ethnicity or race or caste and so, is a crucial factor. In India it is increasingly used to lynch or to be lynched. There is hardly any difference among Faulkner's American white supremacists and Indian Hindu ultranationalists. And there the victim was a Negro, here he may easily be replaced by a Muslim or a Dalit. So there is a strong identical affinity among the lynchers and the lynched. And this trend nakedly demonstrates how one's sense of belonging or un-belonging largely depends on his race or caste or religion or other social identity markers.

Works Cited

1. https://www.thefreshreads.com/lynching-in-dry-september/ accessed Jan 21, 2022.
2. Milica, Iulia Andreea. "Racial Violence in William Faulkner's *Dry September* and Harper Lee's *To Kill A Mocking Bird.*" *Linguaculture*, 1, 2012DOI: 10.2478/v10318-012-0019-1.Available at http://archive.sciendo.com/LINCU/lincu.2012.2012.issue-1/v10318-012-0019-1/v10318-012-0019-1.pdf accessed March 9, 2022.
3. McManus, Dermot. "Dry September by William Faulkner." *The Sitting Bee.* Accessed Aug 13, 2014. Available at http://sittingbee.com/dry-september-william-faulkner/.
4. Ibid.
5. Faulkner, William. "Dry September." *A Norton Anthology: The Literature of the American South.* Ed. William L. Andrews. New York: W. W. Norton & Company, 1998. Print.
6. Ferguson, James. *Faulkner's Short Fiction.* Knoxville: The University of Tennessee Press, 1991. Print.
7. Harrington, Evans and Ann J. Abadie, eds. *Faulkner and The Short Story.* University Press of Mississippi: Jackson and London, 1992. Print.
8. https://www.youtube.com/watch?v=vjBRlRX9Oq8.
9. Abdullah, Aslam. "Lynching of Muslims and Dalits in India." Available at https://www.islamicity.org/20997/lynching-of-muslims-and-dalits-in-india/?gclid=EAIaIQobChMIn63Ww6i69gIVDQ4rCh3i2wDyEAMYASAAEgI2IfD_BwE Accessed March10, 2020.
10. https://scroll.in/article/861826/rajasthan-hate-murder-the-other-tragedy-in-afrazul-khans-murder-is-a-famine-of-compassion-outrage Accessed June 8, 2022.
11. https://scroll.in/topic/56212/karwan-tracks Accessed June 8, 2022.

CHAPTER 12

Poverty, Pandemic and Seasonal Sale of Religious Identity

> What are the roots that clutch, what branches grow
> Out of this stony rubbish? Son of man,
> You cannot say, or guess, for you know only
> A heap of broken images, where the sun beats,
> And the dead tree gives no shelter, the cricket no relief,
> And the dry stone no sound of water.
>
> Thomas Stearns Eliot, *The Waste Land*

Bare Words

The Waste Land (1922), widely regarded as one of the most seminal poetic works of the twentieth century and a central work of modernist poetry, opens with the famous line "April is the cruellest month" and the credit directly goes to 1948 Nobel Prize winner for making this line homely in our literary and cultural parlance. But I claim September is the cruellest month and I am fully aware of the festive mood of the Bengali Hindus across the globe before Durga pujo. Ah! The mellow autumn wind, the mild sun, the river banks and fields spotted with sprightly dance of white bunches of *kaash* flowers. Ma is coming...*aay re chute aay pujor gondho aseche* (come running, for air is filled with the smell of pujo).

Festive Air

Indeed the air of September in Kolkata or any mofussil towns in Bengal is soaked with scent of shiuli, kaash, freebies bonanza, heavy discounts at foodies, malls, showrooms or mobile outlets. Streets are getting repaired, bamboo structures being erected in every street. Channels, portals, webzines, papers, periodicals are giving countdown to the cue of the festive days ahead. Bengali Hindus are busy in shopping at malls, planning holidaying, visiting ancestral homes, etc. Book stalls and magazine stands are stacked with annual *sharodiya* especial issues. Schools and colleges are closed for almost a month. So celebration waits at each home to the full satisfaction of the students and guardians. Leave the measurement of the heights of the pandals to the sponsors, leaders and cultural tag bearers. Leave the inaugural of the pandals to the MPs, MLs, chairmen, secretaries, presidents of thousand public and private charitable bodies and mushrooming clubs.

Sorbojanin Durga Pujo – A Reality Check

The first onslaught is to declare and promote Durga pujo as *sorbojanin,* i.e., meant for everyone, irrespective of caste or creed or other affiliations. What a treacherous lie! A Muslim or a Christian or a Buddhist or an Adivasi has hardly any emotional affinity with Durga pujo. It is quite natural. They are loyal to their individual religious identity. Moreover, Bengali Muslims who comprise of almost 30 per cent of population, have in recent years witnessed the villainous activities of their neighbouring Bengali Hindus who supported National Register of Citizens (NRC) from their very yards and roofs. And Bengali Muslims across the districts, at street corners, at bus stands, before post offices, by railway stations, even at remote village haats have spontaneously staged protest against NRC. The communal divide has become too open in the wake of passing NRC . Friends have been foes overnight. The air is charged with communal tensions. Body languages of friends and relatives and even colleagues have dramatically changed. It seems they have found a remedy to their long pestering malaise. Banish the Muslims from West Bengal and free the land from their scourge! Grasp the land of gold from the traitors! I have written a short story on this theme, available at https://cafedissensusblog.com/2020/02/17/short-shorts-friendship-under-the-cloud-of-the-nrc/ to drive my point home.

West Bengal before 2021 Assembly election for the first time after independence, keeping in mind the tensed days of Babri Masjid demolition of 1992 or Gujrat riots of 2002, has never witnessed such open communal fissures among the two major communities of Bengal whom revolutionary poet Kazi Nazrul Islam (1899-1976) celebrated as *mora eki brinte duti kusum hindu musolman/ muslim tar noyon moni, hindu tahar pran* (we are two buds from the same petal – Hindu and Muslim/ Muslims are eyes to Hindus and Hindus are their souls). The Bengali Muslims have closely watched their Hindu neighbours, brothers and sisters, uncles and aunts to hold meeting at nights to vote for self-declared communal party BJP. The known faces during election days have turned into unknown territories. And now the same people who have left no stones unturned to propagate against Muslims and criminalise them are organising Durga pujos. And the ruling party is giving doles to beat drums and light pandals and preaching them as *sorbojanin.* What a dreaded treachery! What monstrous lies! Months back they are taking each possible step to label peace loving poor peasantary Muslims of Bengal as Bangladeshis, terrorists, jihadists, anti-nationals, etc., and now they are erecting pandals statewide to distribute Ma's *prasad* and blessings. What a mockery! What a double game!

Aryans' Affair

Durga pujo is celebrated by the Aryans, and not by non-Aryans. It is a fatal, sad festival where the killing of the great non-Aryan Asura hero Ravana is celebrated by the Aryans. Let me give a touching anecdote of the lamentation of Asura from Anand Neelakantan's, *Asura: Tales of the Vanquished, the Story of Ravana and His People* (2015):

> My beloved Lanka is being destroyed. I can still see the dying embers in what was once a fine city. My capital, Trikota, was the greatest city in the world. That was before the monkey-man came and set on fire. Trikota burned for days. Shops, homes, palaces, men, women, and babies, everything burned. But we restored it. Almost every able man joined in rebuilding Trikota. Then the monkey-men came with their masters and destroyed everything. Hanuman did that to us. The monkey-man brought us death, destruction and defeat.
>
> I don't want to dwell on that. I should have killed him when my son captured him. Instead, I listened to my younger brother, who plotted against me. But treason and betrayal are nothing new to the Asuras. I was naïve. I foolishly believed that I would always be loved by my brothers and my people. I never imagined that I would be betrayed (pp. 9-10).

Ravana's wailing words testify to the nobility, fidelity, sacrifice and grandeur of his indomitable spirit, his unassailable soul. For the non-Aryans, non-Brahmins, this pujo is a sad occasion to be mourned and, it is much akin to the sacrifice of Hussain Ibn Ali, (Hazrat Imam Hussain) on Ashura day, a day which marks the struggle against oppression and injustice. Let me share some lines from my poem 'September is the Cruellest Month' :

> September is preceded by countrywide cries against NRC,
> Delhi riots, slashed limbs in gutters, pandemic horrors,
> Farmers' protests and barren yards of four hundred plus peasants,
> Job losses, downsizing, homecoming of migrants!

September-sky is filled with calls for Muslims genocide,
Hate speeches of muscle flexing thugs,
The air is thickened with false promises,
Treacherous winds and gory armies of dead nights.

Cultural Politics of Babus of Bengal

The peasantary Bengali Muslims, the poor daily labourers, the daily wage earners, the Adivasis and Dalits of the hills and the jungles have awakened to the ugly reality of babu politics of Bengal. Parties in power or in opposition are solely mooted by upper caste Brahmins interests and advantages. They shed crocodile tears for the plight of the poor and meet out doles to the marginalised. Whoever comes to power, to them September is scented with shiuli and kaash. But in reality it is filled with cries, sighs, sobs and losses of the poor and unfed peasant masses of Bengal. But their sighs get suppressed not by force but with acquiesce. Muslims have no voice. Adivasis have no voice. The leaders of the both communities can be bought and sold like cattle in village haats across *sonar* Bangla, land of gold. And here comes the vicious nexus of Bengali intelligentsia who are born only to bend and touch the feet of powerful minority Brahmins who are at the helm of all state affairs. Exceptions are always there. But in general the Bengali intellectuals like to be wrapped with a chadar of bhadralok who can selflessly and relentlessly act only to her advantages only.

September, the Cruellest Month

September is the cruellest month. It is lean season when peasants are pushed to the walls for no availability of work in fields or kilns or masonry. They borrow rice, dal, oil, salt and other essentials from local grocery shops and count days. Many take loans at exorbitant rates, say 36 per cent, and have to mortgage cycles, kansa dishes, pots and pans. Very few can repay the loans and take their household articles back. September-October bring a seasonal hunger for poor agrarian societies in Bengal and beyond. It is the period after sowing and before harvest. Peasants put all their resources into the sowing, and they desperately wait for the harvest. Rains mean very little vegetable available. There is little work available in agriculture. Other works in construction sites and brick kilns stop during the rains. To top it all, diarrhea and skin diseases afflict the villagers. It is time for hunger and disease.[1]

'Authentic' Entertainment by Adivasis

During Durga pujo I have seen the Adivasi girls, men and women being hired by big puja organisers. They parade the city streets and perform traditional dances with their agile black bodies, and quench the babus' thirst for performing arts. Adivasis sell their culture for a drop of coins, and babus take the full credit for arranging such a circus or show of 'authentic' entertainment by hiring a bunch of santals, mundas, oraons and other tribes from the nearby villages. These poor illiterate Adivasis, living the life of extreme penury, are unaware of Hansda Sowvendra Shekhar's *The Adivasis Will Not Dance* (2015). And it is quite natural for them. They are pariahs, and their struggle is the struggle to have a meal at the end of the day. How can we expect that they will be ashamed of selling their culture during the Durga pujo? Culture is, indeed, a mouthful word for them.

Durga puja is not sorbojanin or meant for all. It is confined to Brahmin babus who either hold white colour jobs or have some established businesses and who have a sway over so called Bengali culture. And the revelry and exhibition of this culture in the month of September is an ugly distortion of hard reality the peasants, the daily workers, the manual and menial workers face because of lack of availability of work. September is a difficult month for them. Bengali culture is too liberal to portray the trajectories of everyday life of the marginal Muslims, Adivasis and the tribals.

Harsh Reality of September of 2021

September of 2021 is quite different as we have lost almost five lakh people in Covid 19. A study said 25,500 children in India lost their mother to Covid 19 while 90,751 lost their father and 12 lost both their parents.[2] The pandemic has starkly exposed India's big divides between the rich and the poor. Even before the lockdowns, three quarters of our population could not afford a healthy diet. And we will never know how many died of starvation because no state governments will admit starvation deaths. It is the month of horror and dismay for lakhs of Bengal poor villagers who become refugees in their own land because of the Ganga erosion. Poverty and plenty go hand in hand. The phenomenal waste in the name of a religious festival whose joys are limited to a section of Bengali people in a poverty-stricken state is especially unpardonable. Politics is always profitable. Durga Puja became a politicized phenomenon long before Mamata Banerjee's Rs 10,000 grant for each of 28,000 community festivals or her party's claim she had been invited to inaugurate 10,000 Pujas. It was reported in 2015 that the Puja industry, growing at a compound annual rate of about 35 per cent, was expected to touch Rs 40,000 crore. Assocham reckons that each year's Puja pumps about Rs 45,000 crore into the economy.[3]

Rising Economic Inequality

On the back of pandemic rises the economic and social inequality. The rise in the fortunes of the very rich during this period, when juxtaposed against the misery of the millions of migrant workers who had to walk back to their villages, is a stark reminder of the extent of economic disparities. To that extent, the latest edition of the World Inequality Report serves as a useful reminder of the concentration of income at the very top of the pyramid. The top 10 per cent earns 57 per cent of the national income. Within the top 10 per cent, the very elite top 1 per cent earns 22 per cent. In comparison, the share of the bottom 50 per cent in national income has declined to 13 per cent.[4]

Keeping these facts in mind I claim September 2021 is the cruellest month. Durga Ma will come and she will go but the lots of the untouchables and the marginalised are not going to change. The sky over their heads is going to be gloomier and duller day by day. So the celebration of a bunch of babus of Kolkata and its outskirts during puja hardly matters to the millions of poor peasants and day labourers of Bengal. Shiuli is scentless to them, and kaash flowers for them never sway heads in glee as in Eliot 'trees give no shelter,' 'stones no sound of water.' It is the season of sale and celebration of babu Hindu identity to the 'others' – the poor, the lowly, the tribals, the Muslims, the autochthonous, the marginals, the peripherals. The season with its pomp and hype showcases the majoritarian annual cultural supremacy and aggression to the common public spaces.

Sale of Religious Identity

The question of identity and belonging based on religious festivals, irrespective of communities, takes a prominent shape in our discourses of daily life and politics. During religious festivals a plain argument like 'the things that touch you, may not touch me' takes a back seat. Instead, we begin to chant *dharma jar jar uthsob sobar* (religion may be for particular community, but celebration is for all). We are too clever to accept the bitter truth. In the name of universality of the religious occasion, it ruthlessly separates people on the basis of the same religious identity. Each religious ritual has its own set of practices. Celebration of a particular religious practice does not necessarily mean the celebration of all religious practices. So, religious celebration is always limited to a set of people, in its scope and reach. It is not inclusive. It is not universal or sorbojonin as is always propagated. It is particular. Identity, whatever colour it may assume, is both adhesive and non-adhesive. It unites people on basis of race, caste, gender, colour, creed, religion, region, language, profession, and ethnicity. It also acts as a potential factor of disunity. From this point, religious festivals, be it the festival of Hindus, Muslims, Christians, Sikhs, or Jains champions a particular identical stand. It also relegates the non-participatory religious people to the passive plains of segregation and separation.

Thus, religious identity may boost and strenthen a particular community's sense of belonging. But it at the same time disorients people of other communities and makes them conscious of their separate identities. Religious celebration is merely a sale of a particular religious identity. It has a huge potential market in India and elsewhere, and marketing religious identity during festivals online and offline is an agreed fact. Be it Hajj pilgrimage or Amaranth yatra, be it Durga puja or Eid or Christmas or Ganesh Chaturthi, sale of religious identity is everywhere. In Friedman's flat world religious symbols, signs are on sale, and the demand is ever increasing among the poor masses. I am a witness to thousand scenes where tall houses of worship with all modern facilities are frowning from the sky over the unending valleys of tarpaulin-covered shacks and shanties of squalor and dirt and soot.

Consumerism in Mecca

Let us have a glimpse of how consumerism has engulfed arteries of the sacred city Mecca from Ziauddin Sardar. He wrote that it is now a city of proliferating bling, a haven of consumerism and opulent tourism.... They call it 'Saudi Las Vegas'. Like any other American city with its gambling casinos and gaudy architecture, has become a playground for the rich. Throughout the year the religious tourists visit partly to pray in the Sacred Mosque but also to shop in its innumerable opulent malls...Many have property around the Sacred Mosque not as an investment but in the hope that it will translate into real estate into paradise. Rich Muslims around the world pay a quick visit first to enhance their prestige and to make them appear more pious to the eyes of the society….Mecca has nothing especial. It is utterly mundane. Everything, from fake watches to plastic bottles of holy 'Zamzam water' is on sale. Crude comforts of consumerism are very dear to Mecca clerics. Ignorance is holy to them, and their open denigration of all the people and things non-Muslim have whetted the zeal of jihadis for killings and massacre…Minarets jostle with skyscrapers; motorways and towers align to face the Kaaba…The sectarian and racial divisions reign supreme. The Saudi clerics with beads in hands instead of giving charity to the poor contempt and curse them.[5]

Religious Festivals and Question of Belonging

By claiming the universality of religious festival we have aggravated the harmony that is supposed to exist among different communities. It is a hugely invested myth made popular in Indian history down the ages by our great men of East, Ramkrishna, Vivekananda, Ram Mohan Roy, Rabindranath, Gandhi, to name only a few. They are all Hindus by birth. So their worldview and outlook were soaked in Indian philosophy of the self. Yes, they were not parochial in their vision. They had big hearts where people from other communities have also found a temporary shelter. But had not they been guided by the Vedanta and the Upanishads? Did not they believe in rebirth or the ways of salvation? Had not they made a quest for God within one's self or *Atma*. Christianity and Islam or Buddhism may have influenced them, and thereby may have coloured their insights. But such remnants of other religions have a peripheral existence. At the core they are Hindus. Moderate or extreme? All we know.

Sale of religious identity, like that of Hajj pilgrims, is to found among the Hindu or Christian or other religious pilgrims. Pilgrimage is an act of marketing to effectively sale identity. It is primarily initiated to make maximum profit out of this religious investment. Pandemic or poverty temporarily hinders this business. But this hindrance to the selling and shopping of religious identity is swept away by the deluge of religious identity enthusiasts.

Conclusion

There is no universality in religious festival, I claim. Each festival is meant for a particular community. Religious festival is a sales-counter for the sale of a particular religious identity, religious signs and symbols. And our country has a huge potential for this emerging festive markets. Religious festival in public spaces does not cement the cultural gaps. It widens them.

Works Cited

1. https://mattersindia.com/2019/10/world-food-day-and-indias-starvation-deaths/. Web. Accessed, Sep. 10, 2021.
2. https://www.indiatoday.in/coronavirus-outbreak/story/covid-orphans-lancet-study-india-death-primary-caregivers-1831040-2021-07-22. Web. Accessed Sep. 12, 2021.
3. https://www.telegraphindia.com/opinion/the-unpardonable-waste-of-durga-puja/cid/1672131. Web. Accessed, Sep. 13, 2021.
4. https://indianexpress.com/article/opinion/columns/covid-pandemic-income-inequality-indian-economy-7669527/. Web. Accessed Sep. 14, 2021.
5. Sardar, Ziauddin. *Mecca: The Sacred City*. New Delhi: Bloomsbury Publishing India, 2014. pp. 348-63. Print.
6. Neelakantan, Anand. *Asura: Tales of the Vanquished, the Story of Ravana and His people.* Mumbai: Platinum Press, 2015. pp. 9-10. Print.
7. Bhowmik, Prabal. "Interplay of Power and Resistance in *The Adivasi Will Not Dance*." *All About Ambedkar: A Journal on Theory and Praxis,* Volume 2, Issue 1, January-April 2021. Available at https://www.allaboutambedkaronline.com/post/interplay-of-power-and-resistance-in-the-adivasi-will-not-dance Accessed June 7, 2022.

CHAPTER 13

The Myth of Hindu-Muslim Bhai-Bhaism: Religious Identity and Contested Belonging

> The bitter truth is that every Indian community has kept itself apart from the others. The traditional approach to diffuse communal tension was the Ram-Rahim or the Ishwar-Allah teyro naam approach, preaching that all religions emphasize love between humans....It is true that a truly religious man has no hatred in him. But such men have become a rarity while those who display their religiosity by emphasizing differences between religions have become a common phenomenon. We are unable to see our own shortcomings but we are eager to see the fatuous in other people's faiths. The Ram-Rahim approach is just a smoke screen.
>
> Khushwant Singh, *The End of India* (2003)

Qazi Sattar was right when he claimed that communalism is a many armed octopus. And just an octopus, when attacked, squirts ink to obscure the vision of its assailant, the communalist spreads canards which put attackers off his trail and make his victims let down their guard. It is wrong and counter-productive to say that communalism is invented in India by the Sanghis. The Congress under Indira Gandhi played its dirty role....Everybody has blood on his hands. One such canard borrowed from die-hard Gandhians is the belief of Hindu-Muslim bhai-bhaism. They argue that we [Indians] are children of the one God who is Ishwar and Allah, Ram and Rahim. Hindus, Muslims and Christians are brothers. *The harsh reality is that wherever people of different races, religions, languages and cultures have co-existed, instead of bhai-bhaism there is tension and turmoil. And if land, property or business is involved, the tension often explodes into violence* (Italics mine). Another canard is that in India there were no communal riots before the introduction of divide and rule policy by the British. The truth is that Hindu-Muslim tensions have existed since Islam came to India. And before Islam there were conflict between Hindus and Jains, Hindus and Buddhists, Dravidians and Aryans.[1]

Every religious or ethnic groups in India can and has been incited to kill and plunder...what happened at Nellie in Assam in 1983...Assamese and Bengalis killed each other, tribals killed non-tribals, Muslims killed Hindus and Christians, and Christians killed Hindus. It was just everyone killing everyone else. Communalism cannot be banished simply by voting BJP out of power. The problem is much larger and deeper...we must not miss the wood for the trees...over two thousand years ago, Buddhism was on the ascendant in India. Emperor Ashoka was the most famous convert to Buddhism. When Brahminical Hinduism gained favour again with ruling dynasties in the ninth and tenth centuries, Buddhists were persecuted and their places of worship demolished. Later during the reign of Muslim rulers, Hindus were discriminated and again their temples destroyed. During the British rule there were Hindu-Muslim riots every now and then. But there was no religious persecution. In the weeks and months followed August 1947 in West Punjab Hindus and Sikhs outdid their fellow goons. In the east, the prolonged Hindu-Muslim riots in Calcutta led to massacres of Muslims in Bihar, followed by massacres of Hindus in Noakhali in East Bengal. Waves of Hindus and Sikhs fled across the borders to safety. Many were butchered on the way.[2]

Religion and community based political parties began to encroach on the political domain from the time Indira Gandhi became Prime Minister. During British rule communal violence was limited to Hindu-Muslim conflicts on religious holidays like Holi, Id-ul-Zuha, the Ganapati festival. Riots occurred in a few riot-prone towns. Today, riots take place between Hindus and Muslims, Hindus and Sikhs, Hindus and Christians, caste Hindus and Harijans, tribals and non-tribals, Bengalis and Assamese, Maharastrians and Kannadigas. The entire country has become riot-prone. *Everone's hand rises against his neighbour because everyone wants what his neighbour has – his land, his job, or his business. Racial, religious and linguistic differences provide the excuse to do so* (Italics mine).[3] Here come the machinations of Sanghis to exploit the rage of the educated jobless Hindu youths, the lumpen elements, and the jealousy and prejudices of the established middle class Hindu traders and to mobilise in the name of Hindu identity against their Muslim neighbours. False rhetoric, enticing lies, fabricated facts through propaganda machines, and even offer of alcohol and hard cash by the Sanghis have been instrumental in building their solid electoral bases in every mohallas of India.

What the Secularists Say

In opinion of famous psychoanalyst Sudhir Kakar, the secularists comprising most of the Western-educated liberal and leftist intelligentsia opine that Hindu and Muslim are relatively recent categories in Indian history. Before the late nineteenth century, overarching religious entities and identities such as Hindu and Muslim did not exist. Among the Hindus there were various sects frequently at odds with each other. And the Indian Muslims did not constitute a monolithic Islamic collectivity. They go on to paint pictures of prevalent Hindu-Muslim symbiosis of the precolonial and early colonial periods. There had been a development of a syncretic popular religion which comingles elements from both Islamic practice and Hindu ritual. And the people revere both the Muslim saints and Hindu holy men.

The secularists, the author argued, make a clear distinction between the terms 'religious' and 'communal.' The term 'communal' is not applied in its Anglo-American lexical sense, meaning someone who is altruistic and civic minded. The term in Indian context gains a huge leverage and refers to one whose exclusive attachment to her or his community is combined with an active hostility against other communities which share the same geographical and political space. Whereas religion is seen solely as a matter of personal faith and reverence for a particular set of icons, rituals and dogmas, communalism is a more collective affair which involves a community's politics and economics as much as its faith. Communalism not only produces identification with a religious community, but also with its political, economic, social and cultural interests and aspirations. And they believe that the interests of one community not only diverge from but are in actual conflicts with the interests of other communities. In this view, the precolonial and early colonial period conflicts between Hindus and Muslims were negligible and they had religious orientation such as the conflicts over the route of religious procession or issues of control over temples and mosques, and so on. Twentieth century conflicts, on the other hand, involve communal ideologies. They are centered basically around clashing economic interests. The secularists are of the opinion that communalism and, the consequent massive violence between Hindus and Muslims was an affair of late nineteenth century colonial aggression and the 'divide and rule' policy of the British. To counter Indian nationalism the British had deliberately fuelled the fire of Muslim communalism. But the basic fabric of India remains syncretic – a commingling of Islamic influences with Hindu traditions. Hindus and Muslims, they argue, are not divided along cultural or social-psychological lines barring the narrow area of personal faith.

For the liberal historian or one with leftist leanings, the story is bathed in a roseate glow of the precolonial golden age of Hindu-Muslim amity. Among Hindus and Muslims there always exists a kind of composite cultural tradition, especially in art, music and architecture. The story is of a gradual drawing closer of Hindus and Muslims in the forms of their daily lives and of an enthusiastic participation in each other's festivals. There is little room for conflict between the communities. The cause of sporadic outbreaks of violence is not religious in origin, but is dictated by local economic interests and political compulsions.

What the Hindu Nationalists Argue

The Hindu nationalists argue, according to Kakar, that a fundamental divide between Hindus and Muslims is a basic fact of Indian history. The conflict between Hindus and Muslims is squarely religious and theological. Its roots lie in Islam's exclusive claim to truth and its refusal to grant equal status to Hindu beliefs and doctrines. Islam's division of people into believers and infidels and the world into areas of peace or *dar-ul-Islam* and of conflict or *dar-ul-harb* which led to terrible cruelties against the Hindu infidels' person and religious shrines over hundreds of years cannot be erased from the Hindu collective memory. The Hindu nationalists also argue that the Muslims continue to persist in intolerance, in the belief that all that is outside the Qur'an is an error, if not abomination. The Hindu nationalists claim that the secularists seem to direct their arguments and appeals only toward the Hindus since they are firmly rejected by the Muslims who seek identity in their own religious tradition and personal laws even when those go against the very fundamentals of a secular state. The roots of Hindu-Muslim conflict lie in Muslim religious intolerance, Muslim failure to outgrow a medieval bigotry, and the inability to learn how to live in a state which is not Muslim-controlled.

To the conservative Hindu nationalists the Hindu saffron and the Muslim green do not mix to create a pale pink, the rift between the two communities is a fundamental fact. They assert that Hindu-

Muslim relations framed by a thousand year –old 'civilisational' conflict in which the Muslims, militarily victorious and politically ascendant for centuries, tried to impose Islamic civilisation on their Hindu subjects through all means, from coercion to bribery and cajolery. And they had limited success. The composite culture was limited to small sections of Hindu populations around the Muslim courts and to court-patronised arts like music and architecture. It also included some Hindus who adopted the Persian inspired language and ways of life of their rulers. But the vast majority of the Hindus kept their civilisational core intact while they resentfully tolerated the Muslim onslaught. And the conflict between the two communities is inevitable. Apart from the economic and political underpinnings, there are many cultural and civilisational differences between the two communities, which sustain the bases of the age old Hindu-Muslim conflict.[4]

One of these religious fault lines – the relationship between India's Hindu majority and the country's smaller religious communities – has particular relevance in public life, especially in recent years under the ruling Bharatiya Janata Party (BJP). The survey finds that Hindus tend to see their religious identity and Indian national identity as closely intertwined: Nearly two-thirds of Hindus (64%) say it is very important to be Hindu to be "truly" Indian.[5]

Bias of Hindu Nationalists

The Hindu nationalists put overemphasis on the tyrannies of ten centuries of Muslim domination. What do they offer about the exploitation and loot of their British colonial masters? They had plundered the wealth of the country and funneled it out of the country. But during the Muslim rule, wealth stayed within the country. Political subjugation and economic exploitation played a lesser role in determining the Hindu reaction because the Hindu collective identity was crystallised around shared symbols and myths, and not on the political and economic structures. Muslims were seen to be mockers of their faith, whereas the British were taken as indifferent elites. The British too ate beef like that of a Hindu's Muslim neighbour. But the Hindus were not hostile to the British for it, as they were in power and their lives were confined to the high walls of barracks and bungalows. But a Muslim butcher with his blood-flecked lungi was a dreadful figure to his Hindu neighbour.

Let us give a much used example of parochialism of a Hindu nationalist writer from Bengal. *Anandmath* (1882), a Bengali novel written by Bankim Chandra Chatterjee outlines the concept of Hindu Rashtra and is considered as the *Gita* by the proponents of Hindu Rashtra. Bankim Chandra played an important role in the degradation of Indian nationalism to communal nationalism and introduced the song 'Vande Mataram' through his novel which equated nationalism to mother worship. *Anandmath* narrates the story of Hindu sanyasi rebellion against Muslims. It romanticizes the attack on Muslims, it describes how the Hindu sanyasis (sanatans) torched Muslim houses and looted everything. The novel also describes how the sanatans killed the Musalman who refused to recite 'I salute thee mother,' the same stand is followed by hindutva terrorists.

Chatterjee was very fond of British rulers and never considered them as people who looted India, and he preached that 'Muslims are our sole enemy.' His love for British masters could be seen in the last lines of *Anandmath*, where when some of the sanatan cadres who have succeeded in overthrowing Muslim rulers now wanted to fight against Britishers, a mystic leader appears and pacifies them that the sanatan virtue could only be restored under the rule of Englishman as King, so the sanatans should not wage war against them. The leader convinces the sanatans that they have become successful by eliminating Muslim rule and now should let the English reign continue. It reads *the Englishman is our ally King. Moreover, none possesses such power who can win the war with the Englishmen ultimately*. The novel glorifies the imperialist masters, who destroyed lives and properties of Indians, and they are depicted as brave and superior souls. Importantly, Bankim Chandra was appointed directly to the post of Deputy Magistrate in the year 1858, the first Indian to be appointed to such a post immediately after 1857. Bankim retired as District Magistrate in the year 1891. He was conferred with the titles of Rai Bahadur and CIE by the British Crown. He was none other than a stooge for British imperialism and part of British exploitation program in India.[6] To the Hindu nationalist a Muslim proves to be an unforgivable enemy as he eats beef and his religion is alien. But the British beef eaters, their Bible are sacred to the Hindu nationalists. Their loot and plunder of nation's wealth is overlooked by the Hindu nationalists out of their innate cowardliness and fear.

The Sustained Chasm

Data journalist Rukmini S finds that a majority of Hindus in India see themselves as very different from their Muslim compatriots (66 per cent), and most Muslims feel the same way, saying they are very different from Hindus (64 per cent). Over a third of Hindu respondents, in a 2019 national survey, considered Muslims to be unpatriotic (although the Muslim respondents did not feel that way about themselves). Hindus, even minorities Sikhs and Jains are comfortable with friends from their respective religions. People from other religions are largely unacceptable as neighbours too. This leads to the ghettoisation of the Muslims (being forced to live with your own community). The work of scholars of Indian religions like David Lorenzen and Andrew Nicholson shows that there was a clear sense of difference between Hindu and Muslim communities long before British rule. Similarly, Hindu-Muslim riots in India date back to hundreds of years before any British official set foot on the subcontinent. In the fourteenth century, the famed Moroccan scholar Ibn Battuta wrote about the state of Hindu-Muslim relations in the south Indian town of Mangalore, …war frequently breaks out between them (the Muslims) and the (Hindu) inhabitants of the town; but the Sultan (the Hindu King) keeps them at peace because he needs the merchants.[7] *Hindu barnashrom prothai e desher samprodayikotar adimotom uthso. Keu keu obossho british samrajjobadkei samprodayikotar jonoyita mone koren. Tara vartiyo itihaser otitke shudhu british shashoner dusho bochorer moddhe simito rakehn bolei ei vulta kore thaken.* (Hindu caste system was the oldest primary source for the birth of communalism in India. Some accused the British to be the primary originator of communalism. They mistook by confining the history of India's past within the British rule of two hundred years.)[8] However regrettable, this state of affairs is not really surprising. Long before the British conquered India, the Hindus had resented their Muslim Mogul masters and those who by conversion followed the same faith. The Muslim for his part had all the scorn of the warrior for those less martial than himself, not untainted with an intellectual inferiority complex vis-à-vis those commercially and politically more astute than he (Frederic M. Bennett).

Cynthia Talbot, a historian who focuses on pre-colonial India claims:

> …no one would deny that modernisation has led to the sharper articulation of identities encompassing broad communities… modern

> identities do not spring fully fashioned out of nowhere. They commonly employ the myths and symbols of earlier forms of identity that may be less clearly formulated and more restricted in circulation but are nonetheless incipient cores of ethnicity.[9]

According to Pew Research Center, despite sharing certain values and religious beliefs – as well as living in the same country, under the same constitution – members of India's major religious communities often don't feel they have much in common with one another. The majority of Hindus see themselves as very different from Muslims (66%), and most Muslims return the sentiment, saying they are very different from Hindus (64%). There are a few exceptions: Two-thirds of Jains and about half of Sikhs say they have a lot in common with Hindus. But generally, people in India's major religious communities tend to see themselves as very different from others.[10]

As Madhavrao Sadashivrao Golwalkar (1906-1973) in his book *We or Our Nationhood Redefine* (sic) (1935) writes, those only are nationalist patriots, who, with the aspiration to glorify the Hindu race and nation next to their heart, are prompted into activity and strive to that goal. All others are either traitors or enemies to the National cause, or, to take a charitable view, idiots (qtd. in Khan).11 Guruji openly wanted to model his Hindu Rashtra or Nation on Hitler's totalitarian and fascist design. He wrote:

> It is worth bearing well in mind how these old Nations solve their minorities problem. They do not undertake to recognise any separate element in their polity. Emigrants have to themselves naturally assimilated in the principal mass of the population, the National Race, by adopting its culture and language and sharing in its aspirations, by losing consciousness of their separate existence, forgetting their foreign origin. If they do not do so, they live merely as outsiders, bound by all the codes and conventions of the Nation, at the sufferance of the Nation and deserving no special protection, far less any privilege of rights. There are only two courses open to the foreign elements, either to merge themselves in the national race and adopt its culture, or to live at its mercy so long as the national race may allow them to do so and to quit the country at the sweet will of the national race. That is the only sound view on the minorities problem. That is the only logical and correct solution. That alone keeps the national life healthy and undisturbed (qtd. in Islam).[12]

Hatred against the minorities is at the core of RSS ideology. While such dehumanising ideologies exist and are openly propagated in each nook and corner of Indian cities and villages by the RSS, BJP and their thousands of political and cultural offshoots, any word on Hindu-Muslim composite culture is bounded to sound empty. The gap between the two religions and their followers is particularly after the victory of BJP in 2014 and 2019 ever widening. Secularists are now mocked by Modi's digital army as 'sickularists.' Hindu nationalists laugh at the name of Nehuru and Gandhi, the father of the nation. Their political agenda, their machinery to make them relevant and demanding in public discourses, their nexus with the corporate power, their success behind the creation of a solid political base of Hindu lumpen class, their continuous attacks on the secular fabric of Indian society, their success in rousing a kind of 'hinduness' among the non-caste lowly Hindus, tribals, Adivasis, their penetration into the so called liberal souls have turned the topic of Hindu-Muslim syncretic relation into a scatological humour.

Vinayak Damodar Savarkar's(1883-1966) Hindutva (1923) claims a Hindu is one who acknowledges Hindustan as his pitrubhumi (fatherland) as well as punyabhumi (holy land). A converted Muslim or a Christian is also welcome back into the Hindu fold provided he accepts the said two prescriptions. Moreover, a Hindu has to love, embrace and own Hindu sanskriti as a whole. This automatically excluded Muslims and Christians, for, while they might have shared a common pitrubhumi with the Hindus, their punyabhumi lay elsewhere. Hindutva also involved the unconditional acceptance of Sanskrit and other Indian languages while there was no place for Urdu or English. While Jains, Buddhists and Sikhs were accepted because their religions were Indian origin, Muslims and Christians and Parsis were excluded on the basis that they were merely communities of numerical minorities. Savarkar was also the first to propound the two-nation theory, referring to the Hindus and Muslims as separate nations.

As Khushwant Singh aptly put, the birth of Hindu nationalism took place in Renaissance Bengal in 1886 with the Hindu melas. The primary objective of these melas was to train young Hindus in the martial arts, the use of lathis, daggars and swords. Non-Hindus were not allowed to participate. Swami Dayanand's establishment of Arya Samaj [even today you can find name of some Hindu paras in Bengal as 'Arya para' or 'Arya palli') and its excessive emphasis on Shuddhi was a step to re-establish the golden age of Hinduism. It encouraged reconversion of Muslims and Christians to its old fold. In Maharstra, Bal Gangadhar Tilak revived Ganapati and Shivaji festivals (Today you may find front gates of many Bengali baniyas's homes decorated with Ganapati idol or the Ganapati bappa ringtone being used in their calling bells and smart phones). In Bengal, anusilan samitis were set up to combat partition of the state. Non-Hindus were not allowed to be its members. Hindu Sabhas, which had initially stood for cow protection, the promotion of Hindi as a national language, formally launched the Hindu Mahasabha in 1922. And with the arrival of V D Savarkar as its president in 1936 it gained a distinctive Hindu ideology, hindutva. The central focus of all the said offshoots of samitis and sakahas and sabhas is on the assertion of Hindu identity and promotion of Hindu ideology. These organisations and its leaders and members had played crucial role in the deterioration of Hindu-Muslim relation. These organisations in the name of Renaissance had actually acted against the interests of the Muslims and lowly Hindus. They basically championed the cause of the Brahmins and acted as divisive forces among the masses of Bengal.

During the BJP regime, the push was that the core identity of a true Hindu be constructed around ancient Hindu lineage, acceptance of militancy, retributive justification of violence and perception of secular acts. Reviving Hinduism through the ancient Indian civilisation theme, the BJP was able to arouse the dormant embers of Hindu pride and retributive violence. Consequently, when the BJP and its allies sounded the clarion call for Hindu militancy, many jumped on the wagon. The BJP put into practice the processes through which traditions and past experiences are used to justify political agendas. Events which followed showed that the agenda of balancing the acts of history was wilfully accepted. Through the agency of Hindu revivalism, an attempt was made to harness the Muslim community and thereby rectify the wrongs suffered by the Hindus when they were under the domination of the Muslims. The project of Hindutva, which basically focuses on the building up of a mass mobilisation geared to the task of forging a new "Hindu" nation, began to take shape, and new symbols were created to operationalise this agenda (Khan and Sen 2009).

Let me quote a couple of my poems to capture the essence of today's Hindu-Muslim relation. First one is titled 'Muslims are to be blamed.' It has two parts. First part holds the prejudiced and pejorative views of Hindu nationalists who are in the habit of dehumanising the Muslim community of the country for each and every faults, be it global warming or abysmal education system of the nation. This view has strong support among the conservative Hindu thinkers and even among the so called libearls.

1

Who are foreigners?
Muslims
Who are aliens?
Muslims
Who lack culture?
Muslims
Who are traitors?
Muslims
Who damaged our education?
Muslims
Who killed our culture?
Muslims
Who looted us?
Muslims
Who raped our women?
Muslims
Who rioted in Gujrat, UP, Delhi?
Muslims
Who divided our land?
Muslims
Who destroyed Kashmir?
Muslims
Who destroyed our forests?
Muslims
Who are behind global warming?
Muslims
Who made a hole in Ozone?
Muslims
Who melted ice in Arctic?
Muslims
Who stole our minerals?
Muslims
Who polluted our seas?
Muslims
Who cause quakes?
Muslims
Who kill you with words?
Muslims
Who spread Corona?
Muslims
Who disturb your sleep?
Muslims
Who betray you?
Muslims
Who are fanatics?
Muslims
Who populate our land?

Muslims
Who spread hate?
Muslims
Who lure our girls?
Muslims
And whom you deeply hate?
Muslims
And so on and on…

2

Who are poor?
Muslims
Who live in ghettos?
Muslims
Who are lynched?
Muslims
Who languish in jails?
Muslims
Who die in custody?
Muslims
Who are primary targets of police?
Muslims
Who inhabit in detention camps?
Muslims
Who build your home?
Muslims
Who plough your lands?
Muslims
Who work in kilns?
Muslims
Who are peasants?
Muslims
Who are daily wagers?
Muslims
Who make your quilt?
Muslims
Who paddle your boat?
Muslims
Who run your mill?
Muslims
Who work at tannery?
Muslims
Who work at garages?
Muslims
Who supply you cheap labourers?
Muslims
Who water your seeds?
Muslims

Who drive you home?
Muslims
Who sew your shoes?
Muslims
Who sell vegetables at your step?
Muslims
Who tailor your wears?
Muslims
Who guard your malls?
Muslims
Who labour like slaves?
Muslims
Who have no voice?
Muslims
Who vote you to power?
Muslims
Who are worst hit by digital divide?
Muslims
Who have no claim to civilised blocks?
Muslims
Who bite dust?
Muslims
And who are falling like dry leaves?
Muslims
And so on and on…

The second part of the poem presents the living reality of the Indian Muslims. They do the all sort of manual and menial jobs. They are in majority in informal sectors. They live in ghettos and slums of the Indian cities and at remote villages. They are a wretched lot. They are the modern slaves. The secularists recognise it. But their Brahmin party bosses hardly take any policy to change the status quo. The secularists in question of Muslim issues hold the same pejorative view as that of their Hindu nationalist counterparts. In today's India fundamentally there are hardly any basic difference among the secularists and the Hindu nationalists in question of Indian Muslim isuues. Only difference is that the secularists acknowledge the pathetic socio-economic conditions of the Indian Muslims whereas the Hindu nationalists put blind eye to this ugly reality and frenziedly beat the 'appeasement' drums to our greatest satisfaction. Moreover, they leisurely enjoy the lower status of the Muslims in socio-economic and cultural spaces.

Let me quote the second poem titled 'Betrayers of Indian Muslim' from my 2022 poetry anthology *Shadows of Mourning,* where I argue that for the dehumanisation and vilification of the Indian

Muslim the RSS or BJP is not solely responsible. In fact many so called secularists and liberals have soft corners for the RSS ideology for making India a Hindu Rasthra. The supporters of RSS ideology have got an unprecedented fillip in the wake of the arrival of Modi in 2014 as country's God. The majority of Hindus, whether they belong to RSS fold or not, have enjoyed many decisions of Modi government, namely the building of Ram temple in Ajodhya, abrogation of article 370 in Kashmir, passing bill for NRC, to name only a few. We have seen such heartening scenes – the sweet being distributed at roadsides, candles lit at homes, thalis banged at rooftops of the so called secularists and liberals. The poem runs thus:

> Today Indian Muslims are falling like autumn leaves,
> Hot election days or calm winter nights
> Spread the same aroma of blood and deaths,
> Alien even to age old 'good' neighbours,
> Barred to beautiful blocks they live and die in ghettos,
> Naked, they are lynched even in resorts,
> A poor race known only for wrong reasons,
> Used, abused, exploited, killed by better brothers.
> A few, however, wear mask of bhadraloks,
> They have achingly mastered the art
> To be quiet in time of crushing quakes, floods or fires.
> The rest, only wagons, carrying filth of masters' fiefdom.
> Who have betrayed the sinless country lovers?
> Poor leaders, shady intelligentsia, paid media and they themselves.
> And now the luxuriant lands and its sunny skies and wide seas,
> Revelling and relishing their routine fall.

We have seen the Modi mania among our good gentle liberal Hindu neighbours. At tea-stall or office, in bus or train or street the bhakts' visibility comes to the fore. Online propaganda machines are put in operation for the rise of 'new India.' Riots held at country's capital, corona took lakhs of lives, lakhs of workers and peasants lost livelihood. But the propaganda machines operated by the dedicated trolls of the party in power have not halted for a second. Without accusing or finding faults of the Muslims they cannot have a wink of sleep. One after another the trivial issues are being raked up simply to make the Muslim community villain to the eyes of the people. Hijab, azan are preposterous excuses. They are the well-researched symbols with which the BJP can profitably play the game of creating a solid political Hindu mass and winning elction. They can drive the hesitant Hindu voters to the 'Hindu' space by spreading innumberable hot stories of islamophobia. It is plain and simple.

I argue that Hindu nationalists are constantly openly and brazenly attacking the Muslim space. And our secularists, especially, caste Marxist babus of West Bengal, are watching the xenophobic scenes like defeated soldiers. In paper they are taking the side of the Muslims but in reality, they are acting against the interests of the Muslims. Muslims have now accepted this mature view. And they are looking out for alternative voice. They believe that the gap between Hindus-Muslims cannot be bridged unless some concrete measures are taken for strengthening the voice of the Muslims. They also believe that both Hindu nationalists and Hindu secularists are happy maintaining the status quo, that is, accepting the second class or third class status of Indian Muslims. The centre is for the Brahmins. Muslims and Christians must be relegated to the margins. Nationalists or secularists have no arguments in the said claim.

So the Hind-Muslim bhai-bhaism is simply a myth. The reality is Hind-Muslim interests clash, and conflicts between the two communities should be acknowledged and alternative politics should be invited in the field of Indian democracy. More we speak about bhai-bhaism without acknowledging and demolishing the divisive and inequal social-economic-cultural factors, more we do harm to Tagore's acclaimed 'idea of India.'

Quest for Truth

Kakar has found fallacies, taking the risk of being labelled either as 'pseudosecularist' or 'cryptofascist' in both the claims of the secularists and the Hindu nationalists. He believes that the secularists have underestimated the extent of the historical rift between Hindus and Muslims. They have tended to downplay the dark side of Hindu-Muslim relations in India. Hindu-Muslim conflicts are not only a product of the colonial period but also occurred in precolonial times. And the conflicts were communal in origin not merely religious. In the medieval period, even the Sufis who are often credited as the originators and bearers of 'composite culture' had serious limitations to their tolerance. In the question of faith they were unequivocal about the superiority of Islam and the hellish fate in store for the Hindu infidels on judgment day. In relation to Hindus it is difficult to distinguish between an orthodox theologian and a liberal mystic. Many a Sufi was openly hostile to the religion and social practices of the Hindus. An average literate Muslim believes that Islam and Hinduism belong to two radically separate and diverse traditions and the twin shall never meet. In the same way the Hindu nationalists have overestimated the existence and strength of overarching Hindu and Muslim religious identities in India's precolonial past. They put excessive emphasis on the doctrinal and cultural differences between Islam and Hindu beliefs for the difficulties in the relations between the two communities. To Kakar Hindu-Muslim rift is as much the consequence of a collision between two collective narcissisms, between two equally grandiose group selves, each convinced of its civilisational superiority, as of differences in matters of faith.

The psychoanalyst points out that there are two overarching histories of Hindu-Muslim relations with many local variations which have been used by various political parties and ideologues. They have been in competition for acquiring political space for many centuries. In times of escalated conflict between the two communities, the Hindu nationalist views on Muslim tyranny assume central space and orchestrate their cultural memory in one particular direction. At this juncture the sayings of the Sufis and saints and sages fall flat. The anecdotes of centuries' harmony and peaceful coexistence between the two communities lose their relevance to the battling communities. However, in times of relative peace and harmony the focus shifts back to the history of commonalities and shared space of daily living and livelihood. Many of the painful cultural memories of both the communities retreat, fade and even annihilate. Communal differences take back seat. And mutual harmony prevails between the two communities. Hostility between the communities is never completely erased. But the degree and intensity of the enmity and consequent violence between the two communities play ebb and flow with the political tides of the land.

The extent of violence in the recent Delhi anti-Muslim riots demonstrates the long-term consequences of the partition, Hindu nationalism, and ultimately how India's government has dealt with this situation. It is crucial to emphasise that Muslims have faced discrimination under Hindu communalism since the end of the Moghul Empire. It has never been as destructive as it has been today, as the religious differences are becoming more apparent and directly challenged. The constant force of violence now prevalent in India showcases how problematic this divide is (Sadia Ahmed).

Works Cited

1. Singh, Khushwant. *The End of India.* New Delhi: Penguin Books, 2003. pp. 79-80. Print.
2. Ibid. pp. 82-92.
3. Ibid.
4. Kakar, Sudhir. *The Colours of Violence.* New Delhi: Penguin Books, 1995. pp.16-20. Print.
5. https://www.pewforum.org/2021/06/29/religion-in-india-tolerance-and-segregation/ Accessed Feb. 25, 2022.
6. https://countercurrents.org/2017/04/bankims-bharat-pro-british-anti-muslim-and-pro-brahminical/ Accessed Feb. 24, 2022.
7. Verghese, Ajay. "British Rule and Hindu-Muslim riots in India: A Reassessment." Available at https://berkleycenter.georgetown.edu/responses/british-rule-and-hindu-muslim-riots-in-india-a-reassessment Accessed Feb. 25, 2022.
8. Sofa, Ahmed. *Bangali Musolmaner Mon.* Dhaka: Hawladar Prokashani, 2018. p. 39. Print.
9. Pillalamarri, Akhilesh. "The Origins of Hindu-Muslim Conflict in South Asia." https://thediplomat.com/2019/03/the-origins-of-hindu-muslim-conflict-in-south-asia/ Accessed Feb. 25, 2022. Web.
10. https://www.pewforum.org/2021/06/29/religion-in-india-tolerance-and-segregation/ Accessed Feb. 25, 2022. Web.
11. Khan, Badre Alam. "Rise of Hindu majoritarianism, making Indian Muslim 'invisible citizen.'" Review of *Visible Muslims, Invisible citizenship: Understanding Islam in Indian Democracy* (2019), Salman Khurshid. https://countercurrents.org/2019/09/rise-of-hindu-majoritarianism-making-indian-muslim-invisible-citizen/ Accessed Feb. 25, 2022. Web.
12. Islam, Shamsul. *Know* the *RSS*. New Delhi: Pharos Media, 2018. p.12. Print.
13. Rukmini S. *Whole Numbers and Half Truths: What Data Can and Cannot Tell us about Modern India.* Context, 2021. [Kindle Basic] Retrieved from amazon.com. [Loc 526].
14. https://thewire.in/communalism/attempt-to-erase-every-aspect-of-life-of-indian-muslims-bebaak-collective-on-communal-riots Accessed June 4, 2022. Web.
15. Khan, Sammyh and Ragini Sen. "Where Are We Going? Perspective on Hindu–Muslim Relations in India." Available at https://www.researchgate.net/publication/227092560_Where_Are_We_Going_Perspective_on_Hindu-Muslim_Relations_in_India Accessed June 4, 2022. Web.
16. Ahmed, Sadia. "Hindu-Muslim Fragmentation: A Consequence of India's Colonial Legacy." Available at https://www.humanrightspulse.com/mastercontentblog/hindu-muslim-fragmentation-a-consequence-of-indias-colonial-legacy Accessed June 4, 2022. Web.
17. Bennett, Frederic M. "Muslim and Hindu." Available at https://www.theatlantic.com/magazine/archive/1958/02/muslim-and-hindu/305462/ Accessed June 7, 2022. Web.

CHAPTER 14

The Myth of Damaging Identity Politics

The damaging identity politics myth creates an *exception* for whiteness, promotes *racial entitlement* via dog whistling ('the wink') and *grievance flipping* and is sustained by appeals to *universalism*.

Basically there are two definitions of identity politics. The first is the effort to secure the rights denied to some on the basis on their identity – defensive identity politics. The second is that which seeks domination on the basis of identity – aggressive identity politics. Aggressive identity politics espoused by the majority is thought to be 'natural and benign.' And identity politics as practised by the blacks, the Asians, the minorities and the disadvantaged is thought to be 'dangerous, indulgent and damaging.'

Exceptionalism

There is a discount applied to rowdy behavior by those we see as our own. In Saudi Arabia, for instance, it was official policy never to use words 'terrorist' or 'terrorism' when referring to religious insurgents waging war against the royal family for the past forty years. Perpetrators were referred to as 'those who have lost their path' or 'the lost ones.' [Similarly the violence against the minorities and the Dalits and women unleashed by the majoritarian India is seen to be natural and harmless. Even the orthodox liberals refuse to speak against it, secretly basking on the glory of their innate identity, *hinduness*. There is nothing wrong in claiming the innate ownership of this Hindu coin. Study the results of West Bengal Assembly Election. What was the election issue? The pride of being non-Muslim, *the appeasement* of the Muslims by the ruling TMC government, the need for solidarity of the Hindu majority for their make-believe grievances. Promises for better health care, better education facility, creation of jobs, were of course printed in party manifestoes. But what have we seen in the campaigns rallies in the streets or on the mobile and TV screens? Bizarre exhibition of majority chauvinism and hooliganism based on their singular religious identity! The whole election is fought on the basis of aggressive identity politics by the BJP. Likewise TMC also plays 'Bangla' identity card].

Defensive identity politics is mistakenly seen as a disruptive influence that divides the electorate and has pushed the white voters into the embrace of the populists. But it is a response against the dominance and ubiquity of a white [majority] identity. As Hannah Arendt said, 'if one is attacked as a Jew, one must defend oneself as a Jew.' When you are attacked and threatened because of your identity, you respond in terms of your identity. [For instance, In Bengal a Muslim is often denied home at posh apartments or posh areas of towns only because she is a Muslim. It is her in-born religious identity against which she can hardly fight. Have the elite Hindu liberals had a second to think over this *negligible* or *minor* issue ever? It is a gross violation of human dignity and the perpetrators are not the village half-literate or illiterate Hindus or the Hindu fanatics. They are the champions of Bengali (Hindu) culture – exclusionary at its best.] David Goodhart, the author of the *Road to Somewhere* has cleared the clouds when he states, 'To put it bluntly – most of us prefer our own kind.' This direct honesty about white racial loyalty [majority Hindu loyalty] is helpful in understanding how minorities are blamed for white [Hindu] tribal behavior.

American academic Mark Lilla in a 2016 op-ed for the *New York Times* asserts: 'liberals should bear in mind that the first identity movement in American politics was the Ku Klux Klan, which still exists. Those who play identity game should be prepared to lose it.' His warning about the damaging effects of identity politics exposes the very heart of the myth. He refuses to believe that white [Hindu] identity politics came first and is aggressive, while identity politics by non-whites [non-Hindus] came second and is defensive. What the damaging identity politics myth is based on is the perception that political motivations of the powerful [majority] are rational and untinged by anything as base as furthering an identity agenda. [Slogans like *sab ka saath, sab ka bikash*, *atmanirvor bharat* vie with *goli maro, khatom karo*. What is the single criterion to kill and to be killed? It is racial or religious identity. Marxists' overemphasis on class identity cannot explain the cause of this crisis.]

Racial Entitlement

The aggressive identity politics constantly harps on false economic anxiety. Multiple researches showed that it was not economic anxiety but prejudices about race, gender and immigration animated support for Trump whose tenure has been characterised by vicious racist and sexist dog whistling. And it hardly impacted his popularity among his base. Trump voters had stronger feelings about the ostensibly declining status of America globally. Dominance at home and abroad meant sitting on top of the totem pole racially. His supporters were not just conservative; they were regressive in that they were strongly motivated by a need to freeze the status quo of their white racial supremacy. They saw in him a saviour of their positions – positions based on race, gender and culture. They were delighted by their leader's racist attacks on Muslims, Mexicans and immigrants.

There are broadly two responses when confronted with proof that white people acted in racial concert: the first is that it is a reaction to changing demographics and the encroachment of the 'others' – 'the browning of America.' The second is that it is benign tribalism – 'people preferring their own.' The phrases 'legitimate concerns,' in the UK and 'economic anxiety' in the USA, are now memes, jokes, ironic comments and religious abuse targeting Muslims and ethnic minorities. A lot of economic anxiety seems to take place on public transport.

The Wink – it's not Race

The damaging identity politics myth is sustained by constant denials that race is an element in white politics, while dog whistling that it is. The white people will deny, in fact, will abhor and object in the strongest terms, that race has anything to do with American politics. The truth is that it is. It is a trick, a wink that has a long and successful history. Steve Bannon, Trump's former strategist in a speech at a French rally bursts: 'Let them call you xenophobes. Let them call you racists. Let them call you nativists. Wear it as a badge of honour.' Is it patriotism or tribalism? In the UK, white entitlement arguments hide behind criticising 'multiculturalism.' By making demands for the return of white spaces as legitimate critiques of the failure of multiculturalism, the issue is removed from race, its edges softened. It becomes how the new arrivals have not integrated and how there needs to be some common ground for a society to function without friction. 'Multiculturalism has failed' is the wink.

Let's study a case. Generation Identity, a Pan European Identitarian movement promotes the values of homeland, freedom and tradition through peaceful activism, political education, and community and cultural activities. They want to create 'a meta political patriotic value base.' These are all good things to be praised. But as the ruse unravels, the more specific the aims become. The three core aims are to 'stop the Islamisation of Europe, oppose globalisation and reverse the Great Replacement.' That would be the 'Great Replacement' of the white indigenous population, one of the founding myths of far-right, neo-Nazi and white nationalist political movement. A disclaimer runs at the bottom of their political statement. The group 'does not provide a platform for any kind of national-socialist or fascists groups or views.' Just a peaceful, non-fascist, non-Nazi, patriotic group, but one that campaigns to repatriate immigrants. This method of gaslighting was continued in America. When Trump, a man with a long record of racist statements was asked by a journalist about his history of clear and explicit prejudice from blocking black tenants from his buildings to fanning flames of the Obama birther myth, he replied that he was 'the least racist person you have ever met.'

White aggressive identity politics is maintained by nailing this implausibility. Its political agenda is to glorify national and racial purity and sell a guarantee of social status based on that racial purity. The goal, the sweet spot of this identity politics, is to achieve a state where a white person can believe that they are good, while also believing that discriminatory policies against non-whites are either necessary or simply being made up. This is a duality that exists at the heart of Anglo-American history. From the seventeenth century, Great Britain invaded, starved and plundered millions of Africans and Asians, while maintaining that barbarity was a necessary civilising mission. Similarly, the United States built its nation on the backs of the black slaves, then in the nineteenth century, ratified a constitution which declared that all men were equal before God.

Grievance Flipping

The dominant identity has been articulating politics in terms of imaginary grievances for as long as there have been minorities demanding anything; from freedom from slavery to freedom from police persecution. While it is non-whites who are accused of overstating their victimhood and triggering that in others, in classic myth fashion, the opposite is true. The flip side of this coddling of white entitlement is a denigration of other groups' expressions of political grievances and accusing them of racism. Their switching between pathos and menace, between plaintiveness and threat, between claiming dispossession and then bringing revenge to bear on those you allege are oppressing you with all the might of your vastly superior resources, is the double think that lies at the heart of the aggressive identity politics myth. White racism, in fact, is a sort of currency. The black studies scholar George Lipsitz calls this 'the possessive investment of whiteness,' which he argues has a 'cash value.' Because it 'accounts for advantages that come to individuals through profits made from housing secured in discriminatory markets through the unequal educational opportunities available to children of different races through insider networks that channel employment opportunities to the relatives and the friends of those who have profited most from present and past racial discrimination and especially through inter-generational transfers of inherited wealth that pass on the spoils of discrimination to succeeding generation.' 'White Americans are encouraged to invest in whiteness to remain true to identity that provides them white resources, power and opportunity,' he adds. A white identity is a trust fund and its currency is grievance that is stolen from others.

The Tool – Universalism

If a single instance will sum up the damaging identity politics myth, it is the anti-Black Lives Matter Slogan, 'All Lives Matter.' Like the heavily memed 'economic anxiety' trope, 'All Lives Matter' has become facetious shorthand, an eye-roll, calling out logic that swerves the issue by using whataboutery. This is the tool of universalism. It sidesteps specific concerns by dismissing them as treatment tantrum thus avoiding engaging with or invalidating them. 'All Lives Matter' does not only suggest that black lives are not lost more brutally and more frequently than white lives, it suggests that to care about black lives is to do so at the expense and exclusion of others. And defensive identity politics has of course some limitations. It has spawned as a culture where it is fashionable to ground one's opinion in their experience 'as a Muslim' or 'as a black man.' It links credibility to identity rather than critical faculties. This is doubly damaging –it cedes and vacates space to the white experience as 'mainstream' and diminishes the authority of the non-whites by serving only as a 'voice ghetto.' There lies the risk of becoming a minority pen for minority voices to write only about minority issues. There is a pressure in the UK publishing houses for delivering 'a certain kind of book' which will conform to a white trade's perception of what is 'authentically' black or Asian. Basically it means non-whites are dictated by the white publishing agencies to write books to perform rage. It is a benign pressure. But it achieves a sinister end which is the sustained marginalisation of ethnic minority voices. This reifies power dynamics in a frustrating self-fulfilling prophecy where 'diversity' is confused with 'representation' – and where campaigning for equal rights ends up as a demand for a seat at the table, while the structure of inequality remains unchanged and the table itself stands on jagged ground. However this is not the fault of representative identity politics. It is the fault of white monopoly on the means of dominant cultural production.

The very origin of the identity politics movement was an effort to find common cause rather than ghettoised demands for equality. The history of the term 'identity politics' and how it was first used illustrates how much it has been corrupted and deliberately misunderstood over the years as divisive and distracting from 'universal' causes. How can someone achieve national patriotism and pride [chanting 'bharat maata' in Indian context], if they feel that their country does not represent them or their interests? It is the left who hardly finds merit in identity politics. They are happy to contrast 'the universalism of class' with 'the narrow, sectional concerns characteristic of so called identity politics.' The loyalty of the minorities is taken for granted by them and they lose ground by remaining narrowly obsessed with the abstract principles of a fight, rather than what is actually happening on the ground. Class is fundamentally about inequality; identity politics is about aspiring to universalism by way of vanquishing inequalities. Economic inequality and identity are inseparable. What is missed by those who are blind to this intersection is that historically, activism based on identity marginalisation has been the most successful way by which class concerns were addressed and lasting economic mobility was secured. For example, on a simpler level, only by campaigning for the admission of black students into universities could they be promoted into white-collar jobs.

The universalism argument assumes that minorities are no longer discriminated against in clear and discreet ways that can be addressed by targeted activism. And so now we must down tools and hold hands for the only remaining cause that should blind us, whatever that is. For some it is nationalism, for others it is class. It is a cousin of the 'progress' myth where women have achieved all the technical legislation wins that can be achieved. Universalism logic imagines successes that are non-existent.

Conclusion

Ideally we should strive to appeal to all and create a solidarity based on common goals. But this ideal world where an identity hierarchy does not exist is a fiction that only exists in the minds of those more preoccupied with the control aspect of universalism. The myth that identity is something that only others do, not white people, is one that has enabled politicians to play on white racial grievance across classes [Hindu grievance across classes in Bengal context] while their liberal counterparts [the left] made the right noises in the direction of the minorities but never genuinely engaged with their causes. And so now, even the cosmetic effort to appeal to non-whites is at risk being abandoned. By doing so, we are doubling down on a mistake which is to allow the populists to set the terms of the debate around identity, and ultimately use it to win votes. This is what US writer Sean McElwee argues: if liberals do not in fact embrace identity politics, they have no future. 'There is simply no electoral benefit to be gained from abandoning identity politics because voters are increasingly sorted in such a way that those who support economically progressive policies are also supportive of racial justice and gender equity.' He concludes 'the path forward will require an understanding of how deeply liberation from patriarchy, white supremacy [majority chauvinism, fascism, and rouge regime] and capitalism are intertwined.'

Defensive identity politics is not the problem. It is, in fact, the only way forward.

Notes

This article is my abridged version of Chapter 4(pp.134-168) titled "The Myth of Damaging Identity Politics" from Nesrine Malik's *We Need New Stories: Challenging the Toxic Myths Behind Our Age of Discontent*. London: Weidenfeld & Nicolson, 2019. Print.

Works Cited

1. https://www.newsclick.in/bjps-anti-muslim-propaganda-manipur-govt-decision-rohingya-refugees-and-more Accessed June 5, 2022. Web.
2. https://economictimes.indiatimes.com/news/politics-and-nation/identity-politics-gaining-ground-in-west-bengal-ahead-of-assembly-polls/articleshow/81291693.cms?from=mdr Accessed June 5, 2022. Web.
3. https://thewire.in/rights/muslims-kolkata-discriminatory-tenancy-problem Accessed June 6, 2022. Web.
4. https://timesofindia.indiatimes.com/city/kolkata/four-doctors-asked-to-vacate-kolkata-flat-for-being-muslims/articleshow/65236711.cms Accessed June 6, 2022. Web.

Index

N

O

P